California Wine Winners

1996

Results of the 1995 Wine Judgings

Edited by
TRUDY AHLSTROM
and
J.T. DEVINE

Printed in the United States of America.

ISBN 1-881796-02-7
ISSN 0883-4423

To order additional copies of this book or copies of any of the previous twelve editions, please send $10.75 to the address below specifying which year's competition results you want to receive.

VARIETAL FAIR
4022 Harrison Grade Road
Sebastopol, CA 95472
707 • 874 • 3105

TABLE OF CONTENTS

INTRODUCTION

This is a simple report of all the medals awarded to California wines in this year's round of wine judgings. Take a look at the inside front cover to see what competitions we cover and how to read the front section. The book covers the 18 most popular varietals, as listed in the Table of Contents.

ORGANIZATION

The first section lists the award winners under specific varietals. Each varietal section is subdivided into groups of nine award winners, eight award winners, seven award winners, etc. The wines are listed alphabetically within these subdivisions, and identified by vintage, appellation and price. Across from each wine a Σ (double gold or special award) G (gold), S (silver), or B (bronze) shows what award was won in each of the competitions.

Johannisberg Riesling, Gewurztraminer and Sparkling wines are further broken down into residual sugar classes, and higher residual sugar wines have their "R.S." noted.

The second part of the book is an alphabetical listing of all the winning wineries, including their addresses. The inside back cover has a key to these listings. Under each winery, the winning wines are listed with the number of awards indicated in parentheses so they can be easily found in the front to see exactly what the medals are. Single-medal winners are listed only in the back, with the award and competition identified.

COMPETITIONS

The competitions start in January and end in July. Since many of the judgings have specific entry requirements (see pages 6 and 7) for the amount of wine to be available at the time of the judging or their fair, many wines entered in the early judgings are too sold out to be entered in the later ones. Keep your copies of this book to compare awards in previous/subsequent years.

The statistics charts will also show you how many of the entered wines win medals in each competition, and how many are gold-plus, gold, silver and bronze. Since this book only covers wines from California, the charts show how many of the total medals were for California wines. And since we don't include every varietal judged (no Gamay, Grenache, Port, etc.) we also list the number of awards from each judging that actually appear in this book.

Some smaller wineries don't enter because of the expense. It is not just the entry fee and paperwork, but also the wine they must give to the competitions if they win. Many of these small producers sell out all their wines every year anyhow. On the other hand, we have seen the ones who choose to compete enter a period of growth and recognition just in the way their medals suggest they should.

On exactly the opposite side are the larger, older wineries who feel they don't need to compete to prove their worth.

We are prohibited not as much by space limitations as by access to information from publishing a list of all the wines entered that did not win a medal. For those reasons, this book cannot be a complete list of who won and who did not win.

POINT COUNTS & REGION COMPARISONS

The first page of each varietal section ranks the top dozen or so winners by weighting the value of each award. Double Golds, Sweepstakes, Best of Class, and other special merit awards = 7 points. (We do not include the best of region and best of region varietal awards from the State Fair for these). Gold = 5 points, Silver = 3 points, and Bronze = 1. The values are arbitrary; it is just another way of looking at the awards.

Also included is a graph that shows which regions of the state took how many points of those weighted medals. The regions refer to those areas where the grapes were grown, not necessarily where the wineries are located:

North Coast.............. Lake, Mendocino, Marin and Solano Co.
Sonoma.................... Sonoma County (11 Appellations).
Napa........................ Napa County (5 Appellations).
Bay Area.................. Alameda, Contra Costa, San Mateo, Santa
.... Clara and Santa Cruz Co.
No. Central Coast... Monterey and San Benito Counties.
So. Central Coast.... San Luis Obispo and Santa Barbara Co.
South Coast.............. L.A., Orange, Riverside, San Diego
and Ventura Counties.
Sierra Foothills.......... Amador, Calaveras, El Dorado, Mariposa,
.... Nevada, Placer, Tuolomne, Yuba Co.
Other......................... All other California Counties
California.................. Non-specified blends from above
appellations.

COMPETITIONS	ENTRIES # Wines #Wineries # in Calif.	MEDALS Total # From CA In book	AWARDS Σ G S B
LOS ANGELES COUNTY FAIR P. O. Box 2250 Pomona, CA 91769 (909) 623-3111	2000 395 307	634 480 445	17 76 148 204
ORANGE COUNTY FAIR P. O. Box 11059 Costa Mesa, CA 92627 (714) 546-8664	2284 ? ?	848 848 693	2 128 224 339
FARMERS FAIR, RIVERSIDE 18700 Lake Perris Drive Perris, CA 92571 (909) 657-4221	1538 289 276	742 628 519	15 45 150 309
SAN FRANCISCO FAIR 455 Golden Gate Avenue #2095 San Francisco, CA 94102 (415) 703-2729	2200 513 330	680 497 422	11 31 161 219
DALLAS MORNING NEWS P. O. Box 38643 Dallas, TX 75238 (214) 319-7000	1520 343 ?	553 403 333	0 28 85 220
CALIFORNIA STATE FAIR P. O. Box 15649 Sacramento, CA 95852 (916) 263-3159	1836 ? ?	722 722 567	23 68 219 257
NEW WORLD INTERNATIONAL P. O. Box 5306 Diamond Bar, CA 91765 (800) 845-9463	1800 417 312	797 623 506	11 121 182 192
RENO-WEST COAST COMP. P. O. Box 837 Reno, NV 89504 (702) 827-7618	1343 258 226	739 664 603	10 73 191 329
SAN DIEGO COMPETITION P. O. Box 880881 San Diego, CA 92168 (619) 421-9463	1741 391 ?	695 582 476	15 43 137 281

1995 Entry Deadline Judging Dates	ENTRY Fee Bottles to Send Min. Produced Min. Inventory at judging	WINNERS Require-ments after Judging	JUDGING SCOPE Geographic Area Covered Judging Categories Entry Restrictions
LOS ANGELES Mid-May June 15-18	$25.00 Six 120 Gal. "Some"	Golds only to sell 2-3 cs. to fair	Any wine from any of the American continents. Some judged in vintage groups. Limit of one entry per class.
ORANGE CO. May 15 June 3-4	No charge Six None "Some"	All winners invited to pour at the fair	California wines available in Orange Co. Judged in price categories. Not all entries voluntary.Current releases only.
RIVERSIDE March 25 May 5-6	$24.00 Four 500 Gal 50 Cases	All entries invited to pour at the fair	Any U.S. wine. Some judged in vintage groups. Chards judged in style groups.
SAN FRAN. June 30 July 22-23	$50.00 Five None 50 Cases	Winners to sell one case to the fair	Any wine in the world. No limit on number of entries. Wines judged in vintag groupings.
DALLAS Dec.19 Jan. 28-29	$55.00 Four 120 Gal. 5 Cases	Golds to give 5 cases for tastings	Any U. S. wine. Limit of 3 entries per category.
STATE FAIR June 9 July 7-9	$25.00 Six 300 Gal. 125 Cases	Golds to sell up to 5 cases for the fair	Any California wine. Wines judged in 10 geogrpahical groups. Limit of 2 entries per class per region.
NEW WORLD Jan 28 Feb. 20-21	$35.00 Six None "Some"	All entries invited to pour at awards	Any wine from the New World. All wines judged in price groups. Must be available to buy in at least one state.
WEST COAST Early April May 3-5	$17.00 Six 500 Gal. 150 Cases	Golds are required to pour at events	Wines from CA, ID, OR, WA and now NY. Some grouped in vintage/price. No limit on number of entries.
SAN DIEGO Early April April 22 & 23	$30.00 Four 300 Gal. No minimum	All winners to donate 1 case for charity sale	Any U. S. vinifera wine. Some judged in vintage groups. No limit on number of entries, except same wine in 2 classes.

GRAND RESERVE

KENDALL-JACKSON

1992

Cabernet Franc

CALIFORNIA

Madroña

1992

EL DORADO

CABERNET FRANC

ESTATE PRODUCED & BOTTLED BY MADROÑA VINEYARDS

CAMINO, CALIFORNIA · ALCOHOL 13.2% BY VOLUME

Cabernet Franc

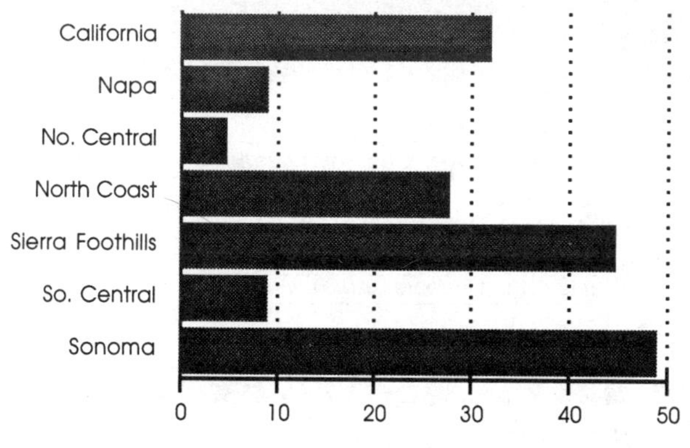

Regional Comparison of Total Points

(Gold-plus=7 Gold=5 Silver=3 Bronze=1)

Highest individual wine totals

19	**IMAGERY SERIES** '92, Alex. Vly., Blue Rock Vnyd., $16.00
14	**KENDALL-JACKSON WINERY** '92, California, Grand Reserve, $20.00
14	**MADRONA VINEYARDS** '92, El Dorado, $11.00
14	**MOUNT KONOCTI** '93, Lake Co., $10.00
12	**GOLD HILL VINEYARD** '90, El Dorado, Est., $12.00
12	**GUENOC WINERY** '91, Lake Co., $14.00
7	**CARMENET WINERY** '92, Sonoma, Moon Mtn. Vnyd., $20.00
7	**COSENTINO WINERY** '92, Napa Co./Sonoma Co., $18.00
7	**LATCHAM VINEYARDS** '93, Sierra Foothills, $10.00

Cabernet Franc	L.A.	Orange	Farmers	San Fran	Dallas	State Fair	New World	W. Coast	San Diego
7 AWARDS									
IMAGERY SERIES '92, Alex. Vly., Blue Rock Vnyd. $16.00		G	S	B	S	S	B		S
6 AWARDS									
GUENOC WINERY '91, Lake Co. $14.00	S		B		B	S		S	B
KENDALL-JACKSON WINERY '92, California, Grand Reserve $20.00	B	G	S		B	S			B
MOUNT KONOCTI '93, Lake Co. $10.00	S	B	B		S	G			B
4 AWARDS									
GOLD HILL VINEYARD '90, El Dorado, Est. $12.00			B			S		B	Σ
MADRONA VINEYARDS '92, El Dorado $11.00		G	S				B		G
3 AWARDS									
BALLENTINE WINES '92, Napa Vly. $15.00	B	B				B			
CARMENET WINERY '92, Sonoma, Moon Mtn. Vnyd. $20.00		S		S	B				
COSENTINO WINERY '92, Napa Co./Sonoma Co. $18.00		B	B				G		
RICHARD L. GRAESER WINERY '91, Napa Vly., Estate $15.00			B		S				B
HAHN ESTATES '93, Santa Lucia Highlands $9.00	B	B				B			
MIRASSOU VINEYARDS '92, California, Family Sel. $7.00			B				S	B	
2 AWARDS									
DRY CREEK VINEYARD '93, Dry Creek Vly. $15.00	B	B							
GUNDLACH-BUNDSCHU WINERY '93, Sonoma Vly., Rhinefarm Vnyd. $14.00		S				S			
JEKEL VINEYARDS '92, Arroyo Seco, Sanctuary Est. $13.00		B					B		
PEPPERWOOD GROVE '92, California, Cask Lot 2					B		G		
PERRY CREEK VINEYARDS '92, El Dorado $11.50							S	S	

Cabernet Franc

L.A.	Orange	Farmers	San Fran	Dallas	State Fair	New World	W. Coast	San Diego	Wine
2 AWARDS									
			B		B				**PRIDE MOUNTAIN VINEYARDS** '93, Sonoma Co. $20.00
		B						B	**RICHARDSON VINEYARDS** '93, Sonoma Vly., Giles Vnyd. $14.50

GREENWOOD
RIDGE
VINEYARDS

ANDERSON VALLEY
CABERNET SAUVIGNON
1992

ESTATE BOTTLED

ALCOHOL 13.5% BY VOLUME

Chateau St. Jean

VINEYARDS AND WINERY

1989

SONOMA COUNTY

Cabernet Sauvignon

RESERVE

Cabernet Sauvignon

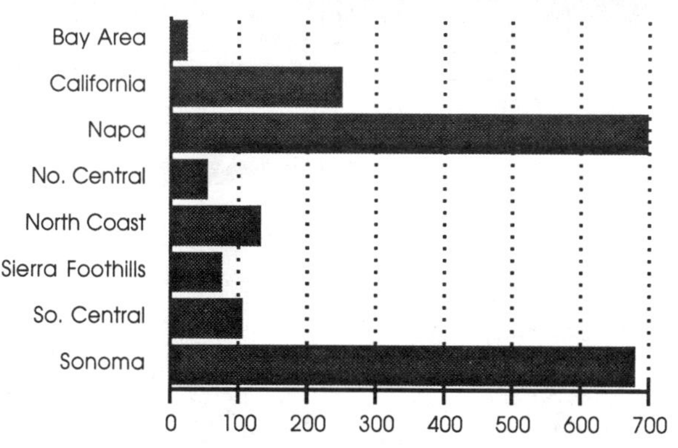

Regional Comparison of Total Points

(Gold-plus=7 Gold=5 Silver=3 Bronze=1)

Highest individual wine totals

30 **GREENWOOD RIDGE VINEYARDS**
'92, Anderson Vly., Estate, $18.00

29 **HESS COLLECTION WINERY**
'91, Napa Vly., Mt. Veeder, Est., $18.00

25 **V. SATTUI WINERY**
'91, Napa Vly., Mario's Reserve, $35.00

24 **CHATEAU ST. JEAN**
'89, Sonoma Co., Reserve, $38.00

23 **CHATEAU ST. JEAN**
'91, Sonoma Co., Cinq Cepages, $18.00

22 **CHATEAU SOUVERAIN**
'92, Alexander Vly., $12.00

20 **A. RAFANELLI WINERY**
'92, Dry Creek Vly., Unfiltered, $18.00

19 **GEYSER PEAK WINERY**
'93, Alexander Vly., $10.00

19 **INDIAN SPRINGS VINEYARDS**
'93, Nevada Co., $10.00

19 **Z D WINES**
'92, Napa Vly., $25.00

18 **DE LOACH VINEYARDS**
'91, Russian River Vly., O.F.S., $25.00

Cabernet Sauvignon

Wine	L.A.	Orange	Farmers	San Fran	Dallas	State Fair	New World	W. Coast	San Diego
9 AWARDS									
HESS COLLECTION WINERY '91, Napa Vly., Mt. Veeder, Est. $18.00	S	G	B	S	B	S	G	S	G
7 AWARDS									
CHATEAU ST. JEAN '91, Sonoma Co., Cinq Cepages $18.00	S	S	G	S	B		G		S
FETZER VINEYARDS '88, Sonoma Co., Reserve $24.00	B	B	B	S		B		B	B
GEYSER PEAK WINERY '93, Alexander Vly. $10.00	Σ		S		S	B	S	B	B
V. SATTUI WINERY '91, Napa Vly., Mario's Reserve $35.00	S		S	B	S		S	G	Σ
Z D WINES '92, Napa Vly. $25.00	G	B		B		S	G	S	B
6 AWARDS									
CHATEAU SOUVERAIN '92, Alexander Vly. $12.00	S	B		S		G	Σ		S
CHATEAU ST. JEAN '89, Sonoma Co., Reserve $38.00	Σ	S		B		G		G	S
ESTRELLA RIVER WINERY '92, California, Prop. Reserve $6.00	B	S	S			B	B	B	
E. & J. GALLO '91, Northern Sonoma, Est. $50.00	S	B		G	G	B		S	
GREENWOOD RIDGE VINEYARDS '92, Anderson Vly., Estate $18.00	Σ			Σ		S	G	G	S
MERIDIAN VINEYARDS '92, Paso Robles $12.00		B			S	S	B	B	S
A. RAFANELLI WINERY '92, Dry Creek Vly., Unfiltered $18.00	S	G		B			G	G	B
SONOMA CREEK WINERY '92, Sonoma Co., Reserve $17.00	S	G				B	B	B	B
STONESTREET WINERY '91, Alexander Vly. $22.00		B		S	B	B		B	B
5 AWARDS									
BARON HERZOG WINE CELLARS '93, California $13.00	B	S	B			B		B	
BEL ARBORS VINEYARD '92, California $7.00		B	B			S	G	B	
BUEHLER VINEYARDS '93, California $9.00	B	B		B		S		S	

Cabernet Sauvignon

5 AWARDS

L.A.	Orange	Farmers	San Fran	Dallas	State Fair	New World	W. Coast	San Diego	Wine
G	B					B	Σ	B	**CHATEAU SOUVERAIN** '91, Alexander Vly., Reserve $16.00
B		B				G	B	G	**CORBETT CANYON VINEYARDS** '92, Sonoma Co., Reserve $9.00
G	B	B					S	S	**DE LOACH VINEYARDS** '93, Russian River Vly., Cuvee $12.00
		B	Σ		G	B	B		**DE LOACH VINEYARDS** '92, Russian River Vly. $15.00
	G	B	B			B	B		**DOUGLASS HILL WINERY** '92, Napa Vly. $15.00
	S		S		S	S	S		**GARY FARRELL** '92, Sonoma Co., Ladi's Vnyd. $20.00
		B			B	B	S	B	**GAINEY VINEYARD** '90, Santa Ynez Vly. $13.00
G	S		B		S		S		**GEYSER PEAK WINERY** '93, Alexander Vly., Reserve $20.00
G	B				Σ	B	B		**GEYSER PEAK WINERY** '92, Alexander Vly., Reserve $20.00
G	B	Σ			B		S		**GUENOC WINERY** '92, Napa Vly., Bella Vista Vnyd. $20.00
B				B		B	B	B	**GUENOC WINERY** '91, Lake Co. $14.00
G	B				G		G	S	**INDIAN SPRINGS VINEYARDS** '93, Nevada Co. $10.00
B		S		G		G	B		**KENDALL-JACKSON WINERY** '91, California, Grand Reserve $30.00
	S	G			S	S		B	**NAPA RIDGE WINERY** '92, Central Coast $8.00
			B		B	B	S	G	**NAPA RIDGE WINERY** '91, North Coast, Reserve $13.00
S	S	S			S		B		**POPPY HILL CELLARS** '92, Napa Vly., Founders Sel. $10.00
		S		B	B		B	B	**RABBIT RIDGE VINEYARDS** '90, Sonoma Co., Est. Reserve $20.00
		B	S		B	G		S	**RAYMOND VINEYARD & CELLAR** '90, Napa Vly., Reserve $26.00
		B		B		G	B	S	**V. SATTUI WINERY** '91, Napa Vly., Preston Vnyd. $25.00
	B		B			S	B	Σ	**SEBASTIANI VINEYARDS** '92, Sonoma Co. $10.00

Cabernet Sauvignon

Wine	L.A.	Orange	Farmers	San Fran	Dallas	State Fair	New World	W. Coast	San Diego
5 AWARDS									
SHAFER VINEYARDS '92, Stag's Leap Dist. $22.00		B	B			S		B	G
RODNEY STRONG VINEYARDS '91, Northern Sonoma, Reserve $30.00	G	S		S				B	G
VILLA MT. EDEN '91, Napa Vly., Grand Reserve $14.00		B	B	S		S		S	
WEINSTOCK CELLARS '93, Alexander Vly. $9.00	S		S	S			S	G	
4 AWARDS									
BAREFOOT CELLARS 'NV, California $4.00	B	G	B			B			
BARON HERZOG WINE CELLARS '93, Chalk Hill, Reserve $11.00		B	B	S		Σ			
BENZIGER FAMILY WINERY '92, Sonoma Co. $13.00			B	S		G			S
BERINGER VINEYARDS '91, Napa Vly., Reserve $45.00	B			G		B			B
CAMELOT VINEYARD '92, Central Coast $11.00			B			S	S	B	
CANYON ROAD CELLARS '92, California $6.00		G	S		B		B		
CHATEAU MARGARITE VINEYARDS '92, Napa Vly. $15.00	G		B			B		G	
CLOS DU BOIS '92, Alexander Vly. $13.00		S				B		B	B
CONN CREEK '91, Napa Vly. $18.00		B	B				B	B	
CYPRESS VINEYARD '92, California $8.00		G		B				S	B
DE LOACH VINEYARDS '91, Russian River Vly., O.F.S. $25.00		G	Σ					B	G
DOMAINE ST. GEORGE '93, California, Vintage Reserve $6.00		B	B			B		B	
DRY CREEK VINEYARD '91, Dry Creek Vly., Reserve $20.00		S	B				G		G
FETZER VINEYARDS '92, California, Valley Oaks $8.00		B				G	B	S	
FETZER VINEYARDS '92, North Coast, Barrel Select $12.00	S					S		S	S

Cabernet Sauvignon

4 AWARDS

L.A.	Orange	Farmers	San Fran	Dallas	State Fair	New World	W. Coast	San Diego	Wine
B		B		B				S	**FOREST GLEN** '92, California, Barrel Select $10.00
	G			B			S	S	**FRANCISCAN OAKVILLE ESTATE** '91, Napa Vly. $15.00
B			B		S			S	**FREEMARK ABBEY** '87, Napa Vly., Sycamore Vnyds. $20.00
	S	G		S			S		**GRGICH HILLS CELLAR** '90, Napa Vly. $24.00
		S		B	B	B			**GROVE STREET WINERY** '92, California, Vineyard Select $7.00
S					S		S	G	**GUENOC WINERY** '92, Napa, Beckstoffer Vnyd., Res. $35.00
	B		B			G	B		**GUNDLACH-BUNDSCHU WINERY** '92, Sonoma, Rhinefarm Vnyd. $15.00
B	B		B				G		**HANNA WINERY** '92, Alexander Vly. $16.00
			B			B	B	B	**HEITZ WINE CELLARS** '90, Napa Vly. $18.00
B	S						G	B	**HOP KILN WINERY** '91, Russian River Vly. $14.00
			S		S	S	S		**KENDALL-JACKSON WINERY** '92, California, Vintner's Reserve $14.00
					B	S	S	B	**LOCKWOOD VINEYARD** '92, Monterey $14.00
			G		B		S	B	**J. LOHR WINERY** '92, Paso Robles, Seven Oaks $12.00
S	B				S			G	**MARKHAM VINEYARDS** '91, Napa Vly. $15.00
		B				S	G	B	**LOUIS M. MARTINI** '90, Sonoma., Monte Rosso Vnyd. $23.00
Σ				B	B			S	**MAZZOCCO VINEYARDS** '91, Sonoma Co. $18.00
B	G			B	S				**MEEKER VINEYARD** '91, Dry Creek., Gold Leaf Cuvee $14.00
		S	B			G		B	**MICHEL-SCHLUMBERGER WINERY** '90, Dry Creek Vly., Reserve $30.00
	B	S			B		B		**MOUNT MADRONA WINERY** '91, Napa Vly. $14.00
	S		B		S	B			**ROBERT PEPI WINERY** '91, Napa Vly., Vine Hill Ranch $18.00

Cabernet Sauvignon

Winery / Wine	L.A.	Orange	Farmers	San Fran	Dallas	State Fair	New World	W. Coast	San Diego
4 AWARDS									
ROBERT PEPI WINERY '89, Napa Vly., Vine Hill Ranch $18.00			B	S				S	S
RANCHO SISQUOC WINERY '92, Santa Maria Vly., Est. $15.00			S	B		S			B
RAYMOND VINEYARD & CELLAR '91, Napa Vly. $17.00					S		B	Σ	S
SEBASTIANI VINEYARDS '91, Sonoma Vly. Cherryblock $25.00		B				S	S		S
SEQUOIA GROVE VINEYARDS '92, Napa Vly., Est. Reserve $18.00	S					S	B		B
ST. CLEMENT VINEYARDS '92, Napa Vly. $23.00		B				B	G	B	
ST. SUPERY VINEYARDS '91, Napa, Dollarhide Ranch $14.00			B			G	G		B
RODNEY STRONG VINEYARDS '91, No.Sonoma, Alex. Crown $20.00	S	S				B		S	
VILLA MT. EDEN '92, California, Cellar Select $8.00	B	B				B			B
WHITEHALL LANE WINERY '91, Napa Vly., Reserve $24.00	B	B			B		S		
WINDSOR VINEYARDS '92, Sonoma Co. $10.00		G	B					B	B
WINDSOR VINEYARDS '91, Mendocino Co. $12.00		B					B	S	B
3 AWARDS									
BANDIERA WINERY '93, Napa Vly. $8.00		G		B				S	
BEAULIEU VINEYARD '92, Rutherford $14.00		S		S		B			
BELVEDERE WINERY '92, Sonoma Co. $12.00		S				B		B	
BENZIGER FAMILY WINERY '90, Sonoma Mtn. $16.00	G	B	B						
BERINGER VINEYARDS '92, Knights Vly. $16.00				S		G		S	
BLOSSOM HILL WINERY 'NV, California $4.00				B		B		B	
BRUTOCAO CELLARS '90, Mendocino, Est. $13.00	G		B					S	

Cabernet Sauvignon

3 AWARDS

L.A.	Orange	Farmers	San Fran	Dallas	State Fair	New World	W. Coast	San Diego	Winery
	B				B			B	**BUEHLER VINEYARDS** '92, Napa Vly. $14.00
S	S			B					**BUENA VISTA** '91, Carneros $12.00
S					S		S		**CAKEBREAD CELLARS** '90, Napa, Rutherford Reserve $40.00
S						B	S		**CALLAWAY VINEYARD & WINERY** '91, California $10.00
B				B		B			**CHALK HILL WINERY** '92, Sonoma Co., Est.
S			B					B	**CLOS FONTAINE DU MONT** '92, Napa Vly., Reserve $32.00
S			B		S				**CONN CREEK** '92, Limited Release $18.00
	B				B	B			**COSENTINO WINERY** '92, Napa Vly. $16.00
	B				S		B		**THOMAS COYNE WINERY** '92, Livermore Vly., Kalthoff Vnyd. $12.00
	B				S			S	**DURNEY VINEYARDS** '91, Carmel Vly., Reserve $32.00
		S	S					B	**EHLERS GROVE WINERY** '93, Napa Vly. $10.00
			S		B			B	**FREEMARK ABBEY** '90, Napa Vly., Boche Vnyds. $25.00
					B	B		B	**GOLD HILL VINEYARD** '91, El Dorado, Estate $11.00
		B			B			G	**RICHARD L. GRAESER WINERY** '91, Napa Vly., Estate $14.00
			B		B			S	**GUENOC WINERY** '92, California $11.00
		S		S		B			**GUENOC WINERY** '91, Napa, Beckstoffer Vnyd, Res. $35.00
	G		S				G		**HEITZ WINE CELLARS** '90, Napa Vly., Trailside Vnyd. $45.00
		B		S				S	**HESS COLLECTION WINERY** '92, California, Hess Select $9.50
		B			S			B	**HUSCH VINEYARDS** '92, Mendocino, No. Field Select $20.00
		G					B	S	**HUSCH VINEYARDS** '91, Mendocino, La Ribera Vnyd. $14.00

Cabernet Sauvignon

	L.A.	Orange	Farmers	San Fran	Dallas	State Fair	New World	W. Coast	San Diego
3 AWARDS									
KENDALL-JACKSON WINERY '90, California, Grand Reserve $30.00	B		B					S	
KENWOOD VINEYARDS '92, Sonoma, Jack London Vnyd. $20.00		S		B				S	
LAMBERT BRIDGE WINERY '92, Sonoma Co. $15.00		G				S		S	
LATCHAM VINEYARDS '91, El Dorado $9.00	S						S	S	
LAVA CAP WINERY '91, El Dorado, Estate $12.00		B				B			G
LEEWARD WINERY '92, Sonoma Co. $15.00		B				B		B	
LOCKWOOD VINEYARD '91, Monterey, Partners Reserve $18.00	S	B					B		
MADRONA VINEYARDS '91, El Dorado $11.00				B		G	B		
LOUIS M. MARTINI '92, North Coast $8.50		B	B						B
MIRASSOU VINEYARDS '91, Monterey, Harvest Reserve $12.00	S							B	B
MONTPELLIER VINEYARDS '92, California $8.00			S			B	B		
NORMAN VINEYARDS '92, Paso Robles $13.00		B				B			B
PARDUCCI WINE CELLARS '91, Mendocino Co. $8.00		B					S		B
PERRY CREEK VINEYARDS '92, El Dorado $10.00						S	B		B
JOSEPH PHELPS VINEYARDS '92, Napa Vly. $20.00	S	B				S			
POPPY HILL CELLARS '92, California, Calif. Selection $8.00		B	B			S			
QUAIL RIDGE CELLARS '89, Napa Vly., Eisele Vnyd., Res. $30.00	B			B		S			
ROUND HILL VINEYARDS '90, Napa Vly., Reserve $14.00			S			B		B	
RUTHERFORD RANCH VINEYARDS '91, Napa Vly. $11.00	S		G			B			

Cabernet Sauvignon

L.A.	Orange	Farmers	San Fran	Dallas	State Fair	New World	W. Coast	San Diego	Winery
3 AWARDS									
		S					B	S	**V. SATTUI WINERY** '91, Napa Vly. $15.00
		B					S	B	**V. SATTUI WINERY** '91, Napa Vly., Suzanne's Vnyd. $20.00
G					S		B		**SIERRA VISTA WINERY** '92, El Dorado, Est. $12.00
	B				B			G	**SILVERADO VINEYARDS** '92, Napa Vly. $19.00
	S				S		S		**ST. FRANCIS VINEYARDS** '93, Sonoma Vly. $10.00
		B		G			B		**STE. CLAIRE** '92, California $11.00
					B	B		B	**STERLING VINEYARDS** '91, Napa, Diamond Mt. Ranch $17.00
			B	G		S			**STONE CREEK WINES** '90, Napa Vly., Chairman's Res. $15.00
S	B				B				**STONY RIDGE WINERY** '93, Napa, Mt. Veeder, Ltd. Rel. $14.00
	S	B			B				**RODNEY STRONG VINEYARDS** '92, Sonoma Co. $10.00
S			S			S			**TULOCAY WINERY** '92, Napa Vly., Cliff Vnyd. $15.00
	B	B		G					**WILD HORSE WINERY** '92, San Luis Obispo $12.00
						S	B	S	**WINDSOR VINEYARDS** '91, Sonoma Co., Signature Series $18.00
2 AWARDS									
							S	S	**ATLAS PEAK VINEYARD** '91, Napa Vly., Atlas Peak $16.00
	B				B				**AUDUBON CELLARS** '92, Napa Vly. $11.00
		S		B					**BEAUCANON COMPANY** '91, Napa Vly. $14.00
	S				B				**BEAULIEU VINEYARD** '92, Napa Vly., Beautour $8.00
				B	B				**BEAULIEU VINEYARD** '91, Napa, Geo. Latour Reserve $40.00
					B			B	**BENICIA CELLARS** 'NV, Napa Vly., Capitol Reserve $12.00

Cabernet Sauvignon

2 AWARDS

Wine	L.A.	Orange	Farmers	San Fran	Dallas	State Fair	New World	W. Coast	San Diego
BENZIGER FAMILY WINERY '91, Sonoma Co. $13.00					G		B		
BERINGER VINEYARDS '91, Knights Vly. $16.00			B				B		
BUENA VISTA '90, Carneros, Grand Reserve $24.00			G						B
CEDAR MOUNTAIN WINERY '92, Livermore, Blanches Vnyd. $20.00				B	S				
CHESTNUT HILL WINERY '92, California, Coastal Cuvee $7.00						B			S
CHIMNEY ROCK WINERY '91, Stag's Leap Dist. $20.00		S							B
CINNABAR VINEYARDS '90, Santa Cruz, Saratoga Vnyd. $20.00			B					B	
CONCANNON VINEYARD '92, Central Coast, Sel. Vnyd. $10.00					S			B	
CRESTON VINEYARDS '91, Paso Robles, Est. $10.00							B	G	
DE MOOR WINERY '90, Napa Vly. $13.00		B	B						
DOMAINE ST. GEORGE '90, Russian River, Premier Cuvee $8.50	B		B						
DOMAINE ST. GEORGE '89, Sonoma Co., Premier Cuvee $8.50							B	B	
DORE WINES '92, California, Floral Series $7.00						B	B		
DRY CREEK VINEYARD '92, Dry Creek Vly. $16.00	B		S						
EHLERS GROVE WINERY '92, Napa Vly. $15.00		B	B						
FALLBROOK WINERY '92, California $7.00			B			S			
FETZER VINEYARDS '91, North Coast, Barrel Select $12.00					B		S		
FIRESTONE VINEYARD '91, Santa Ynez Vly. $20.00			B						B
FORESTVILLE VINEYARD '92, California $6.00			G			B			

Cabernet Sauvignon

L.A.	Orange	Farmers	San Fran	Dallas	State Fair	New World	W. Coast	San Diego	
									2 AWARDS
					B		B		**FRANZIA BROTHERS WINERY** 'NV, California $2.00
		B	S						**GAN EDEN** '89, Alexander Vly. $15.00
	B				B				**GLASS MOUNTAIN** '92, California $9.00
	B					B			**GLEN ELLEN WINERY** '92, California, Proprietor's Res. $5.00
						S		B	**GOLDEN CREEK VINEYARD** '91, Sonoma Co., Reserve
B							B		**GRANITE SPRINGS WINERY** '93, El Dorado $10.00
B					S				**HAGAFEN CELLARS** '89, Napa Vly., Reserve $28.00
		S				B			**HAYWOOD WINERY** '92, California, Vintner's Select $8.00
	B							B	**WILLIAM HILL WINERY** '91, Napa Vly. $14.00
			B			B			**HOPE FARMS** '92, Paso Robles, Est. $13.00
						B	B		**INGLENOOK** 'NV, California, Est. $4.00
B							B		**TOBIN JAMES CELLARS** '93, San Luis Obispo, Star Light $14.00
					G	G			**JUSTIN VINEYARDS** '92, San Luis Obispo, Justin Vnyds. $20.00
	G				S				**MAACAMA CREEK VINEYARDS** '92, Alexander Vly., Est. Reserve $12.00
	B						B		**LOUIS M. MARTINI** '89, Napa Vly., Reserve $15.00
				B				G	**MERRYVALE VINEYARDS** '91, Napa Vly. $23.00
					B	S			**MICHEL-SCHLUMBERGER WINERY** '91, Dry Creek Vly. $18.00
	B				S				**ROBERT MONDAVI WINERY** '93, North Coast $11.00
	B							G	**MONT ST. JOHN** '91, Napa Vly. $14.00
B				B					**NAPA CREEK WINERY** '91, Napa Vly. $10.00

Cabernet Sauvignon

2 AWARDS	L.A.	Orange	Farmers	San Fran	Dallas	State Fair	New World	W. Coast	San Diego
NAVARRO VINEYARDS '91, Mendocino $17.00		S				S			
NAVARRO VINEYARDS '90, Mendocino $16.00			B					B	
NEWLAN VINEYARDS '91, Napa Vly. $16.00				G		B			
NICHELINI VINEYARDS '89, Napa Vly. $12.00			S						B
OAK FALLS '93, Napa Vly. $8.00		S					B		
PEDRONCELLI WINERY '92, Alexander Vly., Fay Vnyd. $14.00	S					S			
PEDRONCELLI WINERY '92, Dry Creek Vly. $9.50		B					B		
PEJU PROVINCE '91, Napa Vly., H.B. Vnyd. $35.00				Σ		S			
R. H. PHILLIPS VINEYARD '93, California, Barrel Cuvee $7.50			S					B	
QUAIL RIDGE CELLARS '90, Napa Vly. $12.00			S				S		
RAYMOND VINEYARD & CELLAR '91, California, Amberhill $9.00					B		G		
RETZLAFF VINEYARDS '92, Livermore Vly., Est. $16.00						B			B
ROSENBLUM CELLARS '92, Napa, Holbrook Mitchell $15.00						B	B		
RUTHERFORD ESTATE CELLARS '92, Napa Vly. $7.00		B							G
RUTHERFORD ESTATE CELLARS '91, Napa Vly. $7.00							G	S	
RUTHERFORD RANCH VINEYARDS '91, Napa Vly., Lot 2 $10.00								S	B
V. SATTUI WINERY '92, Napa Vly., Preston Vnyd. $17.00				S		Σ			
V. SATTUI WINERY '92, Napa Vly., Suzanne's Vnyd. $20.00				B		S			
SAUSAL WINERY '92, Alexander Vly. $14.00						B			S

Cabernet Sauvignon

L.A.	Orange	Farmers	San Fran	Dallas	State Fair	New World	W. Coast	San Diego	Cabernet Sauvignon
									2 AWARDS
				S		G			**SHAFER VINEYARDS** '91, Napa Vly., Stag's Leap $22.00
			S		B				**SIERRA VISTA WINERY** '92, El Dorado, Five Star Reserve $22.00
					S		B		**SINGLE LEAF VINEYARDS** '92, El Dorado, De Casabel $11.00
	S				S				**STEVENOT WINERY** '92, Calaveras Co., Reserve $10.00
				B		S			**SUTTER HOME WINERY** '91, Napa Vly., Reserve $12.00
		S				S			**SYLVESTER VINEYARDS** '92, Paso Robles, Kiara Reserve $8.00
					S	S			**TEMECULA CREST WINERY** '92, Temecula $13.00
				S	B				**TRUCHARD VINEYARDS** '91, Carneros $18.00
				B				B	**M. G. VALLEJO WINERY** '92, California $6.00
	S						S		**VENDANGE** 'NV, California, Autumn Harvest $6.00
	S		S						**VENEZIA** '93, Alexander Vly. $20.00
			B	S					**VICHON WINERY** '91, Napa Vly. $16.00
S							B		**WELLINGTON VINEYARDS** '91, Napa Vly., Mt. Veeder Dist. $16.00
					B			B	**WINDSOR VINEYARDS** '91, River West Vnyd. $14.00
S							S		**STEPHEN ZELLERBACH VINEYARD** '93, California $7.00

RESERVE

Cambria

ESTATE BOTTLED

1993

CHARDONNAY

SANTA MARIA VALLEY CALIFORNIA

ALC 13.8% BY VOL

RESERVE

GEYSER PEAK

1993 Alexander Valley Chardonnay

Chardonnay

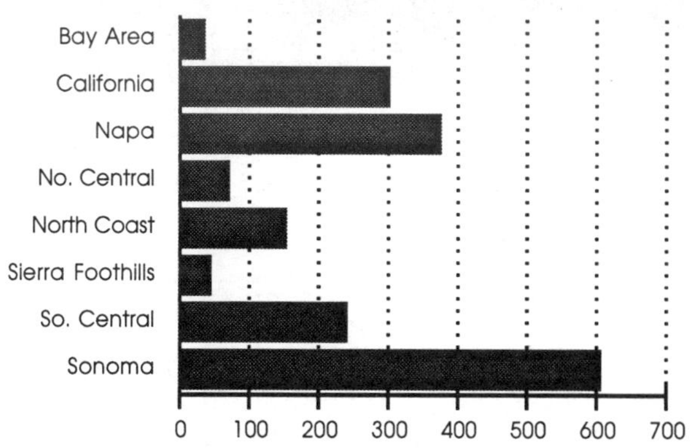

Regional Comparison of Total Points

(Gold-plus=7 Gold=5 Silver=3 Bronze=1)

Highest individual wine totals

30	**CAMBRIA WINERY** '93, Santa Maria Vly., Estate Res., $25.00
24	**GEYSER PEAK WINERY** '93, Alexander Vly., Trione Res., $20.00
24	**GEYSER PEAK WINERY** '93, Sonoma Co., $10.00
24	**KENDALL-JACKSON WINERY** '93, California, LH, R.S. 11.0%, $15.00
21	**CAMELOT VINEYARD** '93, Santa Barbara Co., $12.00
21	**DE LOACH VINEYARDS** '93, Russian River Vly., O.F.S., $25.00
21	**LA CREMA** '93, California, Grand Cuvee, $20.00
19	**WILLIAM HILL WINERY** '93, Napa Vly., $12.00
19	**NAPA RIDGE WINERY** '93, Napa Vly., Reserve, $13.00
19	**VILLA MT. EDEN** '93, Carneros, Grand Reserve, $14.00
18	**FETZER VINEYARDS** '93, Mendocino Co., Bonterra, $9.00

Chardonnay

Chardonnay	L.A.	Orange	Farmers	San Fran	Dallas	State Fair	New World	W. Coast	San Diego
8 AWARDS									
CAMBRIA WINERY '93, Santa Maria Vly., Estate Res. $25.00	S	G	G	S		Σ	G	B	B
CHATEAU SOUVERAIN '93, Sonoma Co., Barrel Ferm. $16.00	B		B	B	B	B	G	B	B
GEYSER PEAK WINERY '93, Alexander Vly., Trione Res. $20.00	G	S	S		S	S	G	B	B
KENDALL-JACKSON WINERY '93, California, LH, R.S. 11.0% $15.00	S	G	B	S		S	G	B	S
7 AWARDS									
ARCIERO WINERY '93, Paso Robles, Est. $9.00	B		S		B	B	B	S	S
DE LOACH VINEYARDS '93, Russian River Vly., O.F.S. $25.00	G	S	S	S			B	G	B
FETZER VINEYARDS '92, Mendocino Co., Reserve $24.00		S	B	S	B	S		S	B
LA CREMA '93, California, Grand Cuvee $20.00	G		S	S	S	B	G	B	
NAPA RIDGE WINERY '93, Napa Vly., Reserve $13.00	G	B	S	S	B		S	S	
J. STONESTREET & SONS '93, Sonoma Co. $21.00		B	B		B	S	S	S	B
6 AWARDS									
CAKEBREAD CELLARS '93, Napa Vly. $22.00	B		S	B		B		S	B
CINNABAR VINEYARDS '93, Santa Cruz, Saratoga Vnyd. $22.00	B	S	B		S		S		B
FETZER VINEYARDS '93, Mendocino Co., Bonterra $9.00		S	B		G	B	G	S	
GEYSER PEAK WINERY '93, Sonoma Co. $10.00		G	Σ			S	S	G	B
HANDLEY CELLARS '92, Dry Creek Vly. $15.00	B	B			B		S	S	S
KENDALL-JACKSON WINERY '93, California, Vintner's Reserve $14.00	G		B	Σ	B		B	S	
MC ILROY WINES '93, Russian Riv., Aquarius Ranch $15.00	B	G	B			S	S	G	
ROBERT PEPI WINERY '92, Napa Vly., Puncheon Ferm. $15.00	S	S		B	B			S	S

Chardonnay

5 AWARDS

L.A.	Orange	Farmers	San Fran	Dallas	State Fair	New World	W. Coast	San Diego	Wine
B	G		B		B		S		**BAILEYANA VINEYARD** '93, Edna Vly., Paragon Vnyd. $13.00
S	S	B	B		S				**BEAULIEU VINEYARD** '92, Napa Vly., Carneros Res. $18.00
B	B	S			B		B		**DAVIS BYNUM WINERY** '93, Russian River Vly. $10.00
Σ			S	S		G	S		**CAMELOT VINEYARD** '93, Santa Barbara Co. $12.00
	B	G				S	S	B	**CANYON ROAD CELLARS** '93, California $6.00
G		S		B	S	S			**CHATEAU SOUVERAIN** '93, Rochioli Vnyd., Reserve $16.00
G	S	S					G	B	**CLOS DU BOIS** '93, Dry Creek, Flintwood $17.00
		B			B	B	B	B	**DE LOACH VINEYARDS** '93, Russian River Vly. $15.00
B	B			G	S			B	**GLORIA FERRER** '93, Carneros, Freixenet Vnyds. $16.00
G	S	B			S	G			**FETZER VINEYARDS** '93, North Coast, Barrel Select $11.00
		S			S	S	B	B	**GAINEY VINEYARD** '93, Santa Barbara Co. $14.00
S	B	B	B				B		**HIDDEN CELLARS** '93, Mendocino, Organic $10.00
	B	G			S	G		G	**WILLIAM HILL WINERY** '93, Napa Vly. $12.00
B	G		B	B	S				**KENDALL-JACKSON WINERY** '93, Santa Maria., Camelot Vnyd. $16.00
	S	S	S	B	S				**LANDMARK VINEYARDS** '93, Sonoma Co., Overlook $13.00
	B	B		B	B		S		**MIRASSOU VINEYARDS** '93, Monterey, Harvest Reserve $12.00
S				B		B	B	B	**RAYMOND VINEYARD & CELLAR** '92, Napa Vly. $13.00
B		S			B		B	G	**J. STONESTREET & SONS** '92, Sonoma Co. $20.00
G	G	S					B	B	**SWANSON VINEYARDS** '93, Napa Vly., Carneros $20.00
G			S			S	G	S	**VILLA MT. EDEN** '93, Carneros, Grand Reserve $14.00

Chardonnay

Wine	L.A.	Orange	Farmers	San Fran	Dallas	State Fair	New World	W. Coast	San Diego
5 AWARDS									
WINDSOR VINEYARDS '93, Sonoma Co., Signature Series $15.00			B		B	S	S	B	
4 AWARDS									
BELVEDERE WINERY '93, Alexander Vly. $10.00			B			B		G	G
BELVEDERE WINERY '93, Sonoma Co. $9.00	S		B		B		G		
BUEHLER VINEYARDS '93, Russian River Vly. $12.00	S	S				B			B
BYRON VINEYARD & WINERY '93, Santa Barbara Co., Reserve $23.00	B	S		S					S
CAMBRIA WINERY '93, S. Maria, Katherine's Vnyd. $18.00				B		B	B	B	
CHATEAU DE BAUN WINERY '93, Russian River Vly. $10.00					B	B	S	B	
CHATEAU ST. JEAN '93, Alexander Vly., Belle Terre $17.00	S				B			B	S
CLOS DU BOIS '93, Alexander Vly., Calcaire $18.00	B	G						G	B
DE LORIMIER VINEYARDS '92, Alexander Vly., Estate $14.00	S	B						B	S
GARY FARRELL '93, Russian River Vly., Allen Vnyd. $18.00				G	B	B		S	
FETZER VINEYARDS '93, California, Sundial $8.00			B				S	S	B
FIELDBROOK WINERY '94, Trinity Co., Meredith Vnyd. $12.00	B	S		B		B			
FIRESTONE VINEYARD '93, Santa Ynez Vly., Barrel Ferm. $12.00			B		B			B	B
FRANCISCAN OAKVILLE ESTATE '93, Napa Vly., Barrel Ferm. $12.00		B					G	G	S
J. FURST '92, California $11.00	S	G						S	B
E. & J. GALLO '93, Northern Sonoma $30.00		G		G		B		B	
GUENOC WINERY '94, Guenoc Vly. $14.00		S	G			B		S	
HAYWOOD WINERY '93, California, Vintner's Select $8.00	B	S					B		B

Chardonnay

4 AWARDS

L.A.	Orange	Farmers	San Fran	Dallas	State Fair	New World	W. Coast	San Diego	Wine
		B			B		B	S	**HESS COLLECTION WINERY** '93, Napa Vly. $15.00
	B		S				B	B	**JORDAN VINEYARD & WINERY** '92, Alexander Vly. $20.00
B	B					B	B		**JOUILLIAN VINEYARDS** '93, Monterey $11.00
S		B					B	B	**KENDALL-JACKSON WINERY** '94, California, Vintner's Reserve $14.00
					B	S	S	B	**KENDALL-JACKSON WINERY** '92, Santa Maria, Camelot Vnyd. $16.00
		B	B				S	B	**CHARLES KRUG WINERY** '93, Napa Vly. $11.00
	S			B	S		G		**LANDMARK VINEYARDS** '93, Alexander Vly., Damaris Res. $19.00
	S	B			G		B		**MERIDIAN VINEYARDS** '93, Edna Vly. $14.00
G	G					G	B		**NAVARRO VINEYARDS** '93, Anderson Vly., Reserve $15.00
B	S			G		B			**FESS PARKER WINERY** '93, Santa Barbara Co., Res. $18.00
	S				S	B	B		**RAYMOND VINEYARD & CELLAR** '93, California, Amberhill $11.00
S				B			B	B	**SEBASTIANI VINEYARDS** '93, Russian River, Dutton Ranch $18.00
	S				B	G	G		**SEBASTIANI VINEYARDS** '93, Sonoma Co. $10.00
B		S				S	B		**SHAFER VINEYARDS** '93, Napa Vly., Barrel Select $16.00
B				S		B	B		**SILVERADO VINEYARDS** '93, Napa Vly. $15.00
		B				B	S	B	**STE. CLAIRE** '92, California, Barrel Select $11.00
S	S		S		B				**TRELLIS VINEYARDS** '93, Sonoma Co. $8.00
S	S			B		G			**VICHON WINERY** '93, California, Coastal Sel. $9.00
	S	S	B			G			**VILLA MT. EDEN** '93, California, Cellar Select $8.00
B	B				S		B		**WINDSOR VINEYARDS** '93, Russian River Vly., Res. $14.00

Chardonnay

Winery	L.A.	Orange	Farmers	San Fran	Dallas	State Fair	New World	W. Coast	San Diego
3 AWARDS									
ARMIDA WINERY '93, Russian River Vly. $12.00			B				B		B
BAREFOOT CELLARS 'NV, California $4.00			B			B			B
BEAULIEU VINEYARD '93, Los Carneros $13.00		B			B		G		
BEAULIEU VINEYARD '93, Napa Vly., Beautour $8.00			B		B		S		
BEL ARBORS VINEYARD '93, California $7.00					B	S		B	
BENZIGER FAMILY WINERY '93, Sonoma, Carneros $16.00		S				G	S		
BENZIGER FAMILY WINERY '92, Carneros, Premier Vnyd. $16.00				S		S	B		
BERINGER VINEYARDS '93, Napa Vly. $10.50			B		B		G		
BERINGER VINEYARDS '93, Napa Vly., Reserve $22.00		S	B						B
CAMELOT VINEYARD '93, Central Coast $11.00				B			S	B	
MAURICE CAR'RIE WINERY '93, Temecula, Reserve $11.00			B	S			B		
CHATOM VINEYARDS '93, Calaveras Co. $10.00			B			B			B
CONCANNON VINEYARD '93, Central Coast, Sel. Vnyd. $10.00			G				B	S	
CORBETT CANYON VINEYARDS '93, Santa Barbara Co., Res. $9.00			B				B	B	
DOMAINE ST. GEORGE '93, Sonoma, Premier Cuvee $8.50		B					S	B	
DRY CREEK VINEYARD '93, Sonoma Co., Barrel Ferm. $13.00		B		B				B	
EDMEADES ESTATE WINERY '93, Mendocino $12.00			G		G		B		
EDNA VALLEY VINEYARD '93, Edna Vly., Estate	G				B		B		
ESTRELLA RIVER WINERY '93, California, Prop. Reserve $6.00	G	B						B	

L.A.	Orange	Farmers	San Fran	Dallas	State Fair	New World	W. Coast	San Diego	Chardonnay
									3 AWARDS
S						B	B		**THOMAS FOGARTY WINERY** '92, Santa Cruz Mtns. $16.00
						S	B	S	**FOREST GLEN** '93, California, Barrel Ferm. $10.00
	B					S		B	**J. FRITZ WINERY** '93, Sonoma Co. $10.00
S	B				S				**GROVE STREET WINERY** '93, Sonoma Co. $7.00
B		S				B			**HACIENDA WINERY** '93, California, Claire De Lune $7.50
B				B	B				**HANDLEY CELLARS** '92, Anderson Vly. $11.00
	G	G			B				**HANNA WINERY** '93, Sonoma Co. $14.00
	B	B						B	**HAUTE CELLARS** 'NV, California $5.00
				B		S		B	**HESS COLLECTION WINERY** '93, California, Hess Select
	G			S			Σ		**KENDALL-JACKSON WINERY** '93, California, Grand Reserve $24.00
S		B	S						**LAURIER VINEYARDS** '92, Sonoma Co. $15.00
B		S						S	**LAVA CAP WINERY** '93, El Dorado, Est., Reserve $15.00
G			S					G	**LOCKWOOD VINEYARD** '92, Monterey, Reserve $17.00
					G		B	B	**MADRONA VINEYARDS** '92, El Dorado, Estate $10.00
	S				S			B	**MARKHAM VINEYARDS** '93, Napa Vly., Barrel Ferm. $14.00
	S			B	B				**LOUIS M. MARTINI** '92, Napa Vly. $9.00
B			B					B	**MERRYVALE VINEYARDS** '93, Napa Vly., Starmont $16.00
	S			B				B	**MICHEL-SCHLUMBERGER WINERY** '92, Dry Creek, Benchland Est. $18.00
G	S			B					**MILL CREEK VINEYARDS** '93, Dry Creek Vly., Estate $12.00
	S	S				B			**NAVARRO VINEYARDS** '93, Mendocino $11.00

Chardonnay

Winery / Wine	L.A.	Orange	Farmers	San Fran	Dallas	State Fair	New World	W. Coast	San Diego
3 AWARDS									
FESS PARKER WINERY '93, Santa Barbara Co. $13.00	G					S	B		
ROBERT PEPI WINERY '91, Napa, Puncheon Ferm. $15.00			B	S					S
PERRY CREEK VINEYARDS '94, El Dorado $9.00	S			B		S			
R. H. PHILLIPS VINEYARD '94, Dunnigan Hills, Cuvee $7.00	G		S	S					
RUTHERFORD ESTATE CELLARS '92, Napa Vly. $7.00	S	S					G		
SONOMA CREEK WINERY '93, Sonoma Vly., Carneros Res. $16.00	B					S		S	
STERLING VINEYARDS '93, Carneros, Winery Lake Vnyd. $19.00	B	S				S			
STEVENOT WINERY '93, Calaveras Co. $9.00				B	B		B		
RODNEY STRONG VINEYARDS '93, Chalk Hill Vnyd. $14.00	S	B						G	
RODNEY STRONG VINEYARDS '93, Sonoma Co. $11.00		S	B				B		
VENTANA VINEYARDS & WINERY '91, Monterey, Gold Stripe $12.00			B				S	B	
WENTE BROS. WINERY '92, Arroyo Seco, Riva Ranch $13.00			B					B	S
WILDHURST VINEYARDS '93, Sonoma Co., Reserve $12.00						S	B		S
WINDSOR VINEYARDS '93, Russian River, Preston Ranch $12.50				S			S		B
YORK MOUNTAIN WINERY '93, San Luis Obispo $12.00		B					S		B
Z D WINES '93, California $22.00		S					G	G	
ZACA MESA WINERY '93, S. Barbara, Chapel Vnyd. $18.00						B	S	B	
2 AWARDS									
ALDERBROOK WINERY '93, Dry Creek Vly. $10.00	S		B						
ARMIDA WINERY '93, Russian River Vly., Reserve $18.00			S		S				

Chardonnay

2 AWARDS

L.A.	Orange	Farmers	San Fran	Dallas	State Fair	New World	W. Coast	San Diego	Chardonnay
	G	B							**ATLAS PEAK VINEYARD** '93, Napa Vly., Atlas Peak Dist. $16.00
	B	S							**BANDIERA WINERY** '94, Napa Vly. $8.00
		B					B		**BELVEDERE WINERY** '93, Russian River Vly. $13.00
		S	B						**BELVEDERE WINERY** '93, Sonoma Co., Preferred Stock $18.00
		B					B		**DAVID BRUCE WINERY** '92, Santa Cruz Mtns., Est. Reserve $30.00
	B						B		**DAVID BRUCE WINERY** '92, Santa Cruz Mtns., Estate $20.00
				B				B	**DAVIS BYNUM WINERY** '93, Russ. Riv., Allen/McIlroy Vnyd. $17.00
	G			B					**BYRON VINEYARD & WINERY** '92, Santa Maria Vly., Est. $25.00
			S		S				**CALLAWAY VINEYARD & WINERY** '93, Temecula, Calla-Lees $10.00
	B	B							**CASTORO CELLARS** '93, San Luis Obispo $10.00
		S						S	**CHALK HILL WINERY** '92, Chalk Hill, Estate $19.00
		S				B			**CHATEAU ST. JEAN** '93, Sonoma Co. $12.00
			B			B			**CRESTON VINEYARDS** '93, Paso Robles, Estate $10.00
B	B								**DORE WINES** '94, California $7.00
				S			S		**DOUGLASS HILL WINERY** '93, Napa Vly $15.00
	B				B				**EDMEADES ESTATE WINERY** '93, Anderson Vly., Dennison Vnyd. $20.00
		S					B		**GARY FARRELL** '93, Russian River, Westside Farms $18.00
B			G						**THOMAS FOGARTY WINERY** '92, Santa Cruz Mtns., Reserve $18.00
	B		B						**FRANCISCAN OAKVILLE ESTATE** '93, Napa Vly., Cuvee Sauvage $30.00
		S			G				**GEYSER PEAK WINERY** '94, Sonoma Co. $10.00

Chardonnay

2 AWARDS	L.A.	Orange	Farmers	San Fran	Dallas	State Fair	New World	W. Coast	San Diego
GRGICH HILLS CELLAR '92, Napa Vly. $24.00		B					B		
GUENOC WINERY '93, Genevieve Magoon, Res. $25.00						G		B	
GUENOC WINERY '93, Guenoc Vly., Estate $14.00	B						S		
HUSCH VINEYARDS '93, Mendocino $11.50			G				S		
JANKRIS VINEYARD '93, Paso Robles $10.00		S	B						
KENWOOD VINEYARDS '93, Sonoma Vly., Beltane Ranch $18.00	S		B						
KINDERWOOD '94, Monterey Co. $6.00	B	S							
KORBEL CHAMPAGNE CELLARS '92, Sonoma Co. $15.00			S						B
KUNDE ESTATE WINERY '94, Sonoma Vly. $14.00		S							S
LA CREMA '93, California, Reserve $12.50		B		B					
LANDMARK VINEYARDS '93, Sonoma Co. $11.00	S							S	
LEEWARD WINERY '93, Central Coast $11.00			S			B			
LOCKWOOD VINEYARD '92, Monterey $14.00							S		G
J. LOHR WINERY '93, Monterey, Riverstone $12.00							S	B	
MERIDIAN VINEYARDS '93, Santa Barbara Co. $10.00						S	B		
MIRASSOU VINEYARDS '92, Monterey Co., Harvest Res. $12.00			B					S	
MONTPELLIER VINEYARDS '93, California $8.00							S	S	
MOUNT MADRONA WINERY '92, Napa Vly. $14.00		S							B
MURPHY-GOODE ESTATE WINERY '93, Alexander Vly. $11.00			S					S	

L.A.	Orange	Farmers	San Fran	Dallas	State Fair	New World	W. Coast	San Diego	Chardonnay
									2 AWARDS
			B			B			**NAPA CREEK WINERY** '92, Napa Vly. $10.00
					S		B		**NAPA RIDGE WINERY** '94, Central Coast $8.00
					B		B		**NEVADA CITY WINERY** '93, Nevada Co., Barrel Ferm. $10.00
				S			B		**PEJU PROVINCE** '93, Napa Vly., Barrel Ferm. $16.00
				B				S	**RAYMOND VINEYARD & CELLAR** '92, Napa Vly., Reserve $18.00
S							B		**ROUND HILL VINEYARDS** '93, California $8.00
				G			B		**V. SATTUI WINERY** '93, Napa Vly., Carsi Vnyd. $17.50
		B			B				**SEQUOIA GROVE VINEYARDS** '93, Napa Vly., Barrel Sel. $16.00
		B			B				**SEQUOIA GROVE VINEYARDS** '93, Napa Vly., Est. Reserve $18.00
					S		B		**SILVER RIDGE VINEYARDS** '92, California, Barrel Ferm. $10.00
	G	G							**SIMI WINERY** '92, Mendo/Sonoma/Napa $13.00
B						B			**ST. SUPERY VINEYARDS** '93, Napa, Dollarhide Ranch $13.00
			B		G				**J. STONESTREET & SONS** '93, Sonoma Co., Reserve $30.00
	B					B			**SYLVESTER VINEYARDS** '93, Paso Robles, Kiara Reserve $8.00
B					B				**TREFETHEN VINEYARDS** '87, Napa Vly., Library Sel. $30.00
S							B		**M. G. VALLEJO WINERY** '94, California $6.00
		B					B		**VAN ROEKEL VINEYARDS** '94, Temecula, A Boire $8.00
							B	B	**VENTANA VINEYARDS & WINERY** '92, Monterey, Est., Gold Stripe $12.00
G				B					**VICHON WINERY** '93, Napa Vly. $14.00
S	B								**WILD HORSE WINERY** '94, Central Coast $13.00

Chardonnay	L.A.	Orange	Farmers	San Fran	Dallas	State Fair	New World	W. Coast	San Diego
2 AWARDS									
WINDSOR VINEYARDS '92, Alex. Vly., Murphy Ranch $12.00							B		S
WINDWALKER VINEYARD '94, El Dorado, Est. $9.00			B						S
ZACA MESA WINERY '94, Santa Barbara, Zaca Vnyd. $13.00				S		B			
STEPHEN ZELLERBACH VINEYARD '94, Calif., Robert Alison Vnyd. $8.00								B	S
STEPHEN ZELLERBACH VINEYARD '94, California $8.00						B			G

Chenin Blanc

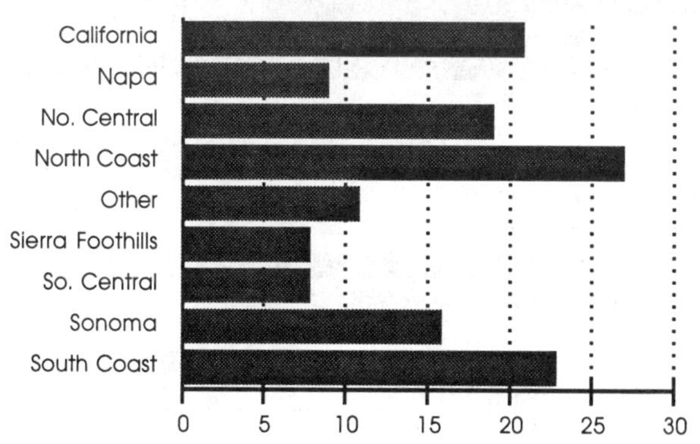

Regional Comparison of Total Points

(Gold-plus=7 Gold=5 Silver=3 Bronze=1)

Highest individual wine totals

Points	Wine
27	**HUSCH VINEYARDS** '94, Mendocino Co., La Ribera, $8.00
13	**CALLAWAY VINEYARD & WINERY** '94, Temecula, $6.00
10	**BARON HERZOG WINE CELLARS** '94, Clarksburg, $6.00
10	**MAURICE CAR'RIE WINERY** '94, Temecula, Soft, $5.00
10	**DRY CREEK VINEYARD** '93, California, $7.00
9	**DRY CREEK VINEYARD** '94, Sonoma Co., $7.00
7	**WINDSOR VINEYARDS** '93, Alexander Vly., $7.00
6	**BERINGER VINEYARDS** '93, Napa Vly., $7.50
6	**MIRASSOU VINEYARDS** '93, Monterey, Family Selection, $6.00
6	**VENTANA VINEYARDS & WINERY** '93, Monterey, Estate, $8.00

Chenin Blanc

Wine	L.A.	Orange	Farmers	San Fran	Dallas	State Fair	New World	W. Coast	San Diego
9 AWARDS									
HUSCH VINEYARDS '94, Mendocino Co., La Ribera $8.00	B	G	G	B	S	S	S	G	B
6 AWARDS									
BARON HERZOG WINE CELLARS '94, Clarksburg $6.00	B	B	B	B		S	S		
5 AWARDS									
CALLAWAY VINEYARD & WINERY '94, Temecula $6.00	S					S	S	S	B
4 AWARDS									
MAURICE CAR'RIE WINERY '94, Temecula, Soft $5.00		S					S	B	S
DRY CREEK VINEYARD '93, California $7.00					B		G	B	S
3 AWARDS									
DRY CREEK VINEYARD '94, Sonoma Co. $7.00	B		B			Σ			
R. H. PHILLIPS VINEYARD '93, California, Dry $5.00	B				B			B	
WINDSOR VINEYARDS '93, Alexander Vly. $7.00			S			B		S	
2 AWARDS									
BERINGER VINEYARDS '93, Napa Vly. $7.50			G		B				
DE MOOR WINERY '93, Napa Vly. $8.00			B						B
DURNEY VINEYARDS '93, Carmel Vly., Estate $9.00	B								B
HACIENDA WINERY '94, California, Clare De Lune $7.00			B			S			
MASTANTUONO WINERY '94, Central Coast $6.00		B				S			
MIRASSOU VINEYARDS '93, Monterey, Family Selection $6.00								S	S
MISSION CANYON CELLARS '93, Santa Barbara $5.50	B	B							
SUTTER HOME WINERY '93, California $4.50	B						B		
VENTANA VINEYARDS & WINERY '93, Monterey, Estate $8.00			S				S		

L.A.	Orange	Farmers	San Fran	Dallas	State Fair	New World	W. Coast	San Diego	Chenin Blanc
									2 AWARDS
		B						B	**WINDWALKER VINEYARD** '93, El Dorado, Estate $6.00

ADLER FELS

1993 SONOMA COUNTY

GEWÜRZTRAMINER

ALCOHOL 11.9% BY VOLUME

1994

GEYSER PEAK

GEWÜRZTRAMINER

NORTH COAST

ALC. 12.3% BY VOL

Gewurztraminer

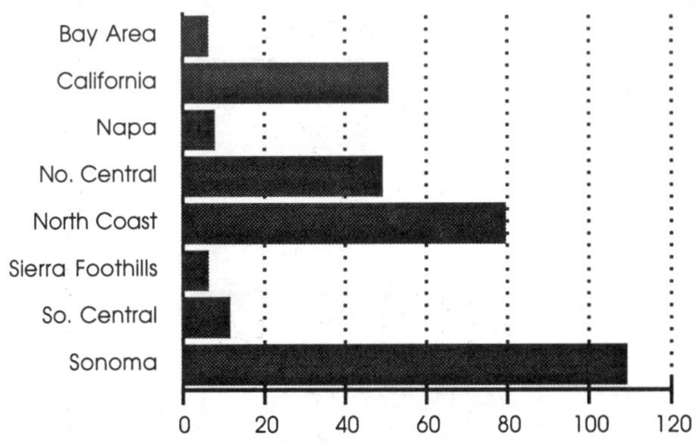

Regional Comparison of Total Points

(Gold-plus=7 Gold=5 Silver=3 Bronze=1)

Highest individual wine totals

28	**ADLER FELS** '94, Sonoma Co., $10.00
23	**GEYSER PEAK WINERY** '94, North Coast, $6.00
20	**FETZER VINEYARDS** '94, California, $7.00
20	**THOMAS FOGARTY WINERY** '94, Monterey, Ventana Vnyd., $12.00
18	**BARGETTO WINERY** '94, Monterey, $9.00
17	**DE LOACH VINEYARDS** '94, Russian River Vly., Est., LH, $14.00
16	**LOUIS M. MARTINI** '93, Russian River Vly., $9.00
15	**NAVARRO VINEYARDS** '93, Anderson Vly., $10.00
9	**FORESTVILLE VINEYARD** '93, California, $5.50
9	**GUNDLACH-BUNDSCHU WINERY** '94, Sonoma, Rhinefarm Vnyd., $8.00
9	**HANDLEY CELLARS** '94, Anderson Vly., $9.00

Gewurztraminer

0 - 3.3 Residual Sugar

	L.A.	Orange	Farmers	San Fran	Dallas	State Fair	New World	W. Coast	San Diego
8 AWARDS									
ADLER FELS '94, Sonoma Co. $10.00		B	S	G	B	G	B	G	Σ
BARGETTO WINERY '94, Monterey $9.00	B	B	S	B		S	S	G	B
FETZER VINEYARDS '94, California $7.00	S	B	S	B	B	G	S		S
7 AWARDS									
GEYSER PEAK WINERY '94, North Coast $6.00	S	G	G		B		S	B	G
6 AWARDS									
DE LOACH VINEYARDS '94, Russian River, Early Harvest $8.00	B	B	B			B		S	B
THOMAS FOGARTY WINERY '94, Monterey, Ventana Vnyd. $12.00	G	B		S		B	S	Σ	
HUSCH VINEYARDS '94, Anderson Vly., Estate $9.00	B	B	B				B	S	B
5 AWARDS									
BARGETTO WINERY '94, Santa Cruz Mtns., Barrel Ferm. $10.00	B	B	B					S	B
NAVARRO VINEYARDS '93, Anderson Vly. $10.00	S		S			S	S	S	
4 AWARDS									
BERINGER VINEYARDS '94, California $8.00	S		B			S		B	
LOUIS M. MARTINI '93, Russian River Vly. $9.00		B	G		S		Σ		
3 AWARDS									
ALDERBROOK WINERY '94, Russian River Vly. $8.00	B		B			S			
ALPEN CELLARS '94, California $6.00	B					B		S	
EDMEADES ESTATE WINERY '94, Anderson Vly. $13.00		B		B				S	
FORESTVILLE VINEYARD '93, California $5.50			G				S	B	
GUNDLACH-BUNDSCHU WINERY '94, Sonoma, Rhinefarm Vnyd. $8.00		S		S				S	
HANDLEY CELLARS '94, Anderson Vly. $9.00	S							G	B

Gewurztraminer

0 - 3.3 Residual Sugar

L.A.	Orange	Farmers	San Fran	Dallas	State Fair	New World	W. Coast	San Diego	Wine
3 AWARDS									
		S					B	B	**WINDSOR VINEYARDS** '94, Sonoma Co., Winemaster Sel. $7.00
2 AWARDS									
B	G								**ALDERBROOK WINERY** '94, Russian River, Barrel Ferm. $10.00
		B						B	**CHATEAU ST. JEAN** '93, Sonoma Co. $8.00
B			S						**CHOUINARD VINEYARD** '94, Monterey $8.00
	S		S						**CONCANNON VINEYARD** '94, Arroyo Seco, Ltd. Bottling $8.00
		G			S				**COSENTINO WINERY** '94, Napa Vly., Estate $12.00
		B				B			**GRAND CRU VINEYARDS** '93, California $7.00
				B		S			**HANDLEY CELLARS** '93, Anderson Vly. $8.00
		B					B		**KENDALL-JACKSON WINERY** '94, California, Vintner's Reserve $10.00
	B					B			**MILL CREEK VINEYARDS** '94, North Coast $8.00
G			B						**NAPA RIDGE WINERY** '94, Central Coast $5.00
				B				B	**NAPA RIDGE WINERY** '93, Central Coast $5.00
B								S	**STONESTREET WINERY** '93, Anderson Vly. $13.00

Gewurztraminer

9.1+ Residual Sugar

L.A.	Orange	Farmers	San Fran	Dallas	State Fair	New World	W. Coast	San Diego	Wine
7 AWARDS									
B	S	S			Σ	B	B	B	**DE LOACH VINEYARDS** '94, Russian River Vly., LH, R.S. 13.5 $14.00
3 AWARDS									
		B				G		B	**CHATEAU ST. JEAN** '92, Johnson Vnyd. SLH, R.S. 21.4 $17.00
2 AWARDS									
			B	G					**HUSCH VINEYARDS** '93, Anderson Vly., LH, R.S. 16.0 $14.00

1994

GEYSER PEAK

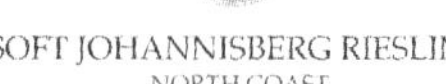

SOFT JOHANNISBERG RIESLING

NORTH COAST

ALC. 9.8% BY VOL.

Johannisberg Riesling

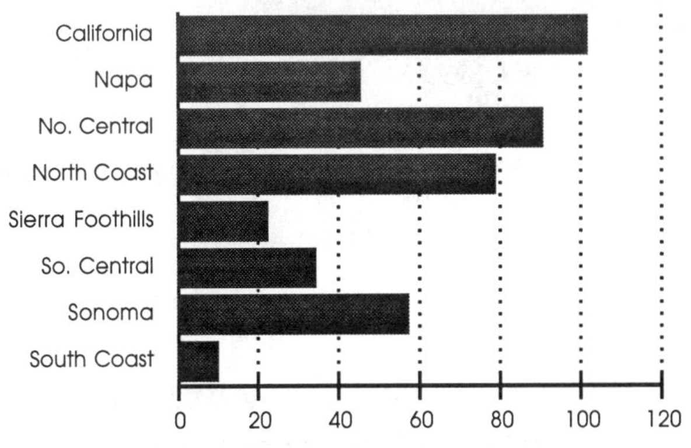

Regional Comparison of Total Points

(Gold-plus=7 Gold=5 Silver=3 Bronze=1)

Highest individual wine totals

26 **J. LOHR WINERY**
'93, Monterey, B. Mist, LH, $10.00

22 **GEYSER PEAK WINERY**
'94, North Coast, Soft, $6.00

20 **KENDALL-JACKSON WINERY**
'93, California, SLH, $15.00

18 **GAINEY VINEYARD**
'94, Santa Ynez Vly., $8.00

18 **GEYSER PEAK WINERY**
'93, Russian River Vly., LH, $16.00

18 **NAVARRO VINEYARDS**
'93, Anderson Vly., LHCS, $20.00

18 **V. SATTUI WINERY**
'94, Napa Vly., Dry, $10.00

17 **BERINGER VINEYARDS**
'94, California, $8.00

16 **FETZER VINEYARDS**
'94, California, $7.00

16 **GEYSER PEAK WINERY**
'94, Russian River Vly., LH, $16.00

16 **KENDALL-JACKSON WINERY**
'93, California, Vintner's Reserve, $10.00

Johannisberg Riesling

0 - 3.0 Residual Sugar

Winery	L.A.	Orange	Farmers	San Fran	Dallas	State Fair	New World	W. Coast	San Diego
8 AWARDS									
GEYSER PEAK WINERY '94, North Coast, Soft $6.00	B	G	Σ	B	S		S	B	B
6 AWARDS									
KENDALL-JACKSON WINERY '93, California, Vintner's Reserve $10.00			B		S	Σ	B	S	B
J. LOHR WINERY '94, Monterey, Bay Mist $7.00		B			S	B	B	S	S
V. SATTUI WINERY '94, Napa Vly., Dry $10.00	G		S	S		S		S	B
5 AWARDS									
BERINGER VINEYARDS '94, California $8.00		S	B	S		S			Σ
HAGAFEN CELLARS '94, Napa Vly. $9.00		B	S			B	B	G	
4 AWARDS									
CONCANNON VINEYARD '94, Arroyo Seco, Sel. Vnyd. $8.00		B	B					S	S
GAINEY VINEYARD '94, Santa Ynez Vly. $8.00		B	G				Σ		G
GREENWOOD RIDGE VINEYARDS '93, Anderson Vly., Estate $8.50		S	B				B	G	
KENDALL-JACKSON WINERY '94, California, Vintner's Reserve $10.00		G	B					B	S
3 AWARDS									
MAURICE CAR'RIE WINERY '94, Temecula $6.00	B		S						B
CHATEAU ST. JEAN '93, Sonoma Co. $8.00			B				B		S
FIRESTONE VINEYARD '93, Santa Ynez Vly. $11.00			B	S				B	
JEKEL VINEYARDS '93, Arroyo Seco, Gravelstone $6.00					S	S	B		
MOUNT KONOCTI '94, Lake Co., White $8.00			S					B	B
PARAISO SPRINGS VINEYARDS '93, Santa Lucia Highlands $7.00			B		B				S
PERRY CREEK VINEYARDS '94, El Dorado $6.00	G					B			S

Johannisberg Riesling

0 - 3.0 Residual Sugar

L.A.	Orange	Farmers	San Fran	Dallas	State Fair	New World	W. Coast	San Diego	Winery
									3 AWARDS
		S				S		B	**VENTANA VINEYARDS & WINERY** '93, Monterey White Riesling $8.00
	S	S						B	**WINDSOR VINEYARDS** '94, Le Baron Vnyd., Est. $7.00
									2 AWARDS
B	S								**CHOUINARD VINEYARD** '94, Monterey $8.00
	B	B							**MADRONA VINEYARDS** '93, El Dorado $7.00
		B				B			**MADRONA VINEYARDS** '92, El Dorado $6.75
	S					B			**NAVARRO VINEYARDS** '93, Anderson Vly. $8.50
	B						B		**OBESTER** '94, Mendocino Co. $7.00
S					S				**RANCHO SISQUOC WINERY** '94, Santa Maria Vly. $8.00
			Σ		B				**V. SATTUI WINERY** '94, Napa Vly., Off Dry $10.00
		B				S			**TEMECULA CREST WINERY** '93, Temecula

Johannisberg Riesling

L.A.	Orange	Farmers	San Fran	Dallas	State Fair	New World	W. Coast	San Diego	Winery
									6 AWARDS
	G	S	B		S		S	B	**FETZER VINEYARDS** '94, California, R.S. 3.1 $7.00
									3 AWARDS
B	G						S		**CONCANNON VINEYARD** '92, Anderson Vly., LH, R.S. 6.9 $9.50
									2 AWARDS
	S					B			**GRAND CRU VINEYARDS** '93, California, R.S. 3.8 $7.00

Johannisberg Riesling

9.1+ Residual Sugar

Winery	L.A.	Orange	Farmers	San Fran	Dallas	State Fair	New World	W. Coast	San Diego
6 AWARDS									
GEYSER PEAK WINERY '94, Russian River Vly., LH, R.S. 19.4 $16.00	G		B	Σ			B	B	B
GEYSER PEAK WINERY '93, Russian River Vly., LH, R.S. 18.5 $16.00			G		B	S	B	B	Σ
KENDALL-JACKSON WINERY '93, California, SLH, R.S. 13.5 $15.00			G	G	B		S	G	B
J. LOHR WINERY '93, Monterey, B. Mist, LH, R.S. 14.4 $10.00	S	G		Σ			S	G	S
5 AWARDS									
WENTE BROS. WINERY '93, Arroyo Seco Vnyd., R.S. 13.6 $18.00			B	B		B		B	B
4 AWARDS									
BARON HERZOG WINE CELLARS '94, Monterey Co., LH, R.S. 15.4 $14.00	G	B		B		S			
NAVARRO VINEYARDS '93, Anderson Vly., LHCS, R.S. 22.2 $20.00	G	G				S	G		
3 AWARDS									
SANTINO WINES '82, El Dorado, DBS, R.S. 42.0 $30.00	B	S				B			
2 AWARDS									
CHATEAU ST. JEAN '90, Alexander Vly., SSLH, R.S. 25.0 $22.50			B					B	
FETZER VINEYARDS '93, California, Reserve, LH,					G		S		
GRGICH HILLS CELLAR '93, Napa Vly., LH, R.S. 11.0 $50.00				B		S			
SANTINO WINES '89, Sonoma Co., DBSH, R.S. 27.7 $11.00		G				S			

1993
Napa Valley

MERLOT

85% Merlot 10% Cabernet Sauvignon 5% Cabernet Franc

Produced & Bottled by Shafer Vineyards, Napa, CA
Alcohol 13.5% by Volume

ESTATE BOTTLED
RUSSIAN RIVER VALLEY
MERLOT
1993

Merlot

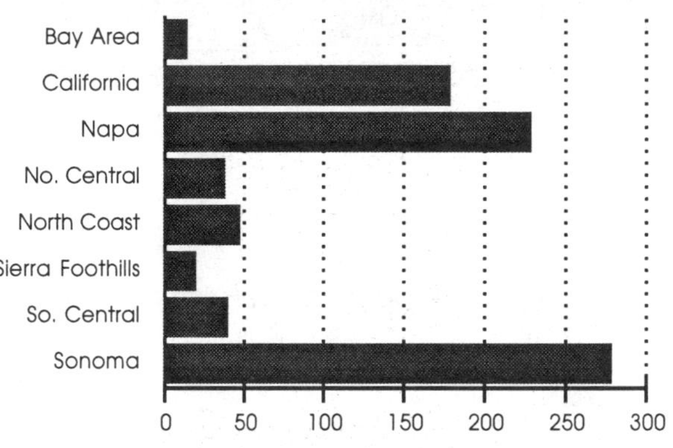

Regional Comparison of Total Points

(Gold-plus=7 Gold=5 Silver=3 Bronze=1)

Highest individual wine totals

23 **SHAFER VINEYARDS**
'93, Napa Vly., $23.00

20 **DE LOACH VINEYARDS**
'93, Russian River Vly., Est., $14.00

17 **GARY FARRELL**
'92, Sonoma Co., Ladi's Vnyd., $20.00

17 **RAYMOND VINEYARD & CELLAR**
'92, Napa Vly., $17.00

17 **RICHARDSON VINEYARDS**
'93, Carneros, Sanciacomo Vnyd., $18.00

16 **BERINGER VINEYARDS**
'91, Howell Mtn., Bancroft Ranch, $28.00

16 **GLEN ELLEN WINERY**
'93, California, Proprietor's Reserve, $5.00

15 **LOUIS M. MARTINI**
'92, North Coast, $9.00

14 **CHATEAU ST. JEAN**
'92, Sonoma Co., $12.00

13 **FOREST GLEN**
'93, California, Barrel Select, $10.00

13 **FRATELLI PERATA WINERY**
'93, Paso Robles, Est., $15.00

13 **KENDALL-JACKSON WINERY**
'92, California, Vintner's Reserve, $15.00

Merlot	L.A.	Orange	Farmers	San Fran	Dallas	State Fair	New World	W. Coast	San Diego
6 AWARDS									
BERINGER VINEYARDS '91, Howell Mtn., Bancroft Ranch $28.00	B		B	B			Σ	S	S
CHATEAU ST. JEAN '92, Sonoma Co. $12.00	B		S	S	S			S	B
DE LOACH VINEYARDS '93, Russian River Vly., Est. $14.00	G		S		B	G	S	S	
5 AWARDS									
GARY FARRELL '92, Sonoma Co., Ladi's Vnyd. $20.00		G		S	S			B	G
FOREST GLEN '93, California, Barrel Select $10.00	Σ		B			B	S	B	
INDIAN SPRINGS VINEYARDS '93, Nevada Co. $12.00	B	B	B					S	B
KENDALL-JACKSON WINERY '92, California, Vintner's Reserve $15.00			S		B		S	S	S
LOUIS M. MARTINI '92, North Coast $9.00		G	B				G	S	B
RAYMOND VINEYARD & CELLAR '92, Napa Vly. $17.00	B	G		S		G		S	
RICHARDSON VINEYARDS '93, Carneros, Sanciacomo Vnyd. $18.00		S		G		S		G	B
SHAFER VINEYARDS '93, Napa Vly. $23.00	S		G	S		Σ		G	
SMITH & HOOK WINERY '92, Santa Lucia Highlands $18.00		B		B		B	G	B	
ST. CLEMENT VINEYARDS '92, Napa Vly. $21.00		B		B		G		B	B
RODNEY STRONG VINEYARDS '92, Sonoma Co. $14.00			B			B	S	B	S
M. G. VALLEJO WINERY '93, California $6.00		G		B		B		S	B
4 AWARDS									
BARGETTO WINERY '93, California $16.00		B				B		B	B
BEL ARBORS VINEYARD '93, California $7.00		B	S				S	S	
BELVEDERE WINERY '92, Sonoma Co. $13.00		B	B				G		S

Merlot

4 AWARDS

L.A.	Orange	Farmers	San Fran	Dallas	State Fair	New World	W. Coast	San Diego	Merlot
S					B	B		B	**DAVIS BYNUM WINERY** '92, Russian River, Laureles Vnyd. $21.00
	S				S	S	B		**CYPRESS VINEYARD** '93, California $9.00
	S				G	G	S		**GLEN ELLEN WINERY** '93, California, Proprietor's Reserve $5.00
	S	B					B	B	**CHARLES KRUG WINERY** '92, Napa Vly. $13.00
	S				B		B	G	**LEEWARD WINERY** '93, Napa Vly. $15.00
	B	S				S	S		**RIVER RUN VINTNERS** '93, California $15.00
B	B			B		S			**RUTHERFORD HILL WINERY** '92, Napa Vly., Reserve XVS $21.00
	B			S		S		B	**STONESTREET WINERY** '92, Alexander Vly. $22.00
	S				B		B	B	**WINDSOR VINEYARDS** '92, Sonoma, Shelton Sig. Series $20.00

3 AWARDS

L.A.	Orange	Farmers	San Fran	Dallas	State Fair	New World	W. Coast	San Diego	Merlot
	S						B	B	**BEAULIEU VINEYARD** '92, Napa Vly., Beautour $8.00
B	G		B						**BENZIGER FAMILY WINERY** '91, Sonoma Mtn., Est. $16.00
			B				B	B	**CANYON ROAD CELLARS** '93, California $8.00
B						B	B		**CRESTON VINEYARDS** '92, Paso Robles $13.00
B	B				Σ				**FETZER VINEYARDS** '93, Mendocino, Barrel Select $12.00
		G	S					G	**FRATELLI PERATA WINERY** '93, Paso Robles, Est. $15.00
	G	B					S		**GRAND CRU VINEYARDS** '93, California $8.00
S			S		S				**HANNA WINERY** '93, Alexander Vly. $16.00
		Σ				S	B		**KENDALL-JACKSON WINERY** '92, California, Grand Reserve $30.00
	B					G		S	**KENWOOD VINEYARDS** '92, Jack London Vnyd. $18.00

Merlot	L.A.	Orange	Farmers	San Fran	Dallas	State Fair	New World	W. Coast	San Diego
3 AWARDS									
LAMBERT BRIDGE WINERY '93, Sonoma Co. $15.00		S				G		S	
MIETZ CELLARS '93, Sonoma Co. $16.50		B	B					S	
NAPA RIDGE WINERY '92, North Coast $9.00		B	S					S	
PARDUCCI WINE CELLARS '93, North Coast $8.00		B		B		B			
RABBIT RIDGE VINEYARDS '92, Carneros, Sangiacomo Vnyd. $15.00			Σ		S		B		
ST. FRANCIS VINEYARDS '92, Sonoma Vly. $18.00		S				G		S	
ST. SUPERY VINEYARDS '92, Napa Vly., Dollarhide Ranch $14.50			B	B				S	
STEVENOT WINERY '93, Sierra Foothills, Reserve $10.00		B			B				G
SWANSON VINEYARDS '92, Napa Vly., Est. $16.00		G	B						B
VILLA MT. EDEN '92, Napa Vly., Grand Reserve $14.00		B					S	S	
VOSS VINEYARDS '92, Napa Vly. $14.00		S			S		B		
WELLINGTON VINEYARDS '92, Sonoma Co. $15.00		G						B	S
2 AWARDS									
ARMIDA WINERY '92, Russian River Vly.							B		B
AZALEA SPRINGS '92, Napa Vly. $22.00		B		S					
BENZIGER FAMILY WINERY '93, Sonoma Co. $14.00		S				S			
BENZIGER FAMILY WINERY '92, Sonoma Co. $14.00					S		B		
BLACKSTONE '93, Napa Vly., Reserve $10.00	B	G							
BLOSSOM HILL WINERY 'NV, California $4.00						B			B
BOGLE VINEYARDS '93, California $8.00		B					S		

Merlot

2 AWARDS

L.A.	Orange	Farmers	San Fran	Dallas	State Fair	New World	W. Coast	San Diego	Merlot
	B							B	**BRUTOCAO CELLARS** '93, Mendocino Co., Estate $15.00
						B	S		**BUENA VISTA** '92, Sonoma, Carneros, Est. $13.00
							B	B	**MAURICE CAR'RIE WINERY** '93, California $9.00
B	S								**CHATEAU JULIEN** '93, Monterey Co., Reserve $10.00
		B					B		**CHATEAU SOUVERAIN** '93, Alexander Vly. $13.00
	S			S					**CLOS DU BOIS** '92, Sonoma Co. $15.00
			B					G	**CRESTON VINEYARDS** '93, Paso Robles $13.00
							B	S	**DEER VALLEY VINEYARDS** '93, California $5.00
		S		B					**DUNNEWOOD VINEYARD** '92, North Coast $8.00
					S			S	**FETZER VINEYARDS** '93, California, Eagle Peak $8.00
					G		B		**FIRESTONE VINEYARD** '93, Santa Ynez Vly. $12.00
						S	B		**FORESTVILLE VINEYARD** '93, California $6.00
S							B		**GEYSER PEAK WINERY** '93, Alexander Vly. $12.00
		S					B		**GOLDEN CREEK VINEYARD** '92, Sonoma Co., Reserve $15.00
				B			B		**GUNDLACH-BUNDSCHU WINERY** '92, Sonoma Vly., Rhinefarm Vnyd. $16.00
		B					S		**HACIENDA WINERY** '93, California $7.50
			B					B	**JAEGER CELLAR** '89, Napa Vly., Inglewood Vnyd. $18.00
					S		S		**TOBIN JAMES CELLARS** '93, Paso Robles, Midnight $15.00
	B				S				**KENDALL-JACKSON WINERY** '93, California, Vintner's Reserve $15.00
B	S								**KINDERWOOD** '93, California $6.00

Merlot	L.A.	Orange	Farmers	San Fran	Dallas	State Fair	New World	W. Coast	San Diego
2 AWARDS									
LAVA CAP WINERY '93, El Dorado, Est. $14.00	B					S			
MONTICELLO VINEYARDS '92, Napa, Corley Fam, Vnyds. $18.00		S							S
MONTPELLIER VINEYARDS '93, California $8.00			S				B		
POPPY HILL CELLARS '93, Napa Vly., Founder's Sel. $11.00		B				B			
PRIDE MOUNTAIN VINEYARDS '93, Napa Vly. $20.00				S		B			
QUAIL RIDGE CELLARS '91, Napa Vly. $14.00				S					B
ROUND HILL VINEYARDS '93, California $8.00		B				Σ			
ROUND HILL VINEYARDS '92, Napa Vly., Reserve $13.00								B	S
SEBASTIANI VINEYARDS '93, Sonoma Co. $11.00								B	S
SILVER RIDGE VINEYARDS '92, California $10.00							B	S	
SILVERADO VINEYARDS '92, Napa Vly. $17.00					B	B			
STORRS WINERY '93, San Ysidro Dist. $17.00				S		G			
TRUCHARD VINEYARDS '92, Carneros $18.00		G				S			
VICHON WINERY '92, Napa Vly. $18.00				B		S			
WHITEHALL LANE WINERY '93, Napa Vly., Leonardini Vnyd. $28.00				G		S			
WHITEHALL LANE WINERY '92, Knight's Vly. $16.00		G						Σ	
WINDSOR VINEYARDS '93, Sonoma Co., Reserve $14.00	B			S					

Guenoc

PETITE SIRAH

NORTH COAST

1991

LILLIE LANGTRY

PROPRIETOR 1888-1906

ALC. 12.5% BY VOL.

Petite Sirah

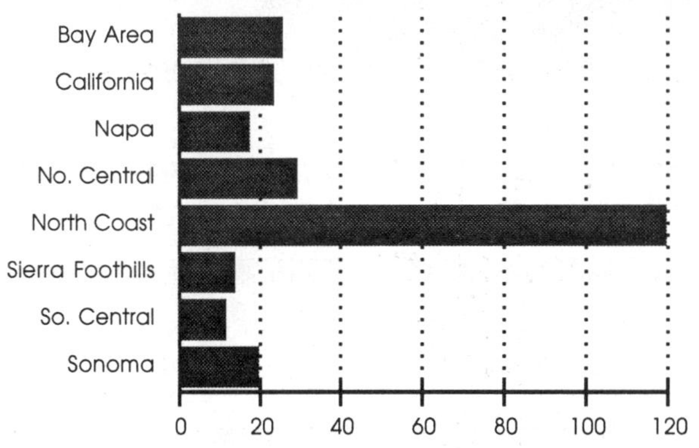

Regional Comparison of Total Points

(Gold-plus=7 Gold=5 Silver=3 Bronze=1)

Highest individual wine totals

30 **GUENOC WINERY**
'91, North Coast, $13.00

21 **FETZER VINEYARDS**
'91, Mendocino Co., Reserve, $13.00

21 **GUENOC WINERY**
'92, North Coast, $13.00

16 **STORRS WINERY**
'93, Santa Cruz Mtns., $16.00

15 **WINDSOR VINEYARDS**
'92, North Coast, $10.00

12 **CHRISTOPHER CREEK**
'91, Russian River Vly., $13.00

11 **BOGLE VINEYARDS**
'93, California, $7.00

11 **CONCANNON VINEYARD**
'93, Central Coast, Sel. Vnyd., $10.00

11 **IMAGERY SERIES**
'92, Paso Robles, Shell Creek, $16.00

10 **CONCANNON VINEYARD**
'92, Livermore, Est. Reserve, $10.00

Petite Sirah

Wine	L.A.	Orange	Farmers	San Fran	Dallas	State Fair	New World	W. Coast	San Diego
8 AWARDS									
GUENOC WINERY '91, North Coast $13.00	Σ	G	B	S	S	S	Σ	B	
7 AWARDS									
FETZER VINEYARDS '91, Mendocino Co., Reserve $13.00	B	G		B		S	S	B	Σ
6 AWARDS									
CONCANNON VINEYARD '92, Livermore, Est. Reserve $10.00	B	B			B	B	S	S	
MIRASSOU VINEYARDS '92, Monterey, Family Sel. $9.00	B	B	B	B				S	B
5 AWARDS									
BOGLE VINEYARDS '93, California $7.00	B	B	Σ			B	B		
CONCANNON VINEYARD '93, Central Coast, Sel. Vnyd. $10.00	B		B	S				S	S
GUENOC WINERY '92, North Coast $13.00	S		G	G		G		S	
WINDSOR VINEYARDS '92, North Coast $10.00	B	S		S				G	S
4 AWARDS									
DAVID BRUCE WINERY '92, California, Vintner's Select $10.00			B				B	B	S
CHRISTOPHER CREEK '91, Russian River Vly. $13.00				S	S	S	S		
CILURZO VINEYARD '94, Temecula $7.00	B	B	B			B			
FOPPIANO VINEYARDS '92, Sonoma Co. $10.00		B				B	B	B	
STORRS WINERY '93, Santa Cruz Mtns. $16.00		S		S		G		G	
3 AWARDS									
DEER PARK WINERY '91, Napa Vly., Howell Mtn. $16.00	B			S					B
GRANITE SPRINGS WINERY '93, El Dorado $10.00	B	S		B					
IMAGERY SERIES '92, Paso Robles, Shell Creek $16.00	S	S			G				
KONRAD ESTATE WINERY '91, Mendocino Co., Est. $11.50		S					S		B

Petite Sirah

L.A.	Orange	Farmers	San Fran	Dallas	State Fair	New World	W. Coast	San Diego	Petite Sirah
									3 AWARDS
		B				B		B	**TRENTADUE WINERY** '92, Sonoma Co. $11.00
									2 AWARDS
							G	S	**FOPPIANO VINEYARDS** '91, Napa, Le Grande Reserve $19.50
				B		B			**LOUIS M. MARTINI** '91, Napa Vly., Reserve
	G		S						**MIRASSOU VINEYARDS** '92, Monterey, Anniversary Sel. $13.50
B							B		**MONTERRA WINERY** '91, Monterey $10.00
	G					B			**PARDUCCI WINE CELLARS** '92, Mendocino Co. $7.00
			S	S					**PARDUCCI WINE CELLARS** '91, Mendocino Co. $7.00

WILD HORSE™
1994
PINOT BLANC
MONTEREY
PRODUCED AND BOTTLED BY WILD HORSE
TEMPLETON, CALIFORNIA BW 5169 ALC. 13.0% BY VOL.

Pinot Blanc

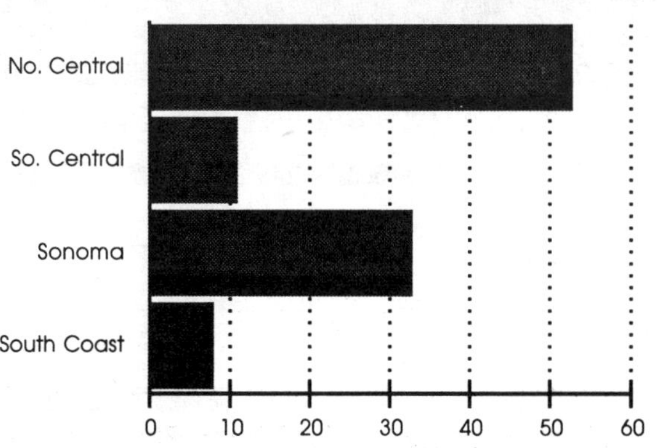

Regional Comparison of Total Points

(Gold-plus=7 Gold=5 Silver=3 Bronze=1)

Highest individual wine totals

19	**WILD HORSE WINERY** '94, Monterey, $13.00
13	**IMAGERY SERIES** '93, Sonoma Mtn., $16.00
10	**LOCKWOOD VINEYARD** '93, Monterey, $10.00
9	**MIRASSOU VINEYARDS** '93, Monterey, Wt. Burgundy, $7.00
8	**J. FRITZ WINERY** '94, Russian River Vly., Melon, $10.00
8	**VAN ROEKEL VINEYARDS** '93, Temecula, $8.00
5	**MURPHY-GOODE ESTATE WINERY** '93, Alexander Vly., Melon De Bourgogne
4	**MAKOR WINERY** '94, Santa Barbara, Bien Nacido, $11.00
4	**MURPHY-GOODE ESTATE WINERY** '94, Alexander Vly., Est., $12.00
4	**VILLA MT. EDEN** '93, Santa Maria, Grand Res., $14.00

Pinot Blanc	L.A.	Orange	Farmers	San Fran	Dallas	State Fair	New World	W. Coast	San Diego
6 AWARDS									
VAN ROEKEL VINEYARDS '93, Temecula $8.00		B	B	B	B	S	B		
5 AWARDS									
IMAGERY SERIES '93, Sonoma Mtn. $16.00	B	G		S	B		S		
MIRASSOU VINEYARDS '93, Monterey, Wt. Burgundy $7.00	B	G	B					B	B
WILD HORSE WINERY '94, Monterey $13.00	B	G	G	B					Σ
4 AWARDS									
LOCKWOOD VINEYARD '93, Monterey $10.00	S	B					S	S	
2 AWARDS									
THOMAS COYNE WINERY '94, Central Coast, Sunol Vnyd. $10.00		B				B			
J. FRITZ WINERY '94, Russian River Vly., Melon $10.00	G			S					
MAKOR WINERY '94, Santa Barbara, Bien Nacido $11.00	S	B							
MIRASSOU VINEYARDS '93, Monterey, Harvest Reserve $12.00	B		B						
MURPHY-GOODE ESTATE WINERY '94, Alexander Vly., Est. $12.00				B		S			
VILLA MT. EDEN '93, Santa Maria, Grand Res. $14.00	B					S			

1992

David Bruce

Santa Cruz Mountains

Pinot Noir

PRODUCED AND BOTTLED BY DAVID BRUCE WINERY
21439 BEAR CREEK RD., LOS GATOS, CA 95030 • (800) 397-9972
ALCOHOL 13% BY VOLUME • CONTAINS SULFITES • 750 ML

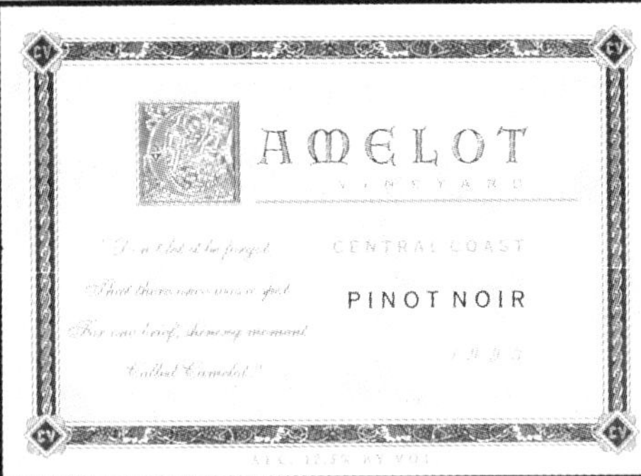

Pinot Noir

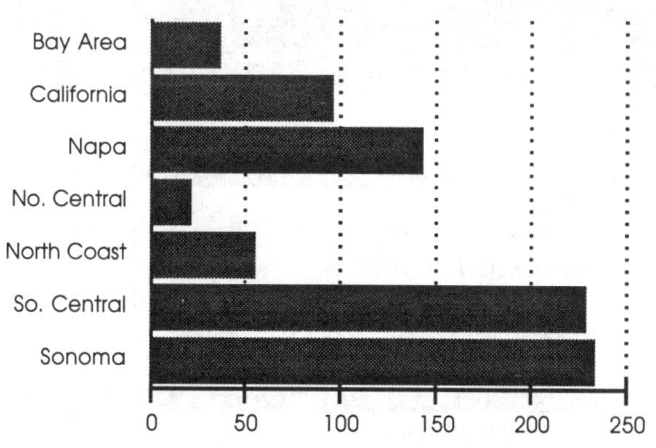

Regional Comparison of Total Points

(Gold-plus=7 Gold=5 Silver=3 Bronze=1)

Highest individual wine totals

25 **DAVID BRUCE WINERY**
'92, Santa Cruz Mtns., Est. Reserve, $35.00

23 **CAMELOT VINEYARD**
'93, Central Coast, $12.00

22 **VILLA MT. EDEN**
'93, Los Carneros, Grand Reserve, $14.00

21 **DAVIS BYNUM WINERY**
'92, Russian River Vly., Ltd. Edition, $28.00

20 **GARY FARRELL**
'93, Santa Barbara, Bien Nacido, $28.00

20 **KENDALL-JACKSON WINERY**
'93, California, Grand Reserve, $30.00

20 **FESS PARKER WINERY**
'93, Santa Barbara Co., Reserve, $20.00

18 **CHATEAU ST. JEAN**
'92, Sonoma Co., $15.00

18 **DE LOACH VINEYARDS**
'92, Russian River Vly., O.F.S., $25.00

18 **LA CREMA**
'93, California, Grand Cuvee, $20.00

18 **STONESTREET WINERY**
'92, Sonoma Co., $21.00

Pinot Noir	L.A.	Orange	Farmers	San Fran	Dallas	State Fair	New World	W. Coast	San Diego
9 AWARDS									
DAVID BRUCE WINERY '92, Santa Cruz Mtns., Est. Reserve $35.00	S	G	S	G	B	S	S	B	B
8 AWARDS									
GARY FARRELL '93, Santa Barbara, Bien Nacido $28.00	B	G	S	S	B	S		B	S
KENDALL-JACKSON WINERY '93, California, Grand Reserve $30.00	S		B	S	B	S	S	S	S
FESS PARKER WINERY '93, Santa Barbara Co., Reserve $20.00	S	S	S	S	B	S	S		B
7 AWARDS									
BENZIGER FAMILY WINERY '92, California $14.00	S		S	S	B	S	B		B
DAVIS BYNUM WINERY '92, Russian River Vly., Ltd. Edition $28.00		B	S		S	S	G	S	S
DAVIS BYNUM WINERY '92, Russian River, Le Pinot $32.00		S	B	B	B	Σ	B		B
CAMELOT VINEYARD '93, Central Coast $12.00	G	G	B		G	S		S	B
6 AWARDS									
DAVID BRUCE WINERY '93, Sonoma Co., Vintner's Select $13.00		S	B			S	B	B	Σ
DE LOACH VINEYARDS '92, Russian River Vly., O.F.S. $25.00	G	B	B				G	S	S
LA CREMA '93, California, Grand Cuvee $20.00			B	S	S	Σ	B		S
FESS PARKER WINERY '93, Santa Barbara Co. $15.00		S		S	B	G	S		B
STONESTREET WINERY '92, Sonoma Co. $21.00		S	B	S		S	G		S
VILLA MT. EDEN '93, Los Carneros, Grand Reserve $14.00		G	B	Σ	S		G	B	
5 AWARDS									
CARNEROS CREEK WINERY '93, Los Carneros $15.00	B	B		S	B	S			
ELKHORN PEAK WINERY '93, Napa, Fagan Creek Vnyds. $21.00		G	S	S			B		B
GARY FARRELL '93, Russian River Vly. $17.00		B		S		S		B	B

Pinot Noir

L.A.	Orange	Farmers	San Fran	Dallas	State Fair	New World	W. Coast	San Diego	Wine
									5 AWARDS
			B	B		S	B	S	**KENDALL-JACKSON WINERY** '93, California, Vintner's Reserve $9.00
	B	B	B			B	B		**LA CREMA** '93, California, Reserve $13.50
B		B			Σ		S	B	**RODNEY STRONG VINEYARDS** '93, River East Vnyd., Estate $15.00
									4 AWARDS
B			S	B		S			**BUENA VISTA** '92, Carneros $10.00
		B				Σ	S	Σ	**CHATEAU ST. JEAN** '92, Sonoma Co. $15.00
	B	B	S				Σ		**CRESTON VINEYARDS** '93, Paso Robles $10.00
		S				S	B	B	**FETZER VINEYARDS** '92, Bien Nacido, Reserve $24.00
B		B			Σ		B		**FETZER VINEYARDS** '92, North Coast, Barrel Select $13.00
		G				S	S	G	**FETZER VINEYARDS** '92, Olivet Vnd., Reserve $24.00
	B	B					G	B	**GREENWOOD RIDGE VINEYARDS** '93, Anderson Vly., Roederer Vn. $15.00
		B			S		B	S	**MONT ST. JOHN** '93, Carneros, Estate $14.00
		S		G		G	B		**NAPA RIDGE WINERY** '93, North Coast $9.00
B	S	G					S		**NAVARRO VINEYARDS** '91, Anderson Vly. $15.00
		S	S		B			B	**OLIVET LANE ESTATE** '93, Russian River Vly. $13.00
B	S				G			S	**STERLING VINEYARDS** '93, Carneros, Winery Lake Vnyd. $18.00
									3 AWARDS
	B					B		G	**BEAULIEU VINEYARD** '93, Carneros $11.00
	S	B						S	**BEAULIEU VINEYARD** '92, Napa Vly., Carneros, Reserve $18.00
			S			S	B		**CAMBRIA WINERY** '93, Santa Maria Vly., Julia's Vnyd. $18.00
	S	B			S				**CAMBRIA WINERY** '92, Santa Maria Vly., Reserve $30.00

Pinot Noir

Pinot Noir	L.A.	Orange	Farmers	San Fran	Dallas	State Fair	New World	W. Coast	San Diego
3 AWARDS									
CHALONE VINEYARD '90, Chalone Vnyd., Est. $30.00	B	S			S				
CHATEAU DE BAUN WINERY '92, Russian River Vly. $10.00		B				B		B	
COSENTINO WINERY '93, Napa Vly. $24.00	Σ	S					G		
HUSCH VINEYARDS '93, Anderson Vly., Est. $15.00						S		B	B
KENWOOD VINEYARDS '93, Russian River Vly. $14.00		B		S				B	
CHARLES KRUG WINERY '93, Napa Vly., Carneros $9.00		B		S					B
LEEWARD WINERY '93, Santa Barbara Co. $15.00						S	S	S	
MIRASSOU VINEYARDS '92, Monterey, Harvest Reserve $12.00			B			B		B	
MONTPELLIER VINEYARDS '93, California $8.00		S					S	S	
RAYMOND VINEYARD & CELLAR '92, Napa Vly. $17.00	S			B		B			
ROCHIOLI VINEYARD '93, Russian River Vly. $18.00		S		S		G			
SANFORD WINERY '93, Santa Barbara Co. $18.00	S			S		G			
SONOMA CREEK WINERY '93, Sonoma Co. $10.00		B						B	B
TROUT GULCH VINEYARDS '91, Santa Cruz Mtns. $16.00	S						G		B
WILD HORSE WINERY '93, Paso Robles, Chev. Sauvage $14.00	S		B						S
YORK MOUNTAIN WINERY '91, San Luis Obispo Co. $10.00	G						G		B
Z D WINES '93, Napa Vly., Carneros $23.00				S		S			B
2 AWARDS									
ACACIA WINERY '93, Carneros $25.00	G	B							
ADELAIDA CELLARS '93, San Luis Obispo $27.00		S						S	

Pinot Noir

L.A.	Orange	Farmers	San Fran	Dallas	State Fair	New World	W. Coast	San Diego	Pinot Noir
									2 AWARDS
			B					B	**ARMIDA WINERY** '93, Russian River Vly. $13.00
					B		B		**BEAULIEU VINEYARD** '93, Napa Vly., Beautour $8.00
			B		S				**DAVID BRUCE WINERY** '93, Russian River Vly., Reserve $25.00
	B						B		**BUENA VISTA** '92, Carneros, Grand Reserve $20.00
G			S						**BYRON VINEYARD & WINERY** '93, Santa Barbara Co. $16.00
	B					B			**CARNEROS CREEK WINERY** '93, Carneros, Fleur De Carneros $9.00
		S			S				**CHATEAU SOUVERAIN** '93, Sonoma, Carneros, Reserve $12.00
	B					S			**JEKEL VINEYARDS** '93, Arroyo Seco, Gravelstone $13.00
		B						S	**MERIDIAN VINEYARDS** '92, Santa Barbara Co. $14.00
				B		B			**ROBERT MONDAVI WINERY** '92, Napa Vly, $15.00
		B					B		**MOSHIN VINEYARDS** '92, Russian River Viy. $15.00
	B	B							**NAVARRO VINEYARDS** '93, Anderson Vly. $9.00
			S		B				**NEWLAN VINEYARDS** '93, Napa Vly. $18.00
S	B								**NICHOLS WINERY** '93, Santa Barbara, Madre Vnyd. $24.00
			B					S	**PARDUCCI WINE CELLARS** '93, Mendocino Co. $7.00
					B			G	**SCHUG CARNEROS ESTATE WINERY** '93, Carneros $16.00
B								B	**SEGHESIO WINERY** '93, Sonoma Co., Home Ranch
B						S			**ROBERT STEMMLER WINERY** '91, Sonoma Co. $20.00
						G	B		**THORNTON WINERY** '93, Brindiamo, Edna Vly. $10.00
	G	B							**VILLA MT. EDEN** '93, California, Cellar Select $8.00

RESERVE ALEXANDRE

GEYSER PEAK

1992 Alexander Valley

Red Meritage

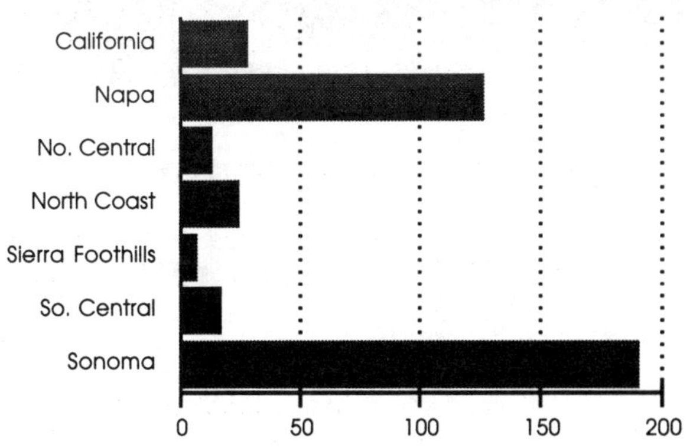

Regional Comparison of Total Points

(Gold-plus=7 Gold=5 Silver=3 Bronze=1)

Highest individual wine totals

Points	Winery
19	**GUENOC WINERY** '91, California, Langtry, $35.00
18	**GEYSER PEAK WINERY** '92, Reserve Alexandre, $25.00
16	**STONESTREET WINERY** '92, Alexander Vly., Legacy, $35.00
14	**GOLDEN CREEK VINEYARD** '92, Sonoma Caberlot, Reserve, $15.00
14	**GUENOC WINERY** '91, Lake Co., $15.00
14	**QUIVIRA VINEYARDS** '91, Dry Creek Vly., Cuvee, $15.00
14	**STONESTREET WINERY** '91, Alexander Vly., Legacy, $35.00
13	**BERINGER VINEYARDS** '92, Knights Vly., $14.00
13	**MOUNT VEEDER WINERY** '91, Napa Vly., Reserve, $40.00
13	**JOSEPH PHELPS VINEYARDS** '91, Napa Vly., Insignia, $50.00
12	**BENZIGER FAMILY WINERY** '90, Sonoma Mtn., A Tribute, $20.00

Red Meritage

Winery / Wine	L.A.	Orange	Farmers	San Fran	Dallas	State Fair	New World	W. Coast	San Diego
8 AWARDS									
GUENOC WINERY '91, Lake Co. $15.00		S	B	B	B	S	B	S	B
7 AWARDS									
GUENOC WINERY '91, California, Langtry $35.00		S	S	B	S		S	S	S
6 AWARDS									
BENZIGER FAMILY WINERY '90, Sonoma Mtn., A Tribute $20.00	B	B	B	B	B	Σ			
DAVIS BYNUM WINERY '91, Sonoma Co., Eclipse $22.00		B	B	B		S	B	B	
CLOS DU BOIS '91, Alexander Vly., Marlstone $20.00		B	S	B	B	G			B
GEYSER PEAK WINERY '92, Reserve Alexandre $25.00	B		Σ	B	S		S	S	
QUIVIRA VINEYARDS '91, Dry Creek Vly., Cuvee $15.00	B		S	S			S	S	B
STONESTREET WINERY '92, Alexander Vly., Legacy $35.00			B	B		G	G	S	B
STONESTREET WINERY '91, Alexander Vly., Legacy $35.00			B	B	B		G	S	S
5 AWARDS									
RUTHERFORD RANCH VINEYARDS '90, Napa Vly., Quintessence $20.00		B	B	B	B			B	
4 AWARDS									
BEAULIEU VINEYARD '91, Napa Vly., Tapestry $20.00	B	B		B				S	
BERINGER VINEYARDS '91, Knights Vly., Prop. Grown $14.00			G		S		S		B
CONCANNON VINEYARD '92, Assemblage, Reserve $15.00	S	S			G			B	
ESTANCIA ESTATES '92, Alexander Vly. $15.00		B		B		S			B
FLORA SPRINGS WINE COMPANY '91, Napa Vly., Trilogy $25.00	B				G		S		S
FRANCISCAN OAKVILLE ESTATE '91, Napa Vly., Magnificat $22.00				B		B		G	S
GOLDEN CREEK VINEYARD '92, Sonoma Caberlot, Reserve $15.00		S	S				G		S

Red Meritage

L.A.	Orange	Farmers	San Fran	Dallas	State Fair	New World	W. Coast	San Diego	Wine
									4 AWARDS
S	B		S					B	**MAZZOCCO VINEYARDS** '91, Dry Creek., Matrix, Estate $28.00
S		S			S			B	**STERLING VINEYARDS** '91, Napa Vly., Reserve $40.00
									3 AWARDS
S					S		Σ		**BERINGER VINEYARDS** '92, Knights Vly. $14.00
B	B				S				**BOEGER WINERY** '91, El Dorado $15.00
B	S							S	**CARMENET WINERY** '90, Sonoma, Moon Mtn. Vnyd. $25.00
		B	G		B				**COSENTINO WINERY** '91, Napa Co., The Poet $25.00
	S	B	S						**DE LORIMIER VINEYARDS** '91, Alexander Vly., Mosaic $18.00
B	G						B		**GEYSER PEAK WINERY** '93, Reserve Alexandre $25.00
			S		B		S		**GUENOC WINERY** '92, Lake Co. $15.00
		B	B		B				**GUENOC WINERY** '90, California, Langtry $35.00
B		S	S						**JUSTIN VINEYARDS** '92, SLO, Isosceles Reserve $24.00
	S						G	G	**MOUNT VEEDER WINERY** '91, Napa Vly., Reserve $40.00
			G		B	Σ			**JOSEPH PHELPS VINEYARDS** '91, Napa Vly., Insignia $50.00
B	S		B						**ST. CLEMENT VINEYARDS** '93, Napa Vly., Oroppas $30.00
		B	B					B	**WINDSOR VINEYARDS** '92, Sonoma Co. $16.00
									2 AWARDS
		B				S			**BEAULIEU VINEYARD** '90, Napa Vly., Tapestry $20.00
	G		B						**CARMENET WINERY** '91, Sonoma, Moon Mtn., Res, $35.00
	S		G						**COSENTINO WINERY** '92, Napa Vly., M. Coz $45.00
	S	G							**FIRESTONE VINEYARD** '91, Santa Ynez Vly., Reserve $20.00

Red Meritage

	L.A.	Orange	Farmers	San Fran	Dallas	State Fair	New World	W. Coast	San Diego
2 AWARDS									
FRANCISCAN OAKVILLE ESTATE '90, Napa Vly., Magnificat $20.00					G		S		
IRON HORSE '91, Alexander Vly., T-T Vnyd. $18.00		B		B					
JEKEL VINEYARDS '90, Arroyo Seco, Sanctuary Est. $13.00		B					B		
KONRAD ESTATE WINERY '91, Mendocino, Melange A Trois $12.00		B						S	
PEJU PROVINCE '92, Napa Vly. $30.00					B	B			
RAYMOND VINEYARD & CELLAR '90, Napa Vly., Reserve $40.00					B			B	
RUBISSOW-SARGENT WINE CO. '90, Napa, Les Trempettes $18.00	B			B					
TOPAZ WINES '91, Napa Vly., Rouge De Trois $16.00				S		G			

CANYON ROAD

SAUVIGNON BLANC

CALIFORNIA

1994

1994

GEYSER PEAK

SAUVIGNON BLANC

SONOMA COUNTY

ALC 12.9% BY VOL.

Sauvignon Blanc

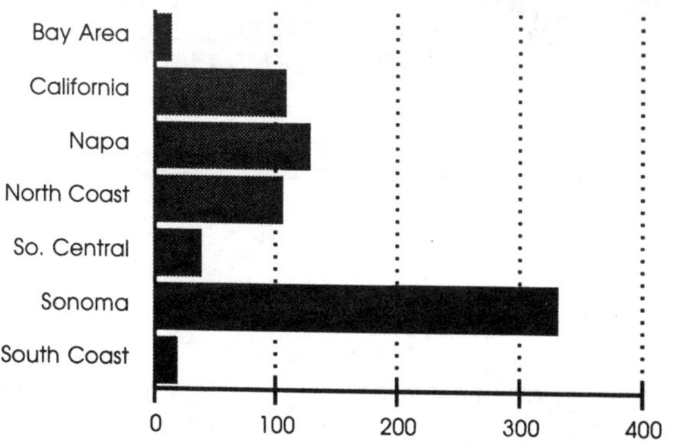

Regional Comparison of Total Points

(Gold-plus=7 Gold=5 Silver=3 Bronze=1)

Highest individual wine totals

26	**CANYON ROAD CELLARS** '94, California, $6.00
23	**GEYSER PEAK WINERY** '94, Sonoma Co., $7.00
17	**GAINEY VINEYARD** '93, Santa Ynez Vly., $9.00
17	**HANDLEY CELLARS** '93, Dry Creek Vly., $8.00
17	**ROCHIOLI VINEYARD** '94, Russian River Vly., Est., $13.00
16	**ADLER FELS** '92, Sonoma Co. Fume, $10.00
16	**DE LORIMIER VINEYARDS** '91, Alex. Vly., Lace, LH, RS 11.5%, $16.00
15	**HANNA WINERY** '94, Sonoma Co., $10.00
14	**COTES DE SONOMA** '94, Sonoma Co., $7.00
13	**GREENWOOD RIDGE VINEYARDS** '93, Anderson Vly., $9.00
13	**GRGICH HILLS CELLAR** '93, Napa Vly., Fume, $13.00
13	**KENDALL-JACKSON WINERY** '93, California, Vintner's Reserve, $9.00

Sauvignon Blanc

Wine	L.A.	Orange	Farmers	San Fran	Dallas	State Fair	New World	W. Coast	San Diego
8 AWARDS									
CANYON ROAD CELLARS '94, California $6.00		S	B	S	B	S	Σ	B	Σ
6 AWARDS									
ADLER FELS '92, Sonoma Co. Fume $10.00	S		S	G		B		S	B
CLOS DU BOIS '94, Sonoma Co. $8.00		B	S	B			S	S	B
DE LORIMIER VINEYARDS '91, Alex. Vly., Lace, LH, RS 11.5% $16.00	S	G	B			B	G		B
5 AWARDS									
ADLER FELS '92, Sonoma, Fume, Organic $10.00	S		B			B		B	B
CONCANNON VINEYARD '93, Livermore Vly. $8.00		B		B	B		S	B	
DRY CREEK VINEYARD '93, Sonoma Co., Fume $9.00		S	B	B		S		B	
GAINEY VINEYARD '93, Santa Ynez Vly. $9.00		S	S				G	G	B
GEYSER PEAK WINERY '94, Sonoma Co. $7.00		G	S			G	S	Σ	
GREENWOOD RIDGE VINEYARDS '93, Anderson Vly. $9.00		S			B	B		S	G
GRGICH HILLS CELLAR '93, Napa Vly., Fume $13.00	B	G				S	S	B	
HANDLEY CELLARS '93, Dry Creek Vly. $8.00		G				S	G	S	B
HANNA WINERY '94, Sonoma Co. $10.00		G	S			B		G	B
KENDALL-JACKSON WINERY '93, California, Vintner's Reserve $9.00			S	S	S			S	B
KENWOOD VINEYARDS '93, Sonoma Co. $9.50		S	B		B		S	S	
MONTEVINA WINERY '93, California, Fume $7.00	B	S				B	G	B	
ROCHIOLI VINEYARD '94, Russian River Vly., Est. $13.00	B	S		G		G			S
4 AWARDS									
BEAULIEU VINEYARD '93, Napa Vly. $8.50			B	B			B	G	

Sauvignon Blanc

L.A.	Orange	Farmers	San Fran	Dallas	State Fair	New World	W. Coast	San Diego	Wine
4 AWARDS									
		B	B				B	G	**CHATEAU SOUVERAIN** '94, Alexander Vly., Barrel Ferm. $7.50
	S			B		G	B		**CHATEAU ST. JEAN** '93, La Petite Etoile Fume $11.00
		S	G		G			B	**COTES DE SONOMA** '94, Sonoma Co. $7.00
			B			G	G	B	**FETZER VINEYARDS** '93, Mendocino Co. Fume $7.00
	G	B					B	B	**FETZER VINEYARDS** '93, Mendocino Co., Barrel Sel. $10.00
S					B		B	B	**GUENOC WINERY** '94, Guenoc Vly., Est. $11.00
	B	B	B				G		**MIRASSOU VINEYARDS** '93, California $5.00
		B			S		B	B	**MOUNT KONOCTI** '93, Lake Co. Fume $8.00
	B	B			G		S		**MURPHY-GOODE ESTATE WINERY** '94, Alexander Vly., Fume $10.00
	S	B					B	B	**NAPA RIDGE WINERY** '93, North Coast $5.00
	B	B		B				B	**ROBERT PEPI WINERY** '93, Napa Vly., Reserve Sel. $20.00
		S	B	S		S			**ROBERT PEPI WINERY** '92, Napa Vly., Reserve Sel. $20.00
	B			S			S	B	**WENTE BROS. WINERY** '93, Livermore Vly., Est. $7.00
	B					S	B	B	**WINDSOR VINEYARDS** '93, Sonoma Co. Fume $8.00
3 AWARDS									
	B			S			B		**ALDERBROOK WINERY** '93, Dry Creek Vly. $8.50
	B			B			B		**BEL ARBORS VINEYARD** '93, California $5.00
B		B					B		**BRUTOCAO CELLARS** '94, Mendocino, Est. $9.00
	B	B					S		**BUENA VISTA** '94, Lake Co. $7.50
				S		B		B	**BUENA VISTA** '93, Lake Co. $7.50

Sauvignon Blanc

Winery	L.A.	Orange	Farmers	San Fran	Dallas	State Fair	New World	W. Coast	San Diego
3 AWARDS									
DAVIS BYNUM WINERY '94, Shone Farm, Fume $8.00			Σ					S	B
CHALK HILL WINERY '93, Chalk Hill, Est. $16.00		S				B			B
CHALK HILL WINERY '92, Chalk Hill, Est. $16.00							B	B	B
CHATEAU ST. JEAN '93, Sonoma Co., Fume $8.00					B		S	B	
DRY CREEK VINEYARD 'NV, Sonoma Co., Soleil, LH $18.00		S			S			B	
WILLIAM HILL WINERY '93, Napa Vly. $9.00		S		S					B
JOUILLIAN VINEYARDS '93, Carmel Vly. $8.50		B					S	B	
KENDALL-JACKSON WINERY '94, California, Vintner's Reserve $9.00		S		B		S			
LAKEWOOD VINEYARDS '93, Clear Lake $9.00						B		B	S
MERIDIAN VINEYARDS '93, California $9.00							B	G	B
MURPHY-GOODE ESTATE WINERY '93, Alexander Vly. Fume, Res. $15.00		B						B	S
ROBERT PEPI WINERY '93, Napa, Two Heart Canopy $11.00					S		S		S
RAYMOND VINEYARD & CELLAR '93, Napa Vly. $9.00		S			B			B	
SAN MARTIN WINERY '93, California $5.00	S	B						G	
ST. CLEMENT VINEYARDS '94, Napa Vly. $11.00		B	B			B			
STEPHEN ZELLERBACH VINEYARD '93, Sonoma Co. $7.00	G					B		B	
2 AWARDS									
AUDUBON CELLARS '92, Napa Vly, LH $10.00	S			S					
BAREFOOT CELLARS 'NV, California $5.00			B					B	
BENZIGER FAMILY WINERY '94, Sonoma Co. Fume $10.00		S				S			

L.A.	Orange	Farmers	San Fran	Dallas	State Fair	New World	W. Coast	San Diego	Sauvignon Blanc
									2 AWARDS
	S		B						**CAKEBREAD CELLARS** '94, Napa Vly. $13.00
	G				B				**CALLAWAY VINEYARD & WINERY** '94, Temecula $8.00
						S	B		**CHATEAU ST. JEAN** '93, Sonoma Co. $7.00
	B	B							**CHATOM VINEYARDS** '93, Calaveras Co. $8.50
	B						G		**DE LOACH VINEYARDS** '94, Russian River Vly. $10.00
	B						G		**DELICATO VINEYARDS** '93, California, Fume $5.50
B							B		**DRY CREEK VINEYARD** '92, Dry Creek, Est. Reserve $14.00
	B		B						**J. FRITZ WINERY** '94, Dry Creek Vly. $9.50
							S	B	**HUSCH VINEYARDS** '94, Mendocino Co. $9.00
	S		B						**JOUILLIAN VINEYARDS** '94, Carmel Vly. $8.50
			G		B				**KENWOOD VINEYARDS** '94, Sonoma Co. $9.00
	B				S				**LOUIS M. MARTINI** '94, Napa Vly. $8.00
			S			S			**MATANZAS CREEK** '93, Sonoma Co. $14.00
	B				G				**MISSION VIEW VINEYARDS** '94, Paso Robles, Fume $9.00
		B						B	**MOUNT KONOCTI** '93, Lake Co. Fume, Reserve $10.00
		B		B					**PEDRONCELLI WINERY** '93, Dry Creek Vly. Fume $8.00
	B						B		**ROBERT PEPI WINERY** '94, Napa, Two Heart Canopy $11.00
	S						B		**PRESTON VINEYARDS & WINERY** '93, Dry Creek, Cuvee De Fume $9.50
		B	B						**QUAIL RIDGE CELLARS** '93, Napa Vly. $9.00
G		S							**QUIVIRA VINEYARDS** '93, Dry Creek Vly. $10.00

Sauvignon Blanc

2 AWARDS	L.A.	Orange	Farmers	San Fran	Dallas	State Fair	New World	W. Coast	San Diego
RUTHERFORD RANCH VINEYARDS '93, Napa Vly. $9.00					B				B
SANTA BARBARA WINERY '93, Santa Ynez, LH, R.S. 18.5% $14.00	B	Σ							
SEGHESIO WINERY '94, Sonoma Co. $7.00	B							S	
SIERRA VISTA WINERY '94, El Dorado, Estate, Fume $8.00		B						B	
SIMI WINERY '93, Sonoma Co. $9.00		G	B						
TRELLIS VINEYARDS '93, Sonoma Co. $6.00				B					S
VAN ROEKEL VINEYARDS '93, Temecula, Fume $7.00					G			G	
VOSS VINEYARDS '94, Napa Vly. $10.00						Σ			B
WILDHURST VINEYARDS '93, Clear Lake, Fume $11.00		B				B			
WINDSOR VINEYARDS '94, Alexander Vly. Fume, Res. $10.00								B	B

LIMITED 1993 BOTTLING

LIVERMORE VALLEY

SÉMILLON

CONCANNON ESTATE VINEYARD

PRODUCED AND BOTTLED BY CONCANNON VINEYARD
LIVERMORE, CALIFORNIA ALC. 14.2% BY VOL. BW 616

Semillon

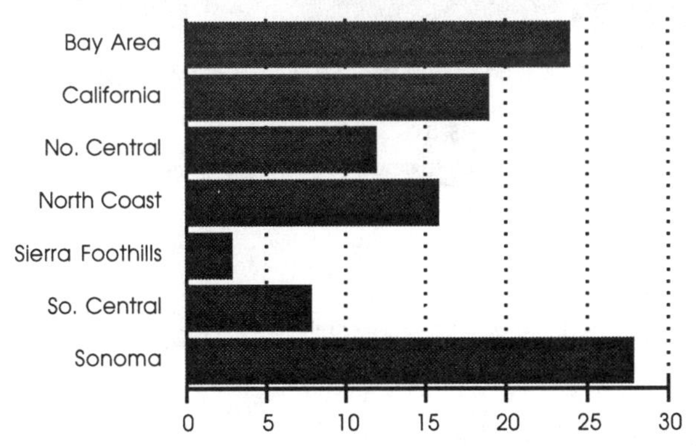

Regional Comparison of Total Points

(Gold-plus=7 Gold=5 Silver=3 Bronze=1)

Highest individual wine totals

Points	Wine
19	**CANYON ROAD CELLARS** '93, Alexander Vly., $8.00
19	**CONCANNON VINEYARD** '93, Livermore Vly., Est., $13.00
13	**GEYSER PEAK WINERY** '94, California, $8.00
12	**CONCANNON VINEYARD** '93, Arroyo Seco, LH, R.S. 15.4%, $10.00
12	**LAKEWOOD VINEYARDS** '93, Clear Lake, $12.00
7	**GAN EDEN** '93, Sonoma Co., $14.00
5	**CRESTON VINEYARDS** '94, Paso Robles, Chevrier, Est., $9.00
5	**DOLCE** '91, California, LH, RS 10.0%, $49.00
4	**NAVARRO VINEYARDS** '93, North Coast, $11.00

Semillon	L.A.	Orange	Farmers	San Fran	Dallas	State Fair	New World	W. Coast	San Diego
9 AWARDS									
CONCANNON VINEYARD '93, Livermore Vly., Est. $13.00	S	B	B	B	B	B	S	G	S
7 AWARDS									
CANYON ROAD CELLARS '93, Alexander Vly. $8.00	S		G	B	G	B	S	B	
GEYSER PEAK WINERY '94, California $8.00	S		B	S		B	B	B	S
6 AWARDS									
CONCANNON VINEYARD '93, Arroyo Seco, LH, R.S. 15.4% $10.00	B	B		B	B		S	G	
LAKEWOOD VINEYARDS '93, Clear Lake $12.00		B	B		B	S	B	G	
5 AWARDS									
GAN EDEN '93, Sonoma Co. $14.00	B	S	B					B	B
3 AWARDS									
CRESTON VINEYARDS '94, Paso Robles, Chevrier, Est. $9.00			B	B				S	
INDIAN SPRINGS VINEYARDS '93, Nevada Co. $8.00						B		B	B
2 AWARDS									
NAVARRO VINEYARDS '93, North Coast $11.00				B			S		
PRESTON VINEYARDS & WINERY '93, Dry Creek Vly. $13.00						B		B	

JORDAN SPARKLING WINE COMPANY

CODORNIU
NAPA
BRUT
MÉTHODE CHAMPENOISE
NAPA VALLEY SPARKLING WINE
ALC 12% VOL
750 ML

Sparkling Wine

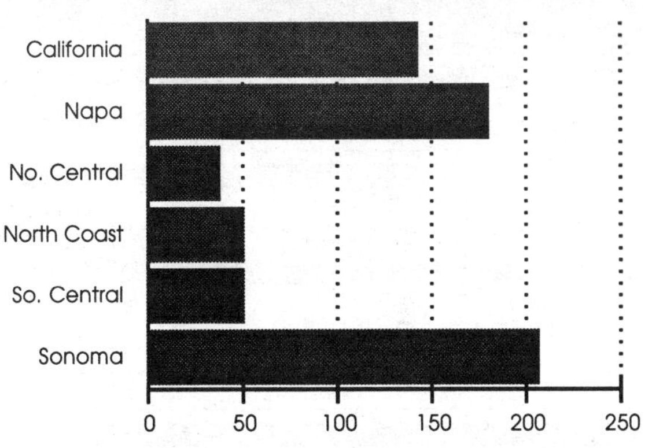

Regional Comparison of Total Points

(Gold-plus=7 Gold=5 Silver=3 Bronze=1)

Highest individual wine totals

Points	Wine
30	**JORDAN VINEYARD & WINERY** '90, Sonoma Co. "J", $23.00
26	**CODORNIU NAPA** 'NV, Napa Vly. Brut, $11.00
22	**S. ANDERSON VINEYARD** '89, Napa Vly., Brut, $18.00
21	**GLORIA FERRER** 'NV, Sonoma Co. Blanc de Noirs, $15.00
19	**BALLATORE CHAMPAGNE CELLARS** 'NV, California, Gran Spumante, $5.00
19	**GLORIA FERRER** '88, Royal Cuvee Brut, $18.00
19	**MUMM NAPA VALLEY** 'NV, Cuvee Napa Blanc De Noirs, $14.00
18	**CHATEAU ST. JEAN** 'NV, Sonoma Co. Blanc De Blanc, $11.00
18	**V. SATTUI WINERY** '92, Napa Vly., Carsi Estate, $15.00
17	**MAISON DEUTZ WINERY** '90, San Luis Obispo, Reserve Brut, $23.00
16	**GLORIA FERRER** 'NV, Sonoma Co., Brut, $15.00

Sparkling Wine	L.A.	Orange	Farmers	San Fran	Dallas	State Fair	New World	W. Coast	San Diego
9 AWARDS									
BALLATORE CHAMPAGNE CELLARS 'NV, California, Gran Spumante $5.00	S	B	B	B	S	S	S	S	B
8 AWARDS									
JORDAN VINEYARD & WINERY '90, Sonoma Co. "J" $23.00	G	B		S	B	B	Σ	G	Σ
7 AWARDS									
GLORIA FERRER 'NV, Sonoma Co. Blanc de Noirs $15.00		G		B	S	S	S	G	B
MUMM NAPA VALLEY 'NV, Cuvee Napa Blanc De Noirs $14.00	G		B	B	B	S	G		S
6 AWARDS									
S. ANDERSON VINEYARD '89, Napa Vly., Brut $18.00	G	S	S		S	S	G		
CODORNIU NAPA 'NV, Napa Vly. Brut $11.00	S		Σ		B	G	G	G	
GLORIA FERRER 'NV, Sonoma Co., Brut $15.00		S		B	S	S	S	S	
HANDLEY CELLARS '89, Anderson Vly. Blanc De Blanc $18.50	S	B		B		S	G		B
KORBEL CHAMPAGNE CELLARS 'NV, California, Rouge $13.00	B				B	S	G	B	S
MIRASSOU VINEYARDS '91, Monterey, 5th Gen. Cuvee $12.00	S	S	S	B		S			B
V. SATTUI WINERY '92, Napa Vly., Carsi Estate $15.00	G		S	S		G		B	B
5 AWARDS									
S. ANDERSON VINEYARD '90, Napa Vly., Blanc De Noirs $20.00	B	S	B				G		S
GLORIA FERRER '88, Royal Cuvee Brut $18.00	S	G		G	S			S	
KORBEL CHAMPAGNE CELLARS 'NV, California, Natural $13.00	S		B			S	S	G	
MAISON DEUTZ WINERY 'NV, San Luis Obispo, Brut Cuvee $14.00			S		B	B		B	B
MAISON DEUTZ WINERY '90, San Luis Obispo, Reserve Brut $23.00	Σ		S			B	G		B
MUMM NAPA VALLEY '89, Carneros, Winery Lake Brut $23.00	B	S			B	G	S		

L.A.	Orange	Farmers	San Fran	Dallas	State Fair	New World	W. Coast	San Diego	Sparkling Wine
									5 AWARDS
G	G	B					B	S	**WINDSOR VINEYARDS** '88, Sonoma Co. Blanc De Noir $13.00
									4 AWARDS
Σ	S	S					G		**CHATEAU ST. JEAN** 'NV, Sonoma Co. Blanc De Blanc $11.00
G	S		B				G		**HANDLEY CELLARS** '89, Anderson Vly. Brut $15.00
		B		B		G	B		**ROBERT HUNTER WINERY** '91, Sonoma Vly., Brut De Noir $25.00
B		B	G		B				**JEPSON VINEYARDS** '89, Mendocino Blanc De Blanc $16.00
B		S				S	S		**KORBEL CHAMPAGNE CELLARS** 'NV, California, Blanc De Noirs $10.00
G		S		B				S	**MAISON DEUTZ WINERY** 'NV, San Luis Obispo, Brut Rose $18.00
S		S	B				S		**MAISON DEUTZ WINERY** 'NV, SLO/SB Blanc De Noirs $16.00
G		B	B				S		**MIRASSOU VINEYARDS** '91, Monterey Co. Brut $12.00
B	B	S			B				**MUMM NAPA VALLEY** '90, Carneros, DVX Brut $32.00
B	B		B	B					**PIPER SONOMA** 'NV, Sonoma Co. Brut $13.50
S		B	B			S			**THORNTON WINERY** '87, Culbertson, Brut Rose $16.00
G	S	B					B		**WENTE BROS. WINERY** 'NV, Arroyo Seco, Grande Brut $10.00
									3 AWARDS
				S			B	B	**CHATEAU DE BAUN WINERY** 'NV, Sonoma Co. Brut Rose $12.00
G		S					S		**CHATEAU ST. JEAN** 'NV, Sonoma Co. Brut $11.00
Σ	G				B				**GLORIA FERRER** '87, Carneros Cuvee Brut $25.00
G	B				B				**HANDLEY CELLARS** '91, Anderson Vly. Brut Rose $18.00
			B		B		B		**MIRASSOU VINEYARDS** '89, Monterey, Au Naturel $15.00
		Σ		S				S	**MUMM NAPA VALLEY** 'NV, Cuvee Napa, Brut Prestige $14.00

Sparkling Wine

Sparkling Wine	L.A.	Orange	Farmers	San Fran	Dallas	State Fair	New World	W. Coast	San Diego
3 AWARDS									
PIPER SONOMA 'NV, Sonoma Co. Blanc De Noir $13.50	Σ	B			S				
SEBASTIANI VINEYARDS '91, Richard Cuneo Cuvee $15.00	S				B			B	
THORNTON WINERY 'NV, Culbertson, Brut $10.00		B	S				G		
THORNTON WINERY 'NV, Culbertson, C. De Frontignan $10.00	S		B						S
TRIBAUT 'NV, California, Blanc De Blanc $9.00		G				G	G		
2 AWARDS									
BRICELAND VINEYARDS 'NV, Humboldt Co., Brut $16.00		S				B			
IMAGERY SERIES '90, Carneros Brut $16.00			B	S					
IRON HORSE '92, Sonoma, Wedding Cuvee $22.00		G		B					
KORBEL CHAMPAGNE CELLARS '91, California, Cuvee Chard, Res. $15.00		G		S					
KORBEL CHAMPAGNE CELLARS '90, California, Cuvee Pinot Noir	G				B				
MIRABELLE CELLARS 'NV, North Coast, Brut $12.00						S	G		
MIRASSOU VINEYARDS '89, Monterey Co., Reserve Brut $15.00				B				B	
PIPER SONOMA '90, Sonoma Co., Sparkling Rose $19.00		S		B					
SCHRAMSBERG VINEYARDS '91, Napa Vly., Cuvee De Pinot $22.00		G				S			
SCHRAMSBERG VINEYARDS '89, Napa Vly., J. Schram $50.00		S					G		
SCHRAMSBERG VINEYARDS '87, Napa Vly., Blanc De Noirs $24.00				B			G		
THORNTON WINERY 'NV, Culbertson, Blanc De Noir $10.00			S	B					
THORNTON WINERY '94, Culbertson, Artist Ser. Cuvee $12.00					B		G		
THORNTON WINERY '88, Culbertson, Brut Reserve $18.00					B		G		

L.A.	Orange	Farmers	San Fran	Dallas	State Fair	New World	W. Coast	San Diego	Sparkling Wine
									2 AWARDS
		B	B						**THORNTON WINERY** '88, Culbertson, Natural $16.00
					B	G			**TRIBAUT** 'NV, California, Brut $9.00
B	B								**WINDSOR VINEYARDS** 'NV, California, Lot 2, Extra Dry $8.00
			S		B				**WINDSOR VINEYARDS** '90, Sonoma, Lib. Reserve Brut $16.00
		B					B		**WINDSOR VINEYARDS** '88, Sonoma Co. Brut $12.50

1 9 9 2

Tepusquet Vineyard

S Y R A H

SANTA MARIA VALLEY, CALIFORNIA

ALC 13.5% BY VOL

EBERLE

1993

PASO ROBLES

SYRAH

FRALICH VINEYARD

PRODUCED AND BOTTLED BY
EBERLE WINERY, PASO ROBLES, CALIFORNIA
ALCOHOL 13.3% BY VOLUME

Syrah

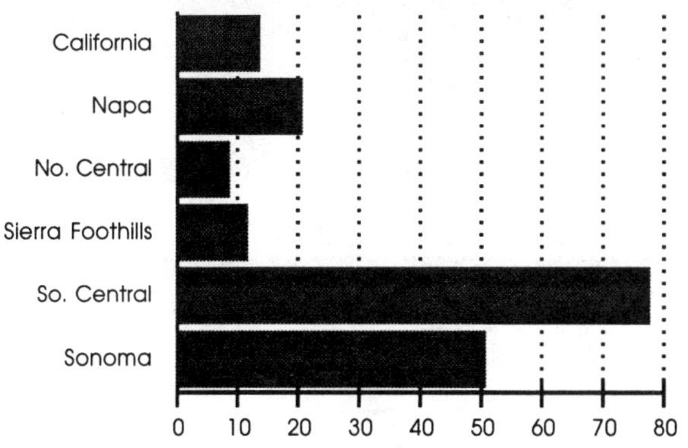

Regional Comparison of Total Points

(Gold-plus=7 Gold=5 Silver=3 Bronze=1)

Highest individual wine totals

28 **CAMBRIA WINERY**
'92, Santa Maria, Tepusquet Vnyd., $30.00

25 **EBERLE WINERY**
'93, Paso Robles, Fralich Vnyd., $16.00

12 **GEYSER PEAK WINERY**
'93, Alexander Vly., Reserve, $30.00

11 **SWANSON VINEYARDS**
'92, Napa Vly., $25.00

10 **PRESTON VINEYARDS & WINERY**
'92, Dry Creek Vly., Est., $18.00

10 **SIERRA VISTA WINERY**
'92, El Dorado, Estate, $16.00

10 **TRUCHARD VINEYARDS**
'93, Napa Vly., Carneros, $18.00

9 **GEYSER PEAK WINERY**
'93, Alexander Vly. Shiraz, $10.00

9 **MOUNT PALOMAR WINERY**
'93, California, Rey Sol, $8.00

9 **RIVER RUN VINTNERS**
'93, Monterey, Ventana Vnyd., $15.00

8 **ZACA MESA WINERY**
'93, Santa Barbara, Zaca Vnyds., $12.00

Syrah

Syrah	L.A.	Orange	Farmers	San Fran	Dallas	State Fair	New World	W. Coast	San Diego
7 AWARDS									
EBERLE WINERY '93, Paso Robles, Fralich Vnyd. $16.00		B		G	S	G	S	G	S
6 AWARDS									
CAMBRIA WINERY '92, Santa Maria, Tepusquet Vnyd. $30.00	Σ	Σ	S		B		S	Σ	
5 AWARDS									
GEYSER PEAK WINERY '92, Alexander Vly., Reserve $30.00		B	S	B	B				B
MOUNT PALOMAR WINERY '93, California, Rey Sol $8.00	B		B			S	S		B
RIVER RUN VINTNERS '93, Monterey, Ventana Vnyd. $15.00		S	B	S			B	B	
4 AWARDS									
GEYSER PEAK WINERY '93, Alexander Vly., Reserve $30.00		G		G		B		B	
PRESTON VINEYARDS & WINERY '92, Dry Creek Vly., Est. $18.00		S			B	S		S	
SIERRA VISTA WINERY '92, El Dorado, Estate $16.00		S				S		S	B
TRUCHARD VINEYARDS '93, Napa Vly., Carneros $18.00		B			B	G		S	
VAN ROEKEL VINEYARDS '93, Temecula, Estate $6.00			S			B		B	B
3 AWARDS									
ALDERBROOK WINERY '93, Russian River Vly. $14.00		S	S		B				
GEYSER PEAK WINERY '93, Alexander Vly. Shiraz $10.00		G				B			S
KENDALL-JACKSON WINERY '91, California, Grand Reserve $20.00		B	B					S	
SWANSON VINEYARDS '92, Napa Vly. $25.00			Σ	B				S	
2 AWARDS									
FESS PARKER WINERY '93, Santa Barbara Co. $15.00	B	B							
ZACA MESA WINERY '93, Santa Barbara, Zaca Vnyds. $12.00		G				S			

Knights Valley
ESTABLISHED 1876
Beringer
1992
KNIGHTS VALLEY
Sauvignon Blanc & Semillon
Meritage
PROPRIETOR GROWN
Our Knights Valley Meritage wine is made from
56% Sauvignon Blanc and 44% Semillon

CONCANNON
VINEYARD
RESERVE
1993
assemblage
LIVERMORE VALLEY
SAUVIGNON BLANC 51%
SEMILLON 49%

White Meritage

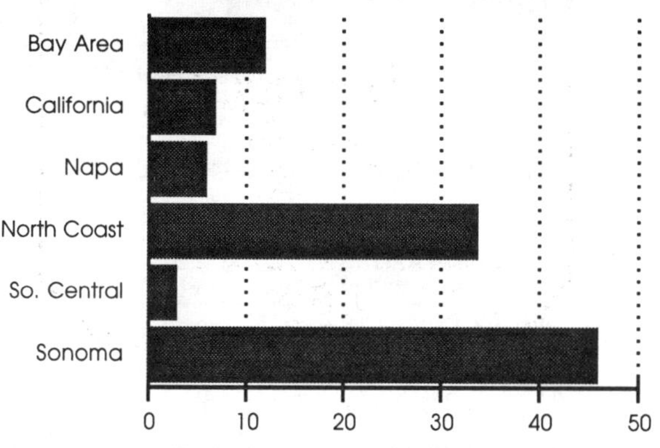

Regional Comparison of Total Points

(Gold-plus=7 Gold=5 Silver=3 Bronze=1)

Highest individual wine totals

13	**BERINGER VINEYARDS** '92, Knights Vly., $9.00
12	**BENZIGER FAMILY WINERY** '92, Sonoma Mtn. Est., Tribute, $16.00
11	**CONCANNON VINEYARD** '93, Livermore Vly., Assemblage, $15.00
11	**GUENOC WINERY** '93, Guenoc Vly., Langtry, $17.00
10	**LAKEWOOD VINEYARDS** '93, Clear Lake, Chevriot, $12.00
8	**DE LORIMIER VINEYARDS** '92, Alexander Vly., Spectrum, $10.00
7	**GUENOC WINERY** '94, Guenoc Vly., Langtry, $17.00
7	**VENEZIA** '94, Alex. Vly., Nuovo Mondo, $20.00
6	**BERINGER VINEYARDS** '93, Knights Vly., $9.00
5	**COSENTINO WINERY** '94, Napa Vly., The Novelist, $16.00
5	**LAKEWOOD VINEYARDS** '92, Clear Lake, Chevriot, $12.00

White Meritage

Wine	L.A.	Orange	Farmers	San Fran	Dallas	State Fair	New World	W. Coast	San Diego
6 AWARDS									
LAKEWOOD VINEYARDS '93, Clear Lake, Chevriot $12.00		B	S			B	S	B	B
5 AWARDS									
BERINGER VINEYARDS '92, Knights Vly. $9.00	S		B	S	B	G			
CONCANNON VINEYARD '93, Livermore Vly., Assemblage $15.00			B			B	Σ	B	B
GUENOC WINERY '93, Guenoc Vly., Langtry $17.00	G		B				B	S	B
LAKEWOOD VINEYARDS '92, Clear Lake, Chevriot $12.00	B		B		B		B	B	
4 AWARDS									
BENZIGER FAMILY WINERY '92, Sonoma Mtn. Est., Tribute $16.00		S	G			S	B		
BERINGER VINEYARDS '93, Knights Vly. $9.00	B	S				B		B	
DE LORIMIER VINEYARDS '92, Alexander Vly., Spectrum $10.00		S	B			B	S		
3 AWARDS									
COSENTINO WINERY '94, Napa Vly., The Novelist $16.00	B	B				S			
GUENOC WINERY '94, Guenoc Vly., Langtry $17.00	G			B		B			
VENEZIA '94, Alex. Vly., Nuovo Mondo $20.00		G		B		B			
2 AWARDS									
CARDINALE WINERY '94, California, Royale $15.00				S		B			

1994

VINEYARDS

White Zinfandel

CALIFORNIA

White Zinfandel

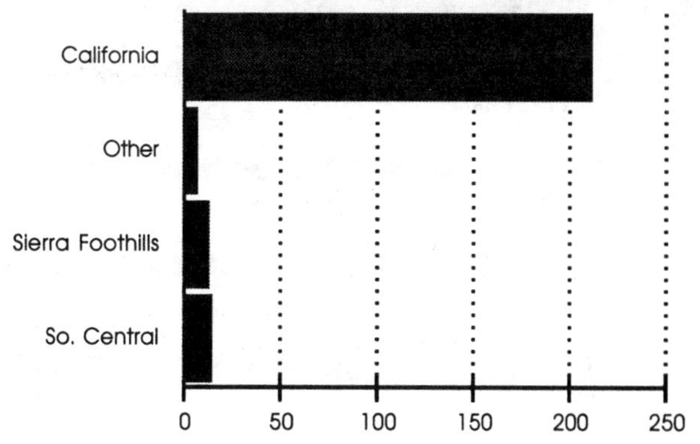

Regional Comparison of Total Points

(Gold-plus=7 Gold=5 Silver=3 Bronze=1)

Highest individual wine totals

26	**FETZER VINEYARDS** '94, California, $7.00
25	**BEL ARBORS VINEYARD** '94, California, $5.00
19	**WEINSTOCK CELLARS** '94, California, $7.00
18	**BERINGER VINEYARDS** '94, California, $5.00
18	**V. SATTUI WINERY** '94, California, $8.00
14	**GLEN ELLEN WINERY** '94, California, Prop.Reserve, $4.00
13	**CYPRESS VINEYARD** '94, California, $6.00
10	**DELICATO VINEYARDS** '94, California, $5.00
9	**RUTHERFORD ESTATE CELLARS** '94, California, $6.00
9	**M. G. VALLEJO WINERY** '94, California, $5.00

White Zinfandel	L.A.	Orange	Farmers	San Fran	Dallas	State Fair	New World	W. Coast	San Diego
9 AWARDS									
BEL ARBORS VINEYARD '94, California $5.00	B	G	S	B	B	B	G	G	S
8 AWARDS									
FETZER VINEYARDS '94, California $7.00	B	B	G		B	S	G	G	G
7 AWARDS									
WEINSTOCK CELLARS '94, California $7.00	S	G	B		B	Σ		B	B
6 AWARDS									
BERINGER VINEYARDS '94, California $5.00	G	G			B	B	S	S	
GLEN ELLEN WINERY '94, California, Prop.Reserve $4.00	S	B		B	B		G		S
V. SATTUI WINERY '94, California $8.00			G	S	B		G	S	B
5 AWARDS									
CYPRESS VINEYARD '94, California $6.00		S		B	B		G	S	
4 AWARDS									
DELICATO VINEYARDS '94, California $5.00	S				B		G	B	
DORE WINES '94, California $6.00	S			B			B	S	
NAPA RIDGE WINERY '94, Lodi $5.00	S		B			S	B		
3 AWARDS									
BARON HERZOG WINE CELLARS '94, California $6.00		G	B					B	
CASTORO CELLARS '94, San Luis Obispo Co. $6.00			B					B	B
GRAND CRU VINEYARDS '94, California $7.00			B				B	B	
RUTHERFORD ESTATE CELLARS '94, California $6.00		G		S		B			
M. G. VALLEJO WINERY '94, California $5.00	B	B				Σ			
2 AWARDS									
ARCIERO WINERY '93, Paso Robles, Estate $5.50							G	S	

White Zinfandel

2 AWARDS

L.A.	Orange	Farmers	San Fran	Dallas	State Fair	New World	W. Coast	San Diego	White Zinfandel
		B			B				**BAREFOOT CELLARS** 'NV, California $4.00
		B					B		**MAURICE CAR'RIE WINERY** '94, Temecula $4.00
		S						B	**CRESTON VINEYARDS** '94, Paso Robles $6.00
	B						B		**GROVE STREET WINERY** '94, California $4.50
		B					S		**MONTEVINA WINERY** '94, Amador Co. $6.50
	S	S							**MONTPELLIER VINEYARDS** '94, California $7.00
B							S		**SAN MARTIN WINERY** '94, California $5.00
		B			B				**SANTINO WINES** '94, Amador Co., White Harvest $6.00
					G		B		**SINGLE LEAF VINEYARDS** '94, El Dorado $6.00

GREENWOOD
RIDGE
VINEYARDS
SONOMA COUNTY
ZINFANDEL
1993
SCHERRER VINEYARDS
ALCOHOL 13.5% BY VOLUME

GARY FARRELL
1993
COLLINS VINEYARD
RUSSIAN RIVER VALLEY
ZINFANDEL
PRODUCED AND BOTTLED BY GARY FARRELL
HEALDSBURG, CA CONTAINS SULFITES TABLE WINE

Zinfandel

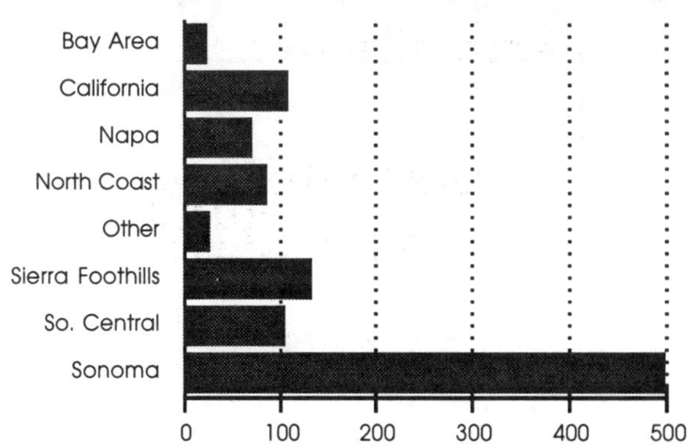

Regional Comparison of Total Points

(Gold-plus=7 Gold=5 Silver=3 Bronze=1)

Highest individual wine totals

36 **GREENWOOD RIDGE VINEYARDS**
'93, Sonoma, Scherrer Vnyd., $14.00

28 **MC ILROY WINES**
'93, Russian Riv.., Porter Bass Vnyd., $15.00

24 **GARY FARRELL**
'93, Russian River, Collins Vnyd., $15.00

22 **CASTORO CELLARS**
'92, Paso Robles, $10.00

18 **BELVEDERE WINERY**
'91, Dry Creek Vly., $11.00

18 **J. FRITZ WINERY**
'93, Dry Creek, 80 Yr. Old Vines, $12.00

16 **CLOS DU BOIS**
'93, Sonoma Co., $13.00

16 **KENDALL-JACKSON WINERY**
'92, California,Grand Reserve, $20.00

15 **EBERLE WINERY**
'93, Paso Robles, Sauret Vnyd., $13.00

15 **ROSENBLUM CELLARS**
'93, Sonoma Co., Old Vines, $13.00

14 **PRESTON VINEYARDS & WINERY**
'93, Dry Creek Vly., Est., $12.00

14 **QUIVIRA VINEYARDS**
'93, Dry Creek Vly., $14.00

Zinfandel	L.A.	Orange	Farmers	San Fran	Dallas	State Fair	New World	W. Coast	San Diego
9 AWARDS									
EBERLE WINERY '93, Paso Robles, Sauret Vnyd. $13.00	B	B	B	G	B	S	B	B	B
8 AWARDS									
GARY FARRELL '93, Russian River, Collins Vnyd. $15.00	B	S	Σ	S		B	G	S	B
GREENWOOD RIDGE VINEYARDS '93, Sonoma, Scherrer Vnyd. $14.00	G	G	G	S	S	G	G	G	
6 AWARDS									
BELVEDERE WINERY '91, Dry Creek Vly. $11.00	Σ	B	B	B			S		G
CASTORO CELLARS '92, Paso Robles $10.00	G	G	S	S				S	S
DE LOACH VINEYARDS '93, Russian River Vly. $13.00		B	B	B	B	S	B		
MC ILROY WINES '93, Russian Riv.., Porter Bass Vnyd. $15.00	Σ	G	Σ	B				G	S
MONTEVINA WINERY '93, Amador Co. $7.00	B	S	S	S		B		B	
QUIVIRA VINEYARDS '93, Dry Creek Vly. $14.00	S		B	S		S		B	S
ROSENBLUM CELLARS '93, Contra Costa Co. $11.00		S	B		S	S	S	B	
5 AWARDS									
BARON HERZOG WINE CELLARS '93, Sonoma Co. $12.00			S	S		B		B	G
FETZER VINEYARDS '92, Mendocino Co., Barrel Sel. $9.00		B		B	S		G	B	
FETZER VINEYARDS '91, Mendocino Co., Reserve $13.00	S	B					B	B	B
GUNDLACH-BUNDSCHU WINERY '93, Sonoma, Rhinefarm Vnyd. $14.00	S	B				S		B	B
HOP KILN WINERY '93, Sonoma Co., Primitivo $18.00		B	B	S		G		B	
ROSENBLUM CELLARS '93, Sonoma Co., Old Vines $13.00		G	B			G		B	S
4 AWARDS									
BENZIGER FAMILY WINERY '92, Sonoma Co. $14.00			B	B			B		S

Zinfandel

4 AWARDS

L.A.	Orange	Farmers	San Fran	Dallas	State Fair	New World	W. Coast	San Diego	Zinfandel
		B	B	B			G		**DAVIS BYNUM WINERY** '92, Russian River Vly. $12.00
G			Σ		S			B	**CLOS DU BOIS** '93, Sonoma Co. $13.00
	B	G	B				B		**EDMEADES ESTATE WINERY** '92, North Coast $12.50
			B		B		S	G	**FRANCISCAN OAKVILLE ESTATE** '93, Napa Vly. $11.00
G	G				S			G	**J. FRITZ WINERY** '93, Dry Creek, 80 Yr. Old Vines $12.00
S					G	S	B		**GRANITE SPRINGS WINERY** '92, El Dorado, Est. $8.00
				B	B		B	B	**KENDALL-JACKSON WINERY** '92, California, Vintner's Reserve $13.00
S	S					G	G		**KENDALL-JACKSON WINERY** '92, California,Grand Reserve $20.00
B	B						S	B	**KENWOOD VINEYARDS** '92, Sonoma Vly. $12.00
G		B	S				B		**MEEKER VINEYARD** '93, Dry Creek, Gold Leaf Cuvee $13.00
B		S	B			B			**NAVARRO VINEYARDS** '93, Mendocino $15.00
		B	B		Σ			B	**NICHELINI VINEYARDS** '91, Napa Vly., Nichelini Vnyd. $12.00
S		S	G				S		**PRESTON VINEYARDS & WINERY** '93, Dry Creek Vly., Est. $12.00
		B				G	G	B	**RABBIT RIDGE VINEYARDS** '93, Dry Creek Vly. $10.00
S	S	B			G				**A. RAFANELLI WINERY** '93, Dry Creek Vly. $13.00
	G	S				S	S		**RIVER RUN VINTNERS** '93, California, LH, R.S. 7.0% $15.00
	G		S		S		B		**ROSENBLUM CELLARS** '93, Mt. Veeder, Brandlin Ranch $19.00
S	G				S			S	**SAUSAL WINERY** '93, Alexander Vly. $9.00
					G	B	S	B	**SONOMA CREEK WINERY** '93, Sonoma Co. $10.00
	S			B	B		B		**STORRS WINERY** '92, Beauregard Ranch $15.00

Zinfandel	L.A.	Orange	Farmers	San Fran	Dallas	State Fair	New World	W. Coast	San Diego
4 AWARDS									
WINDSOR VINEYARDS '92, Sonoma, Shelton Sig. Series $14.00	S						B	B	B
3 AWARDS									
DAVID BRUCE WINERY '92, San Luis Obispo, Vintners Sel. $10.00	S			B				S	
CLAUDIA SPRINGS WINERY '93, Mendocino, Pacini Vnyd. $14.00		B	B	S					
COSENTINO WINERY '93, Sonoma Co., The Zin $18.00		B	S				B		
DUNNEWOOD VINEYARD '92, Sonoma $7.00			S		S		S		
EDMEADES ESTATE WINERY '93, Mendocino Co., Zeni Vnyd. $20.00	B						G		B
FORESTVILLE VINEYARD '93, California $6.00	S	B	S						
GRGICH HILLS CELLAR '91, Sonoma Co. $14.00			S					B	B
GUENOC WINERY '91, California $10.00			B	B	B				
KENDALL-JACKSON WINERY '93, California, Vintner's Reserve $13.00	B		B	B					
MEEKER VINEYARD '92, Sonoma Co., Third Rack $8.00						S	S	B	
PEIRANO ESTATE VINEYARDS '92, Lodi, Est. $10.00	B					B		S	
ROSENBLUM CELLARS 'NV, California, Cuvee X $8.00			G					S	B
ROUND HILL VINEYARDS '92, Napa Vly. $8.00					B			B	B
SANTINO WINES '89, Amador Co., Dry Berry Select $11.00	Σ					S	B		
SIERRA VISTA WINERY '93, El Dorado, Est. $10.00	G							S	S
SILVER HORSE VINEYARDS '92, Paso Robles $12.00		S						Σ	S
STORRS WINERY '93, Santa Cruz Mtns. $16.00	S	B		G					
STORYBOOK MOUNTAIN VINEYARDS '92, Napa Vly. $14.00		S	S						B

L.A.	Orange	Farmers	San Fran	Dallas	State Fair	New World	W. Coast	San Diego	Zinfandel
									3 AWARDS
B					B			B	**TULOCAY WINERY** '92, Napa Vly., Casanova Vnyd. $11.00
G					B		S		**VILLA MT. EDEN** '93, California, Cellar Select $8.00
B		B						B	**YORK MOUNTAIN WINERY** '91, San Luis Obispo Co. $9.00
									2 AWARDS
			S		Σ				**BOEGER WINERY** '93, El Dorado, Walker Vnyd. $12.00
B					S				**BOEGER WINERY** '92, El Dorado $10.00
				B	B				**BRUTOCAO CELLARS** '93, Mendocino, Hopland Ranch $12.00
		S						G	**CHESTNUT HILL WINERY** '91, California, Old Vines Cuvee $8.00
	S			G					**CLINE CELLARS** '93, Contra Costa Co. $10.00
B					B				**DE MOOR WINERY** '93, Napa Vly. $12.00
S								B	**DEER PARK WINERY** '91, Napa Vly., Howell Mtn. $14.00
			B		B				**DELICATO VINEYARDS** '93, California $6.00
				S				Σ	**DRY CREEK VINEYARD** '92, Sonoma Co., Old Vines $15.00
S						G			**ESTRELLA RIVER WINERY** '93, California, Prop. Reserve $6.00
		B					B		**FOPPIANO VINEYARDS** '93, Dry Creek Vly. $9.50
	S						B		**HAYWOOD WINERY** '92, Sonoma, Los Chamizal Vnyd. $14.00
		G				G			**HAYWOOD WINERY** '92, Sonoma, Rocky Terrace, Est. $18.00
S				S					**HAYWOOD WINERY** '91, Sonoma, Los Chamizal Vnyd. $14.00
		B					B		**HIDDEN CELLARS** '93, Mendocino, Organic $10.00
						G	B		**HOP KILN WINERY** '92, Russian River Vly. $14.00

Zinfandel

2 AWARDS

Wine	L.A.	Orange	Farmers	San Fran	Dallas	State Fair	New World	W. Coast	San Diego
JANKRIS VINEYARD '93, Paso Robles, Est. $9.50			B						B
LATCHAM VINEYARDS '93, El Dorado, Reserve $10.00				B		B			
MADRONA VINEYARDS '93, El Dorado $9.00				S		S			
MADRONA VINEYARDS '92, El Dorado, Estate $8.50		B						B	
MAZZOCCO VINEYARDS '93, Sonoma Co. $14.00	B			S					
MAZZOCCO VINEYARDS '92, Sonoma Co. $14.00			B		B				
MEEKER VINEYARD '93, Sonoma Co., Cuvee $10.00			B					S	
MERIDIAN VINEYARDS '90, Paso Robles $13.00	S		S						
MIRASSOU VINEYARDS '92, Central Coast, Family Sel. $6.00						S		B	
MISSION VIEW VINEYARDS '93, Paso Robles $12.00				B		G			
MONTEVINA WINERY '93, Amador Co., Brioso $7.50		B		S					
NEVADA CITY WINERY '93, Sierra Foothills $10.00						B		B	
PEDRONCELLI WINERY '93, Dry Creek, Pedroni-Bushnell $12.00	S							B	
A. RAFANELLI WINERY '92, Dry Creek Vly. $13.00					B		G		
RIVER RUN VINTNERS '92, California							B	G	
ROSENBLUM CELLARS '93, Alex. Vly., Harris-Kratka Vnyd. $15.00						B		B	
ROSENBLUM CELLARS '93, Paso Robles, R. Sauret Vnyd. $11.50			B					G	
SANTA BARBARA WINERY '92, Santa Ynez, La Fond Vnyd. $11.00	B	B							
V. SATTUI WINERY '91, Napa Vly., Howell Mtn. $16.00			S				G		

L.A.	Orange	Farmers	San Fran	Dallas	State Fair	New World	W. Coast	San Diego	Zinfandel
									2 AWARDS
B								S	**SEGHESIO WINERY** '93, Sonoma Co., Home Ranch $9.00
						S		Σ	**SONOMA CREEK WINERY** '93, Sonoma Vly., Old Vines
	S			B					**SONORA WINERY** '92, Sonoma, Passalacqua Vnyd. $10.00
	S						G		**ST. FRANCIS VINEYARDS** '93, Sonoma Vly., Old Vines $16.00
						G	B		**RODNEY STRONG VINEYARDS** '92, Russian Riv., River West Vnyd. $14.00
B								S	**SUTTER HOME WINERY** '90, Amador Co., Reserve
		S				Σ			**VILLA MT. EDEN** '92, California, Cellar Select $8.00
	S						B		**WHITE OAK VINEYARDS** '92, Sonoma Co. $9.00
B					S				**WILDHURST VINEYARDS** '92, Clear Lake $9.00
		B			S				**WINDSOR VINEYARDS** '92, Sonoma Co. $8.00

ALL VARIETALS

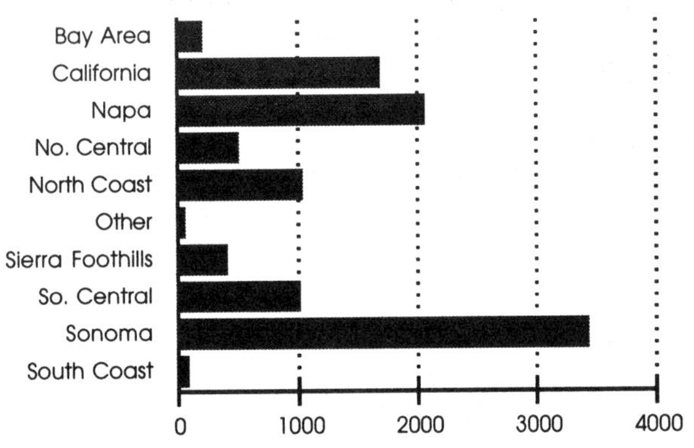

Regional Comparison of Total Points

(Gold-plus=7 Gold=5 Silver=3 Bronze=1)

Grand Total Points for Wineries

Points	Winery
291	**KENDALL-JACKSON WINERY** 421 Aviation Blvd., Santa Rosa CA 95403
281	**GEYSER PEAK WINERY** 22281 Chianti Rd., Geyserville CA 95441
273	**FETZER VINEYARDS** 13325 So. Hwy. 101, Hopland CA 95449
223	**GUENOC WINERY** 21000 Butts Cyn.Rd., Middletown CA
160	**CHATEAU ST. JEAN** 8555 Sonoma Hwy., Kenwood CA 95452
159	**WINDSOR VINEYARDS** 11455 Old Redwood Hwy., Healdsburg CA
154	**DE LOACH VINEYARDS** 1791 Olivet Rd., Santa Rosa CA 95401
153	**BERINGER VINEYARDS** 2000 Main Street, St Helena CA 94574
145	**V. SATTUI WINERY** 1111 White Lane, St Helena CA 94574
130	**CONCANNON VINEYARD** 4590 Tesla Road, Livermore CA 94550
115	**NAVARRO VINEYARDS** 5601 Highway 128, Philo CA 95466
114	**MIRASSOU VINEYARDS** 3000 Aborn Rd., San Jose CA 95135

111 **BENZIGER FAMILY WINERY**
1883 London Ranch Rd., Glen Ellen CA

109 **VILLA MT. EDEN**
620 Oakville Cross Rd., Oakville CA 94562

103 **STONESTREET WINERY**
4611 Thomas Road, Healdsburg CA 95448

100 **GREENWOOD RIDGE VINEYARDS**
5501 Highway 128, Philo CA 95466

99 **GARY FARRELL**
P.O. Box 342, Forestville CA 95436

96 **NAPA RIDGE WINERY**
2000 Main Street, St Helena CA 94574

87 **CLOS DU BOIS**
19410 Geyserville Ave., Geyserville CA

86 **CHATEAU SOUVERAIN**
400 Souverain Road, Geyserville CA 95441

83 **BEAULIEU VINEYARD**
1960 St. Helena Highway, Rutherford CA

82 **DRY CREEK VINEYARD**
3770 Lambert Bridge, Healdsburg CA

82 **HUSCH VINEYARDS**
4400 Highway 128, Philo CA 95466

82 **RAYMOND VINEYARD & CELLAR**
849 Zinfandel Lane, St Helena CA 94574

81 **GLORIA FERRER**
23555 Carneros Hwy. 121, Sonoma CA

80 **HANDLEY CELLARS**
3151 Highway 128, Philo CA 95466

79 **RODNEY STRONG VINEYARDS**
11455 Old Redwood Hwy., Healdsburg CA

78 **DAVIS BYNUM WINERY**
8075 Westside Rd., Healdsburg CA 95448

76 **CAMBRIA WINERY**
5475 Chardonnay Lane, Santa Maria CA

71 **CANYON ROAD CELLARS**
22281 Chianti Rd., Geyserville CA 95441

70 **DAVID BRUCE WINERY**
21439 Bear Creek Road, Los Gatos CA

68 **KORBEL CHAMPAGNE CELLARS**
13250 River Road, Guerneville CA 95446

ABBEY D'OR

4620 Hog Canyon Rd. San Miguel 93451
Chenin Blanc,'94, Paso Robles $6.00 (B-Orange)

ACACIA WINERY

2750 Las Amigas Road Napa 94559
Chardonnay,'92, Carneros Reserve (B-Dallas)
Chardonnay,'93, Carneros $11.00 (B-Orange)
Pinot Noir,'93, Carneros $25.00 (2)
Zinfandel,'93, Napa, Caviste, Old Vines $11.00 (B-Orange)

ADELAIDA CELLARS

2170 Adelaida Rd. Paso Robles 93446
Chardonnay,'91, San Luis Obispo $17.00 (B-New World)
Pinot Noir,'93, San Luis Obispo $27.00 (2)
Zinfandel,'92, San Luis Obispo $15.00 (G-L.A.)

ADLER FELS

5325 Corrick Lane Santa Rosa 95405
Chardonnay,'92, Sonoma, Coleman Res. $12.00 (B-New World)
Gewurztraminer,'94, Sonoma Co. $10.00 (8)
Sauvignon Blanc,'92, Sonoma Co. Fume $10.00 (6)
Sauvignon Blanc,'92, Sonoma, Fume, Organic $10.00 (5)

ALDERBROOK WINERY

2306 Magnolia Drive Healdsburg 95448
Chardonnay,'93, Dry Creek Vly. $10.00 (2)
Gewurztraminer,'94, Russian River Vly. $8.00 (3)
Gewurztraminer,'94, Russian River, Barrel Ferm. $10.00 (2)
Sauvignon Blanc,'93, Dry Creek Vly. $8.50 (3)
Sauvignon Blanc,'94, Dry Creek Vly. $8.50 (B-Orange)
Semillon,'92, Santa Clara Vly. $8.00 (S-San Fran)
Syrah,'93, Russian River Vly. $14.00 (3)
Zinfandel,'92, Dry Creek Vly. $12.00 (B-New World)
Zinfandel,'93, Dry Creek Vly. $12.00 (G-State Fair)

ALEXANDER VALLEY VINEYARDS

8644 Highway 128 Healdsburg 95448
Cabernet Sauvignon,'87, Alexander Vly. $18.00 (B-San Fran)
Cabernet Sauvignon,'92, Wetzel Fam. Vnyd. $15.00 (B-Orange)

ROBERT ALLISON WINERY

Address Not Available
Chardonnay,'94, California (G-L.A.)

ALPEN CELLARS

P.O. Box 3966 Trinity Center 96091
Gewurztraminer,'94, California $6.00 (3)
Johannisberg Riesling,'94, Trinity Co. $6.00 (S-State Fair)

ALTAMURA VINEYARD

4240 Silverado Trail Napa 94558
Cabernet Sauvignon,'90, Napa Vly. $25.00 (G-San Fran)

AMADOR FOOTHILL WINERY

12500 Steiner Road Plymouth 95669
Zinfandel,'91, Shenandoah, Ferrero Vnyd. $10.00 (B-State Fair)

S. ANDERSON VINEYARD

1473 Yountville Cross Road   Yountville   94599

Sparkling Wine,'89, Napa Vly., Brut $18.00 (6)
Sparkling Wine,'90, Napa Vly., Blanc De Noirs $20.00 (5)
Sparkling Wine,'90, Napa Vly., Brut $20.00 (S-San Fran)

ANGELINE

Address Not Available

Zinfandel,'92, California, Old Vine Cuvee   (B-L.A.)

ARCIERO WINERY

P. O. Box 1287   Paso Robles   93447

Chardonnay,'93, Paso Robles, Est. $9.00 (7)
Petite Sirah,'92, Paso Robles, Est. $9.00 (B-Orange)
White Zinfandel,'93, Paso Robles, Estate $5.50 (2)

ARMIDA WINERY

2201 Westside Road   Healdsburg   95448

Chardonnay,'93, Russian River Vly. $12.00 (3)
Chardonnay,'93, Russian River Vly., Reserve $18.00 (2)
Merlot,'92, Russian River Vly.   (2)
Pinot Noir,'93, Russian River Vly. $13.00 (2)

ATLAS PEAK VINEYARD

3700 Soda Canyon Rd.   Napa   94558

Cabernet Sauvignon,'91, Napa Vly., Atlas Peak $16.00 (2)
Chardonnay,'93, Napa Vly., Atlas Peak Dist. $16.00 (2)

AUDUBON CELLARS

600 Addison Street   Berkeley   94710

Cabernet Sauvignon,'92, Napa Vly. $11.00 (2)
Sauvignon Blanc,'92, Napa Vly, LH $10.00 (2)
Sauvignon Blanc,'94, Napa Vly., Juliana Vnyd. $9.00 (B-Farmers)

AZALEA SPRINGS

Address Not Available

Merlot,'92, Napa Vly. $22.00 (2)

B

WILLIAM BACCALA

Address Not Available

Merlot,'91, Napa Vly. $13.00 (B-W. Coast)

BAILEY & BROCK CELLARS

5500 Highway 128   Philo   95466

Sparkling Wine,'NV, Central Coast, Brut Rose $15.00 (B-Farmers)

BAILEYANA VINEYARD

3031 Lopez Drive   San Luis Obispo   93401

Chardonnay,'93, Edna Vly., Paragon Vnyd. $13.00 (5)

BAILY VINEYARD & WINERY

36150 Pauba Road   Temecula   92592

Chardonnay,'93, Temecula, Greer Vnyd.   (B-New World)
Johannisberg Riesling,'94, Mother's Vnyd. $8.00 (B-Farmers)

BALLATORE CHAMPAGNE CELLARS

P. O. Box 1130   Modesto   95353

Sparkling Wine,'NV, California, Gran Spumante $5.00 (9)

BALLENTINE WINES

2820 St. Helena Hwy. St Helena 94574

Cabernet Franc,'92, Napa Vly. $15.00 (3)
Merlot,'92, California (B-New World)

BANDIERA WINERY

155 Cherry Creek Rd. Cloverdale 95425

Cabernet Sauvignon,'93, Napa Vly. $8.00 (3)
Chardonnay,'93, Napa Vly. $8.00 (G-New World)
Chardonnay,'94, Napa Vly. $8.00 (2)
Sauvignon Blanc,'94, Napa Vly. (B-New World)

BAREFOOT CELLARS

134-A Lystra Court Santa Rosa 95403

Cabernet Sauvignon,'NV, California $4.00 (4)
Chardonnay,'NV, California $4.00 (3)
Sauvignon Blanc,'NV, California $5.00 (2)
White Zinfandel,'NV, California $4.00 (2)

BARGETTO WINERY

3535 N. Main Street Soquel 95073

Chardonnay,'93, Central Coast, Cypress $10.00 (B-Orange)
Chardonnay,'93, Santa Cruz Mtns. $16.00 (B-Orange)
Gewurztraminer,'94, Monterey $9.00 (8)
Gewurztraminer,'94, Santa Cruz Mtns., Barrel Ferm. $10.00 (5)
Merlot,'92, San Ysidro (B-Dallas)
Merlot,'93, California $16.00 (4)

BARON HERZOG WINE CELLARS

12378 Saratoga-Sunnyvale Rd. Saratoga 95070

Cabernet Sauvignon,'93, California $13.00 (5)
Cabernet Sauvignon,'93, Chalk Hill, Reserve $11.00 (4)
Chardonnay,'93, California $11.00 (S-Orange)
Chenin Blanc,'94, Clarksburg $6.00 (6)
Johannisberg Riesling,'93, Monterey Co., LH $14.00 (B-Farmers)
Johannisberg Riesling,'94, Monterey Co., LH $14.00 (4)
Sauvignon Blanc,'93, Sonoma Co. (B-New World)
White Zinfandel,'94, California $6.00 (3)
Zinfandel,'93, Sonoma Co. $12.00 (5)

BEAUCANON COMPANY

1695 St. Helena Hwy. St Helena 94574

Cabernet Sauvignon,'91, Napa Vly. $14.00 (2)

BEAULIEU VINEYARD

1960 St. Helena Highway Rutherford 94573

Cabernet Sauvignon,'90, Latour Reserve $40.00 (S-State Fair)
Cabernet Sauvignon,'91, Latour Reserve $40.00 (2)
Cabernet Sauvignon,'91, Napa Vly., Rutherford $11.00 (S-Farmers)
Cabernet Sauvignon,'92, Napa Vly., Beautour $8.00 (2)
Cabernet Sauvignon,'92, Rutherford $14.00 (3)
Chardonnay,'92, Napa Vly., Carneros Res. $18.00 (5)
Chardonnay,'93, Los Carneros $13.00 (3)
Chardonnay,'93, Napa Vly., Beautour $8.00 (3)
Chardonnay,'94, California, Beautour $8.00 (B-San Fran)
Merlot,'92, Napa Vly., Beautour $8.00 (3)
Pinot Noir,'92, Napa Vly., Carneros, Reserve $18.00 (3)
Pinot Noir,'93, Carneros $11.00 (3)
Pinot Noir,'93, Napa Vly., Beautour $8.00 (2)

Red Meritage,'90, Napa Vly., Tapestry $20.00 (2)
Red Meritage,'91, Napa Vly., Tapestry $20.00 (4)
Sauvignon Blanc,'93, Napa Vly. $8.50 (4)
Sauvignon Blanc,'94, Napa Vly., Beautour $7.00 (B-W. Coast)

BEL ARBORS VINEYARD

13325 So. Highway 101 Hopland 95449

Cabernet Sauvignon,'92, California $7.00 (5)
Chardonnay,'93, California $7.00 (3)
Merlot,'93, California $7.00 (4)
Sauvignon Blanc,'93, California $5.00 (3)
White Zinfandel,'94, California $5.00 (9)

BELL VINEYARDS

Address Not Available

Cabernet Sauvignon,'91, Baratelle Vnyd. $40.00 (S-San Fran)

BELVEDERE WINERY

4035 Westside Road Healdsburg 95448

Cabernet Sauvignon,'90, Preferred Stock $18.00 (B-W. Coast)
Cabernet Sauvignon,'92, Sonoma Co. $12.00 (3)
Chardonnay,'92, Alexander Vly. $10.00 (S-Dallas)
Chardonnay,'93, Alexander Vly. $10.00 (4)
Chardonnay,'93, Russian River Vly. $13.00 (2)
Chardonnay,'93, Sonoma Co. $9.00 (4)
Chardonnay,'93, Sonoma Co., Preferred Stock $18.00 (2)
Merlot,'92, Sonoma Co. $13.00 (4)
Zinfandel,'91, Dry Creek Vly. $11.00 (6)

BENICIA CELLARS

4740 E. Second St. #33 Benicia 94510

Cabernet Sauvignon,'NV, Napa Vly., Capitol Reserve $12.00 (2)

BENZIGER FAMILY WINERY

1883 London Ranch Rd. Glen Ellen 95442

Cabernet Sauvignon,'90, Sonoma Mtn. $16.00 (3)
Cabernet Sauvignon,'91, Sonoma Co. $13.00 (2)
Cabernet Sauvignon,'92, Sonoma Co. $13.00 (4)
Chardonnay,'92, Carneros, Premier Vnyd. $16.00 (3)
Chardonnay,'93, Sonoma, Carneros $16.00 (3)
Merlot,'91, Sonoma Mtn., Est. $16.00 (3)
Merlot,'92, Sonoma Co. $14.00 (2)
Merlot,'93, Sonoma Co. $14.00 (2)
Pinot Noir,'92, California $14.00 (7)
Red Meritage,'90, Sonoma Mtn., A Tribute $20.00 (6)
Sauvignon Blanc,'94, Sonoma Co. Fume $10.00 (2)
White Meritage,'92, Sonoma Mtn. Est., Tribute $16.00 (4)
Zinfandel,'92, Sonoma Co. $14.00 (4)

BERINGER VINEYARDS

2000 Main Street St Helena 94574

Cabernet Sauvignon,'91, Knights Vly. $16.00 (2)
Cabernet Sauvignon,'91, Napa Vly., Reserve $45.00 (4)
Cabernet Sauvignon,'92, Knights Vly. $16.00 (3)
Chardonnay,'93, Napa Vly. $10.50 (3)
Chardonnay,'93, Napa Vly., Reserve $22.00 (3)
Chenin Blanc,'93, Napa Vly. $7.50 (2)
Chenin Blanc,'94, Napa Vly. $7.00 (B-State Fair)
Gewurztraminer,'93, California $8.00 (B-Dallas)

Gewurztraminer,'94, California $8.00 (4)
Johannisberg Riesling,'94, California $8.00 (5)
Merlot,'91, Howell Mtn., Bancroft Ranch $28.00 (6)
Red Meritage,'91, Knights Vly., Prop. Grown $14.00 (4)
Red Meritage,'92, Knights Vly. $14.00 (3)
Sauvignon Blanc,'92, Napa Vly. $7.50 (G-New World)
White Meritage,'92, Knights Vly. $9.00 (5)
White Meritage,'93, Knights Vly. $9.00 (4)
White Zinfandel,'94, California $5.00 (6)
Zinfandel,'91, Napa Vly. $8.50 (B-Dallas)
Zinfandel,'92, North Coast $7.50 (S-W. Coast)

BETTINELLI

1241 Adams St., #1029 St Helena 94574

Cabernet Sauvignon,'92, Napa Vly. $13.00 (S-Orange)
Chardonnay,'92, Napa Vly. $11.00 (B-Dallas)
Chardonnay,'93, Napa Vly. $11.00 (G-Orange)

BLACKSTONE

Address Not Available

Chardonnay,'94, Monterey Co., Reserve $7.00 (B-Orange)
Merlot,'93, California, Reserve (B-L.A.)
Merlot,'93, Napa Vly., Reserve $10.00 (2)
Zinfandel,'92, California (B-New World)

BLOSSOM HILL WINERY

P. O. Box 99 Madera 93639

Cabernet Sauvignon,'NV, California $4.00 (3)
Chardonnay,'NV, California, Reserve (B-New World)
Merlot,'NV, California $4.00 (2)
White Zinfandel,'NV, California, Reserve (S-New World)

BOEGER WINERY

1709 Carson Road Placerville 95667

Merlot,'93, El Dorado $14.00 (B-San Fran)
Red Meritage,'91, El Dorado $15.00 (3)
Zinfandel,'92, El Dorado $10.00 (2)
Zinfandel,'93, El Dorado, Walker Vnyd. $12.00 (2)

BOGLE VINEYARDS

37675 County Road 144 Clarksburg 95612

Cabernet Sauvignon,'93, California $6.00 (S-Farmers)
Chardonnay,'94, California $6.00 (S-Orange)
Chenin Blanc,'93, Clarksburg $6.00 (B-State Fair)
Merlot,'93, California $8.00 (2)
Petite Sirah,'93, California $7.00 (5)
Zinfandel,'93, California $7.00 (B-L.A.)

BOUCHAINE VINEYARDS

1075 Buchli Station Rd. Napa 94559

Chardonnay,'92, Carneros (B-Dallas)
Gewurztraminer,'93, Russian River Vly., Dry (S-Dallas)

BRICELAND VINEYARDS

5959 Briceland Rd. Redway 95560

Johannisberg Riesling,'94, Bourassa Vnyd. $9.00 (S-State Fair)
Sparkling Wine,'NV, Humboldt Co., Brut $16.00 (2)

DAVID BRUCE WINERY

21439 Bear Creek Road Los Gatos 95030

Cabernet Sauvignon,'92, Mendo/S. Clara, Res. $18.00 (S-Orange)
Chardonnay,'92, California, Vintner Select $12.00 (B-San Diego)
Chardonnay,'92, Santa Cruz Mtns., Est. Reserve $30.00 (2)
Chardonnay,'92, Santa Cruz Mtns., Estate $20.00 (2)
Chardonnay,'92, Santa Cruz, Split Rail Vnyd. $20.00 (S-San Fran)
Petite Sirah,'92, California, Vintner's Select $10.00 (4)
Pinot Noir,'92, Santa Cruz Mtns., Est. Reserve $35.00 (9)
Pinot Noir,'92, Sonoma, Vintner Select $13.00 (B-Dallas)
Pinot Noir,'93, Russian River Vly., Reserve $25.00 (2)
Pinot Noir,'93, Sonoma Co., Vintner's Select $13.00 (6)
Zinfandel,'92, San Luis Obispo, Vintners Sel. $10.00 (3)

BRUTOCAO CELLARS

2300 Highway 175 Hopland 95449

Cabernet Sauvignon,'90, Mendocino, Est. $13.00 (3)
Chardonnay,'93, Mendocino, Bliss Vnyd. (S-New World)
Merlot,'93, Mendocino Co., Estate $15.00 (2)
Pinot Noir,'93, Anderson Vly., Reserve $20.00 (B-San Fran)
Sauvignon Blanc,'93, Mendocino $9.00 (B-W. Coast)
Sauvignon Blanc,'94, Mendocino, Est. $9.00 (3)
Zinfandel,'93, Mendocino, Hopland Ranch $12.00 (2)

BUEHLER VINEYARDS

820 Greenfield Rd. St Helena 94574

Cabernet Sauvignon,'92, Napa Vly. $14.00 (3)
Cabernet Sauvignon,'93, California $9.00 (5)
Chardonnay,'93, Russian River Vly. $12.00 (4)
White Zinfandel,'94, Napa Vly. $6.00 (B-San Diego)

BUENA VISTA

27000 Ramal Road Sonoma 95476

Cabernet Sauvignon,'90, Carneros, Grand Reserve $24.00 (2)
Cabernet Sauvignon,'91, Carneros $12.00 (3)
Chardonnay,'91, Carneros, Grand Reserve $20.00 (B-Farmers)
Chardonnay,'92, Carneros $10.00 (S-L.A.)
Chardonnay,'93, Carneros $10.00 (B-Orange)
Merlot,'92, Sonoma, Carneros, Est. $13.00 (2)
Pinot Noir,'92, Carneros $10.00 (4)
Pinot Noir,'92, Carneros, Grand Reserve $20.00 (2)
Pinot Noir,'93, Carneros $10.00 (S-Orange)
Sauvignon Blanc,'93, Lake Co. $7.50 (3)
Sauvignon Blanc,'94, Lake Co. $7.50 (3)

BURGESS CELLARS

1108 Deer Park Road St Helena 94574

Cabernet Sauvignon,'91, Napa Vly. $18.00 (B-San Fran)

BUTTONWOOD FARM

1500 Alamo Pintado Rd. Solvang 93463

Sauvignon Blanc,'93, Santa Ynez Vly. $11.50 (B-Orange)

BYINGTON WINERY

21850 Bear Creek Rd. Los Gatos 95030

Cabernet Sauvignon,'91, Smith Reichle Vnyd. (B-New World)
Cabernet Sauvignon,'92, Bates Ranch $20.00 (B-State Fair)
Chardonnay,'93, Santa Cruz, Redwood Hill (B-Dallas)
Pinot Noir,'91, Santa Barbara, Bien Nacido (S-New World)

DAVIS BYNUM WINERY

8075 Westside Rd. Healdsburg 95448

Chardonnay,'93, Russ. Riv., Allen/McIlroy Vnyd. $17.00 (2)
Chardonnay,'93, Russian River Vly. $10.00 (5)
Merlot,'92, Russian River, Laureles Vnyd. $21.00 (4)
Pinot Noir,'92, Russian River Vly., Ltd. Edition $28.00 (7)
Pinot Noir,'92, Russian River, Le Pinot $32.00 (7)
Red Meritage,'91, Sonoma Co., Eclipse $22.00 (6)
Sauvignon Blanc,'94, Shone Farm, Fume $8.00 (3)
Zinfandel,'92, Russian River Vly. $12.00 (4)

BYRON VINEYARD & WINERY

5230 Tepusquet Road Santa Maria 93454

Chardonnay,'92, Santa Maria Vly., Est. $25.00 (2)
Chardonnay,'93, Santa Barbara Co. $15.00 (G-State Fair)
Chardonnay,'93, Santa Barbara Co., Reserve $23.00 (4)
Pinot Noir,'92, Santa Barbara Co. $16.00 (B-Dallas)
Pinot Noir,'92, Santa Barbara, Reserve $25.00 (B-Dallas)
Pinot Noir,'93, Santa Barbara Co. $16.00 (2)
Sauvignon Blanc,'94, Santa Barbara Co. $10.00 (B-State Fair)

C

CAKEBREAD CELLARS

8300 St. Helena Hwy. Rutherford 94573

Cabernet Sauvignon,'90, Napa, Rutherford Reserve $40.00 (3)
Chardonnay,'93, Napa Vly. $22.00 (6)
Sauvignon Blanc,'94, Napa Vly. $13.00 (2)

CALLAWAY VINEYARD & WINERY

32720 Rancho California Temecula 92390

Cabernet Sauvignon,'91, California $10.00 (3)
Chardonnay,'92, Temecula, Calla-Lees $10.00 (B-New World)
Chardonnay,'93, Temecula, Calla-Lees $10.00 (2)
Chenin Blanc,'94, Temecula $6.00 (5)
Sauvignon Blanc,'94, Temecula $8.00 (2)

CAMBRIA WINERY

5475 Chardonnay Lane Santa Maria 93454

Chardonnay,'93, S. Maria, Katherine's Vnyd. $18.00 (4)
Chardonnay,'93, Santa Maria Vly., Estate Res. $25.00 (8)
Pinot Noir,'92, Santa Maria Vly., Reserve $30.00 (3)
Pinot Noir,'93, Santa Maria Vly., Julia's Vnyd. $18.00 (3)
Syrah,'92, Santa Maria, Tepusquet Vnyd. $30.00 (6)

CAMELOT VINEYARD

5680 Tepusquet Canyon Rd. Santa Maria 93454

Cabernet Sauvignon,'92, Central Coast $11.00 (4)
Chardonnay,'93, Central Coast $11.00 (3)
Chardonnay,'93, Santa Barbara Co. $12.00 (5)
Pinot Noir,'93, Central Coast $12.00 (7)

CANYON ROAD CELLARS

22281 Chianti Rd. Geyserville 95441

Cabernet Sauvignon,'92, California $6.00 (4)
Chardonnay,'93, California $6.00 (5)
Merlot,'93, California $8.00 (3)
Sauvignon Blanc,'94, California $6.00 (8)
Semillon,'93, Alexander Vly. $8.00 (7)

MAURICE CAR'RIE WINERY

34225 Rancho California Temecula 92390

Cabernet Sauvignon,'93, Temecula $8.00 (B-Farmers)
Chardonnay,'93, Temecula, Reserve $11.00 (3)
Chenin Blanc,'94, Temecula, Soft $5.00 (4)
Johannisberg Riesling,'94, Temecula $6.00 (3)
Merlot,'93, California $9.00 (2)
Sauvignon Blanc,'93, Temecula $5.00 (S-W. Coast)
Syrah,'93, Temecula (B-Dallas)
White Zinfandel,'94, Temecula $4.00 (2)

CARDINALE WINERY

P. O. Box 328 Oakville 94562

White Meritage,'94, California, Royale $15.00 (2)

CARMENET WINERY

1700 Moon Mountain Road Sonoma 95476

Cabernet Franc,'92, Sonoma, Moon Mtn. Vnyd. $20.00 (3)
Chardonnay,'92, Carneros, Sangiacomo Ranch $16.00 (B-Orange)
Red Meritage,'90, Sonoma, Moon Mtn. Vnyd. $25.00 (3)
Red Meritage,'91, Sonoma Vly., Moon Mtn. $25.00 (S-San Fran)
Red Meritage,'91, Sonoma, Moon Mtn., Res, $35.00 (2)
White Meritage,'93, Edna Vly., Paragon Vnyd. (S-L.A.)

CARNEROS CREEK WINERY

1285 Dealy Lane Napa 94559

Pinot Noir,'93, Carneros, Fleur De Carneros $9.00 (2)
Pinot Noir,'93, Los Carneros $15.00 (5)

CARTLIDGE & BROWN

Address Not Available

Chardonnay,'93, California $7.50 (G-Orange)
Pinot Noir,'92, California $7.50 (B-Farmers)
Pinot Noir,'93, California $7.50 (G-Orange)

CASTLE VINEYARDS

Address Not Available

Merlot,'93, Sonoma Vly. $17.00 (S-San Fran)

CASTORO CELLARS

1480 No. Bethel Road Templeton 93465

Cabernet Sauvignon,'91, Paso Robles (B-Dallas)
Cabernet Sauvignon,'91, Paso Robles, Reserve $12.00 (B-Orange)
Cabernet Sauvignon,'92, Paso Robles $10.00 (B-State Fair)
Chardonnay,'93, San Luis Obispo $10.00 (2)
Pinot Noir,'93, Santa Barbara Co. $10.50 (S-Orange)
White Zinfandel,'94, San Luis Obispo Co. $6.00 (3)
Zinfandel,'92, Paso Robles $10.00 (6)

CEDAR BROOK WINERY

Address Not Available

Cabernet Sauvignon,'93, Napa Vly. (S-L.A.)
Chardonnay,'93, Santa Barbara, Reserve (B-New World)
Chardonnay,'94, Napa Vly. (B-L.A.)
Pinot Noir,'92, California (S-New World)

CEDAR MOUNTAIN WINERY

7000 Tesla Road Livermore 94550

Cabernet Sauvignon,'91, Livermore, Blanches Vnyd. (B-Dallas)
Cabernet Sauvignon,'92, Livermore, Blanches Vnyd. $20.00 (2)

CHALK HILL WINERY

10300 Chalk Hill Rd. Healdsburg 95448

Cabernet Sauvignon,'91, Chalk Hill, Est. $18.50 (B-Orange)
Cabernet Sauvignon,'92, Sonoma Co., Est. (3)
Chardonnay,'92, Chalk Hill, Estate $19.00 (2)
Chardonnay,'93, Chalk Hill, Estate $18.50 (B-Orange)
Sauvignon Blanc,'92, Chalk Hill, Est. $16.00 (3)
Sauvignon Blanc,'93, Chalk Hill, Est. $16.00 (3)

CHALONE VINEYARD

P.O. Box 855 Soledad 93960

Pinot Blanc,'93, Estate (S-Dallas)
Pinot Noir,'90, Chalone Vnyd., Est. $30.00 (3)

CHATEAU DE BAUN WINERY

5007 Fulton Road Fulton 95439

Chardonnay,'93, Russian River Vly. $10.00 (4)
Pinot Noir,'92, Russian River Vly. $10.00 (3)
Pinot Noir,'92, Sonoma, Chateau Rouge $5.00 (B-W. Coast)
Sparkling Wine,'NV, Sonoma Co. Brut $12.00 (B-San Diego)
Sparkling Wine,'NV, Sonoma Co. Brut Rose $12.00 (3)

CHATEAU JULIEN

8940 Carmel Valley Rd. Carmel 93922

Cabernet Sauvignon,'91, Monterey, Res. $15.00 (G-Orange)
Merlot,'93, Monterey Co., Reserve $10.00 (2)

CHATEAU MARGARITE VINEYARDS

Address Not Available

Cabernet Sauvignon,'92, Napa Vly. $15.00 (4)

CHATEAU POTELLE

3875 Mt. Veeder Rd. Napa 94558

Cabernet Sauvignon,'90, Napa Vly., Cuvee 95 $18.00 (B-Orange)
Chardonnay,'94, Napa Vly/Central Coast $10.00 (B-Farmers)
Sauvignon Blanc,'93, Napa Vly. $9.00 (G-Farmers)
Sauvignon Blanc,'94, Napa Vly. $9.00 (B-San Diego)

CHATEAU SOUVERAIN

400 Souverain Road Geyserville 95441

Cabernet Sauvignon,'91, Alexander Vly., Reserve $16.00 (5)
Cabernet Sauvignon,'92, Alex. Vly., Res. $16.00 (S-State Fair)
Cabernet Sauvignon,'92, Alexander Vly. $12.00 (6)
Chardonnay,'93, Rochioli Vnyd., Reserve $16.00 (5)
Chardonnay,'93, Sonoma Co., Barrel Ferm. $16.00 (8)
Merlot,'93, Alexander Vly. $13.00 (2)
Pinot Noir,'93, Sonoma, Carneros, Reserve $12.00 (2)
Sauvignon Blanc,'94, Alexander Vly., Barrel Ferm. $7.50 (4)
Zinfandel,'93, Dry Creek Vly. $9.50 (S-San Fran)

CHATEAU ST. JEAN

8555 Sonoma Hwy. Kenwood 95452

Cabernet Sauvignon,'89, Sonoma Co., Reserve $38.00 (6)
Cabernet Sauvignon,'91, Sonoma Co., Cinq Cepages $18.00 (7)
Chardonnay,'93, Alexander Vly., Belle Terre $17.00 (4)
Chardonnay,'93, Sonoma Co. $12.00 (2)
Gewurztraminer,'92, Russian Riv., Johnson Vnyd. SLH $17.00 (3)
Gewurztraminer,'93, Sonoma Co. $8.00 (2)
Gewurztraminer,'94, Sonoma Co. $8.00 (B-W. Coast)

Johannisberg Riesling,'90, Alexander Vly., SSLH $22.50 (2)
Johannisberg Riesling,'93, Sonoma Co. $8.00 (3)
Johannisberg Riesling,'94, Sonoma Co. $8.00 (B-W. Coast)
Merlot,'92, Sonoma Co. $12.00 (6)
Pinot Blanc,'92, Alex. Vly., Robt. Young Vnyd. $12.00 (S-Farmers)
Pinot Noir,'92, Sonoma Co. $15.00 (4)
Sauvignon Blanc,'93, La Petite Etoile Fume $11.00 (4)
Sauvignon Blanc,'93, Sonoma Co. $7.00 (2)
Sauvignon Blanc,'93, Sonoma Co., Fume $8.00 (3)
Sparkling Wine,'NV, Sonoma Co. Blanc De Blanc $11.00 (4)
Sparkling Wine,'NV, Sonoma Co. Brut $11.00 (3)

CHATOM VINEYARDS

7449 Esmeralda Rd San Andreas 95249

Chardonnay,'93, Calaveras Co. $10.00 (3)
Sauvignon Blanc,'93, Calaveras Co. $8.50 (2)

CHESTNUT HILL WINERY

Address Not Available

Cabernet Sauvignon,'92, California, Coastal Cuvee $7.00 (2)
Chardonnay,'94, California, Coastal Cuvee $8.00 (S-San Diego)
Zinfandel,'91, California, Old Vines Cuvee $8.00 (2)

CHEVAL SAUVAGE

Address Not Available

Pinot Noir,'93, Paso Robles $35.00 (G-Orange)

CHIMNEY ROCK WINERY

5350 Silverado Trail Napa 94558

Cabernet Sauvignon,'91, Stag's Leap Dist. $20.00 (2)
Chardonnay,'93, Carneros (S-L.A.)
Sauvignon Blanc,'94, Napa Vly., Fume $11.00 (B-Orange)

CHOUINARD VINEYARD

33853 Palomares Rd. Castro Valley 94552

Gewurztraminer,'94, Monterey $8.00 (2)
Johannisberg Riesling,'94, Monterey $8.00 (2)

CHRISTOPHER CREEK

641 Limerick Lane Healdsburg 95448

Petite Sirah,'91, Russian River Vly. $13.00 (4)
Syrah,'91, Russian River Vly. $14.00 (B-Farmers)

CILURZO VINEYARD

41220 Calle Contento Temecula 92592

Cabernet Sauvignon,'92, Temecula $10.00 (B-State Fair)
Petite Sirah,'92, Temecula $10.00 (B-Farmers)
Petite Sirah,'94, Temecula $7.00 (4)
Red Meritage,'92, Temecula $11.00 (B-Farmers)
Sauvignon Blanc,'93, Temecula, Luiseno Vnyd. $8.00 (B-Orange)

CINNABAR VINEYARDS

23000 Congress Spg. Rd. Saratoga 95071

Cabernet Sauvignon,'89, Saratoga Vnyd. $20.00 (B-Farmers)
Cabernet Sauvignon,'90, Saratoga Vnyd. $20.00 (2)
Cabernet Sauvignon,'92, Saratoga Vnyd. $20.00 (B-San Fran)
Chardonnay,'93, Saratoga Vnyd. $22.00 (6)

CLAUDIA SPRINGS WINERY

2160 Guntley Road Philo 95466

Zinfandel,'93, Mendocino, Pacini Vnyd. $14.00 (3)

CLINE CELLARS

24737 Arnold Drive Sonoma 95476

Zinfandel,'93, Contra Costa Co. $10.00 (2)

CLONINGER CELLARS

1645 River Road Soledad 93960

Cabernet Sauvignon,'92, Monterey (S-New World)
Chardonnay,'91, Monterey $10.00 (B-San Diego)

CLOS DANIELLE

Address Not Available

Merlot,'93, Napa Vly. (B-New World)

CLOS DU BOIS

19410 Geyserville Ave. Geyserville 95441

Cabernet Sauvignon,'91, Briarcrest $18.00 (B-San Diego)
Cabernet Sauvignon,'92, Alexander Vly. $13.00 (4)
Chardonnay,'93, Alexander Vly., Barrel Ferm. $13.00 (S-New World)
Chardonnay,'93, Alexander Vly., Calcaire $18.00 (4)
Chardonnay,'93, Dry Creek, Flintwood $17.00 (5)
Chardonnay,'94, Alexander Vly., Barrel Ferm. $13.00 (B-San Diego)
Merlot,'92, Sonoma Co. $15.00 (2)
Pinot Noir,'93, Sonoma Co. $13.00 (B-W. Coast)
Red Meritage,'91, Alexander Vly., Marlstone $20.00 (6)
Sauvignon Blanc,'94, Sonoma Co. $8.00 (6)
Zinfandel,'93, Sonoma Co. $13.00 (4)

CLOS DU VAL WINERY

5330 Silverado Trail Napa 94558

Cabernet Sauvignon,'90, Napa Vly., Reserve $45.00 (S-Orange)
Merlot,'92, Stags Leap Dist. $30.00 (B-San Fran)
Red Meritage,'90, Napa Vly., Reserve $35.00 (B-San Fran)
Zinfandel,'91, Stags Leap Dist. $15.00 (B-San Fran)

CLOS FONTAINE DU MONT

P. O. Box 3989 Napa 94558

Cabernet Sauvignon,'92, Napa Vly., Reserve $32.00 (3)

CLOS LA CHANCE

Address Not Available

Cabernet Sauvignon,'92, Santa Cruz Mtns. $28.00 (B-Orange)

CLOS PEGASE

1060 Dunaweal Lane Calistoga 94515

Merlot,'92, Napa Vly. $16.50 (S-Orange)

COASTAL CELLARS

Address Not Available

Cabernet Sauvignon,'90, California $6.00 (B-L.A.)

CODORNIU NAPA

1345 Henry Road Napa 94558

Sparkling Wine,'NV, Napa Vly. Brut $11.00 (6)

CONCANNON VINEYARD

4590 Tesla Road Livermore 94550

Cabernet Franc,'93, Paso Robles (S-L.A.)
Cabernet Sauvignon,'92, Central Coast, Sel. Vnyd. $10.00 (2)
Chardonnay,'93, Central Coast, Sel. Vnyd. $10.00 (3)
Chardonnay,'93, Livermore Vly., Reserve $15.00 (G-New World)
Gewurztraminer,'94, Arroyo Seco, Ltd. Bottling $8.00 (2)

Johannisberg Riesling,'92, Anderson Vly., LH $9.50 (3)
Johannisberg Riesling,'94, Arroyo Seco, Sel. Vnyd. $8.00 (4)
Merlot,'93, Livermore Vly. $13.00 (S-W. Coast)
Petite Sirah,'92, Livermore, Est. Reserve $10.00 (6)
Petite Sirah,'93, Central Coast, Sel. Vnyd. $10.00 (5)
Red Meritage,'92, Assemblage, Reserve $15.00 (4)
Sauvignon Blanc,'93, Livermore Vly. $8.00 (5)
Semillon,'93, Arroyo Seco, LH, R.S. 15.4% $10.00 (6)
Semillon,'93, Livermore Vly., Est. $13.00 (9)
White Meritage,'92, Livermore, Assemblage $15.00 (B-Dallas)
White Meritage,'93, Livermore Vly., Assemblage $15.00 (5)

CONN CREEK

8711 Silverado Trail St Helena 94574

Cabernet Sauvignon,'91, Napa Vly. $18.00 (4)
Cabernet Sauvignon,'92, Limited Release $18.00 (3)
Merlot,'90, Napa Vly., Barrel Select $14.00 (B-Dallas)

CORBETT CANYON VINEYARDS

2195 Corbett Canyon Rd. San Luis Obispo 93406

Cabernet Sauvignon,'92, Sonoma Co., Reserve $9.00 (5)
Chardonnay,'93, Santa Barbara Co., Res. $9.00 (3)
Merlot,'92, California, Coastal Classic $7.00 (B-Dallas)
Merlot,'93, California,Coastal Classic $7.00 (B-San Fran)
Pinot Noir,'92, Santa Barbara, Reserve $9.00 (S-New World)

COSENTINO WINERY

7415 St. Helena Hwy. Yountville 94599

Cabernet Franc,'92, Napa Co./Sonoma Co. $18.00 (3)
Cabernet Sauvignon,'91, Napa Vly., Res. $30.00 (B-State Fair)
Cabernet Sauvignon,'92, Napa Vly. $16.00 (3)
Chardonnay,'93, Napa Vly. $16.00 (B-State Fair)
Chardonnay,'93, Napa Vly., The Sculptor $24.00 (B-New World)
Gewurztraminer,'94, Napa Vly., Estate $12.00 (2)
Merlot,'86, Napa, Crystal Valley Cellars $35.00 (S-San Fran)
Merlot,'93, Napa Vly. $21.00 (B-L.A.)
Pinot Noir,'93, Napa Vly. $24.00 (3)
Red Meritage,'91, Napa Co., The Poet $25.00 (3)
Red Meritage,'92, Napa Vly., M. Coz $45.00 (2)
White Meritage,'94, Napa Vly., The Novelist $16.00 (3)
Zinfandel,'93, Sonoma Co., The Zin $18.00 (3)

COTES DE SONOMA

P. O. Box 2386 So San Francisco 94083

Cabernet Sauvignon,'93, Sonoma $9.00 (B-San Fran)
Chardonnay,'94, Sonoma Co. $8.00 (B-Farmers)
Sauvignon Blanc,'94, Sonoma Co. $7.00 (4)

THOMAS COYNE WINERY

51 E. Vallecitos Road Livermore 94550

Cabernet Sauvignon,'92, Livermore Vly., Kalthoff Vnyd. $12.00 (3)
Merlot,'92, California $10.00 (S-W. Coast)
Merlot,'92, Sonoma Co. $14.00 (B-W. Coast)
Merlot,'93, El Dorado, Quartz Hill Vnyd. $14.00 (S-State Fair)
Pinot Blanc,'94, Central Coast, Sunol Vnyd. $10.00 (2)
Red Meritage,'91, Sonoma Co., Cabernets $16.00 (B-Orange)
Zinfandel,'93, Sonoma, Amarone, LH, 12.0% $10.00 (G-Orange)

CRESTON VINEYARDS

679 Calf Canyon Hwy. Creston 93432

Cabernet Sauvignon,'91, Paso Robles, Est. $10.00 (2)
Chardonnay,'93, Paso Robles, Estate $10.00 (2)
Merlot,'92, Paso Robles $13.00 (3)
Merlot,'93, Paso Robles $13.00 (2)
Pinot Noir,'93, Paso Robles $10.00 (4)
Semillon,'93, Paso Robles, Chevrier Blanc $9.00 (S-Dallas)
Semillon,'94, Paso Robles, Chevrier, Est. $9.00 (3)
White Zinfandel,'94, Paso Robles $6.00 (2)
Zinfandel,'93, Paso Robles $10.00 (B-Farmers)

CYPRESS VINEYARD

1000 Lenzen Avenue San Jose 95126

Cabernet Sauvignon,'92, California $8.00 (4)
Merlot,'93, California $9.00 (4)
Sauvignon Blanc,'94, California $8.00 (B-San Fran)
White Zinfandel,'94, California $6.00 (5)

D

DE LOACH VINEYARDS

1791 Olivet Rd. Santa Rosa 95401

Cabernet Sauvignon,'91, Russian River Vly., O.F.S. $25.00 (4)
Cabernet Sauvignon,'92, Russian River Vly. $15.00 (5)
Cabernet Sauvignon,'93, Russian River Vly., Cuvee $12.00 (5)
Chardonnay,'93, Russian Riv., Sonoma Cuvee $12.00 (B-W. Coast)
Chardonnay,'93, Russian River Vly. $15.00 (5)
Chardonnay,'93, Russian River Vly., O.F.S. $25.00 (7)
Gewurztraminer,'94, Russian River Vly., Est., LH $14.00 (7)
Gewurztraminer,'94, Russian River, Early Harvest $8.00 (6)
Merlot,'93, Russian River Vly., Est. $14.00 (6)
Pinot Noir,'92, Russian River Vly., O.F.S. $25.00 (6)
Pinot Noir,'93, Russian River Vly. $12.00 (B-State Fair)
Sauvignon Blanc,'94, Russian River Vly. $10.00 (2)
Sauvignon Blanc,'94, Russian River Vly., Fume $10.00 (S-W. Coast)
Zinfandel,'93, Russian River Vly. $13.00 (6)

DE LORIMIER VINEYARDS

2001 Highway 128 Geyserville 95441

Chardonnay,'92, Alexander Vly., Estate $14.00 (4)
Red Meritage,'91, Alexander Vly., Mosaic $18.00 (3)
Sauvignon Blanc,'91, Alex. Vly., Lace, LH, RS 11.5% $16.00 (6)
White Meritage,'92, Alexander Vly., Spectrum $10.00 (4)

DE MOOR WINERY

7481 St. Helena Hwy. Oakville 94562

Cabernet Sauvignon,'90, Napa Vly. $13.00 (2)
Chenin Blanc,'93, Napa Vly. $8.00 (2)
Zinfandel,'93, Napa Vly. $12.00 (2)

DE NATALE VINEYARDS

11020 Eastside Rd. Healdsburg 95448

Cabernet Sauvignon,'93, Napa Vly. $12.50 (B-Orange)
Chardonnay,'93, Russian River Vly., Est. (B-New World)

DEER PARK WINERY

1000 Deer Park Rd. Deer Park 94576

Petite Sirah,'91, Napa Vly., Howell Mtn. $16.00 (3)

Zinfandel,'91, Napa Vly., Howell Mtn. $14.00 (2)

DEER VALLEY VINEYARDS

P.O. Box 780 Gonzales 93926

Cabernet Sauvignon,'92, Monterey $5.00 (B-San Diego)
Merlot,'93, California $5.00 (2)

DELICATO VINEYARDS

12001 S. Hwy. 99 Manteca 95336

Chardonnay,'93, California $6.00 (B-Orange)
Sauvignon Blanc,'93, California, Fume $5.50 (2)
White Zinfandel,'94, California $5.00 (4)
Zinfandel,'93, California $6.00 (2)

DIAMOND G WINERY

Address Not Available

Cabernet Sauvignon,'93, California $5.00 (B-W. Coast)

DOLCE

Address Not Available

Semillon,'91, California, LH, RS 10.0% $49.00 (G-Orange)

DOMAINE CARNEROS

1240 Duhig Road Napa 94558

Sparkling Wine,'89, Carneros, Blanc De Blanc $25.00 (B-Dallas)
Sparkling Wine,'90, Carneros, Blanc De Blanc $25.00 (G-Orange)
Sparkling Wine,'91, Carneros, Brut $18.00 (G-Orange)
Sparkling Wine,'NV, Carneros, Brut (B-Dallas)

DOMAINE CHANDON

California Drive Yountville 94599

Sparkling Wine,'NV, Napa, Rose Cuvee 29 $18.00 (S-San Fran)

DOMAINE MICHEL

4155 Wine Creek Rd. Healdsburg 95448

Cabernet Sauvignon,'92, Sonoma Co. (B-San Diego)
Chardonnay,'93, Dry Creek Vly. $10.00 (B-Orange)

DOMAINE ST. GEORGE

1141 Grant Avenue Healdsburg 95448

Cabernet Sauvignon,'89, Sonoma Co., Premier Cuvee $8.50 (2)
Cabernet Sauvignon,'90, Russian River, Premier Cuvee $8.50 (2)
Cabernet Sauvignon,'93, California, Vintage Reserve $6.00 (4)
Chardonnay,'93, Sonoma, Premier Cuvee $8.50 (3)
Merlot,'93, Alexander Vly., Cuvee Res. $10.00 (B-San Diego)

DORE WINES

42 Miller Avenue Mill Valley 94941

Cabernet Sauvignon,'92, California, Floral Series $7.00 (2)
Chardonnay,'94, California $7.00 (2)
Sauvignon Blanc,'93, California $6.00 (B-W. Coast)
White Zinfandel,'94, California $6.00 (4)

DOUGLASS HILL WINERY

Address Not Available

Cabernet Sauvignon,'92, Napa Vly. $15.00 (5)
Chardonnay,'93, Napa Vly $15.00 (2)

DRY CREEK VINEYARD

3770 Lambert Bridge Healdsburg 95448

Cabernet Franc,'93, Dry Creek Vly. $15.00 (2)
Cabernet Sauvignon,'91, Dry Creek Vly., Reserve $20.00 (4)

Cabernet Sauvignon,'92, Dry Creek Vly. $16.00 (2)
Chardonnay,'91, Sonoma Co., Reserve $15.00 (B-Dallas)
Chardonnay,'92, Dry Creek, Reserve $15.00 (S-Orange)
Chardonnay,'93, Sonoma Co., Barrel Ferm. $13.00 (3)
Chenin Blanc,'93, California $7.00 (4)
Chenin Blanc,'94, Sonoma Co. $7.00 (3)
Merlot,'91, Dry Creek Vly., Reserve $20.00 (B-Dallas)
Merlot,'92, Dry Creek Vly. $16.00 (S-New World)
Merlot,'93, Sonoma Co. $16.00 (S-State Fair)
Sauvignon Blanc,'92, Dry Creek, Est. Reserve $14.00 (2)
Sauvignon Blanc,'93, Sonoma Co., Fume $9.00 (5)
Sauvignon Blanc,'NV, Sonoma Co., Soleil, LH $18.00 (3)
Zinfandel,'92, Sonoma Co., Old Vines $15.00 (2)
Zinfandel,'93, Sonoma Co., Old Vines $15.00 (B-San Fran)

DUNNEWOOD VINEYARD

2399 N. State Street Ukiah 95482

Chardonnay,'93, North Coast $8.00 (B-New World)
Merlot,'92, North Coast $8.00 (2)
Merlot,'93, North Coast $9.00 (S-W. Coast)
Zinfandel,'92, Sonoma $7.00 (3)

DURNEY VINEYARDS

P. O. Box 221670 Carmel 93922

Cabernet Sauvignon,'91, Carmel Vly., Reserve $32.00 (3)
Cabernet Sauvignon,'92, Carmel Vly. $23.50 (B-Orange)
Chenin Blanc,'93, Carmel Vly., Estate $9.00 (2)
Pinot Noir,'92, Carmel Vly. $23.00 (S-L.A.)

E

EBERLE WINERY

128 Fairview Paso Robles 93446

Cabernet Sauvignon,'91, Paso Robles $16.00 (B-W. Coast)
Chardonnay,'93, Paso Robles, Estate $12.00 (B-Orange)
Syrah,'93, Paso Robles, Fralich Vnyd. $16.00 (7)
Zinfandel,'93, Paso Robles, Sauret Vnyd. $13.00 (9)

EDMEADES ESTATE WINERY

5500 Highway 128 Philo 95466

Chardonnay,'93, Anderson Vly., Dennison Vnyd. $20.00 (2)
Chardonnay,'93, Mendocino $12.00 (3)
Gewurztraminer,'94, Anderson Vly. $13.00 (3)
Zinfandel,'92, North Coast $12.50 (4)
Zinfandel,'93, Mendocino Co., Zeni Vnyd. $20.00 (3)

EDNA VALLEY VINEYARD

2585 Biddle Ranch Rd. San Luis Obispo 93401

Chardonnay,'93, Edna Vly., Estate (3)
Pinot Noir,'92, Edna Vly., Paragon, Res. $22.00 (S-Orange)
Pinot Noir,'93, Edna Vly., Estate $15.00 (G-Orange)

EHLERS GROVE WINERY

Address Not Available

Cabernet Sauvignon,'92, Napa Vly. $15.00 (2)
Cabernet Sauvignon,'93, Napa Vly. $10.00 (3)
Chardonnay,'93, California (B-L.A.)
Sauvignon Blanc,'94, Napa Vly. $9.50 (G-Farmers)

ELKHORN PEAK WINERY

Address Not Available

Pinot Noir,'93, Napa, Fagan Creek Vnyds. $21.00 (5)

ESTANCIA ESTATES

1178 Galleron Road Rutherford 94573

Cabernet Sauvignon,'92, Alexander Vly. $10.00 (B-W. Coast)
Chardonnay,'93, Monterey $9.00 (B-Dallas)
Pinot Noir,'93, Monterey Co. $10.00 (S-W. Coast)
Red Meritage,'91, Alexander Vly. $15.00 (S-Dallas)
Red Meritage,'92, Alexander Vly. $15.00 (4)
White Meritage,'93, Monterey $12.00 (B-State Fair)

ESTRELLA RIVER WINERY

P. O. Box 30496 Paso Robles 93446

Cabernet Sauvignon,'92, California, Prop. Reserve $6.00 (6)
Chardonnay,'93, California, Prop. Reserve $6.00 (3)
Chenin Blanc,'94, Calif., Prop. Reserve $5.00 (B-L.A.)
Sauvignon Blanc,'93, Calif., Prop. Reserve $5.00 (B-L.A.)
White Zinfandel,'94, Calif., Prop. Reserve $4.50 (B-New World)
Zinfandel,'93, California, Prop. Reserve $6.00 (2)

F

FALCONER WINE CELLARS

Address Not Available

Chardonnay,'93, Russian River Vly. $13.00 (B-Orange)
Sparkling Wine,'84, SLO, Blanc De Blanc (B-L.A.)

FALLBROOK WINERY

2554 Via Rancheros Fallbrook 92028

Cabernet Sauvignon,'92, California $7.00 (2)
Pinot Noir,'92, California $7.00 (S-State Fair)

FALLENLEAF VINEYARD

3370 White Alder Sonoma 95476

Sauvignon Blanc,'94, Sonoma Vly. $9.00 (G-State Fair)

FANUCCHI VINEYARDS

Address Not Available

Zinfandel,'94, Russian River, Old Vines $23.00 (B-San Fran)

FARELLA-PARK VINEYARDS

2224 N. Third Street Napa 94558

Cabernet Sauvignon,'92, Napa Vly. $24.00 (S-San Fran)

GARY FARRELL

P.O. Box 342 Forestville 95436

Cabernet Sauvignon,'92, Sonoma Co., Ladi's Vnyd. $20.00 (5)
Chardonnay,'93, Russian River Vly., Allen Vnyd. $18.00 (4)
Chardonnay,'93, Russian River, Westside Farms $18.00 (2)
Merlot,'92, Sonoma Co., Ladi's Vnyd. $20.00 (5)
Pinot Noir,'93, Russian River Vly. $17.00 (5)
Pinot Noir,'93, Santa Barbara, Bien Nacido $28.00 (8)
Zinfandel,'93, Russian River, Collins Vnyd. $15.00 (8)

FENESTRA WINERY

2954 Kilkare Road Sunol 94586

Cabernet Sauvignon,'89, Monterey $14.00 (S-L.A.)
Cabernet Sauvignon,'91, Livermore Vly. $11.00 (B-Orange)
Chardonnay,'93, Livermore, Toy Vnyd. $12.00 (B-Orange)

Merlot,'92, Livermore Vly. $13.00 (S-State Fair)
Semillon,'92, Livermore Vly. $9.00 (B-San Diego)

FERRARI-CARANO

8761 Dry Creek Rd. Healdsburg 95448

Cabernet Sauvignon,'91, Sonoma Co. $15.50 (B-Orange)
Sauvignon Blanc,'94, Sonoma Co. $11.00 (B-Orange)

GLORIA FERRER

23555 Carneros Hwy. 121 Sonoma 95476

Chardonnay,'93, Carneros, Freixenet Vnyds. $16.00 (5)
Pinot Noir,'93, Carneros, Freixenet Vnyds. $16.00 (B-State Fair)
Sparkling Wine,'87, Carneros Cuvee Brut $25.00 (3)
Sparkling Wine,'88, Royal Cuvee Brut $18.00 (5)
Sparkling Wine,'NV, Sonoma Co. Blanc de Noirs $15.00 (7)
Sparkling Wine,'NV, Sonoma Co., Brut $15.00 (6)

FETZER VINEYARDS

13325 So. Highway 101 Hopland 95449

Cabernet Sauvignon,'88, Sonoma Co., Reserve $24.00 (7)
Cabernet Sauvignon,'91, North Coast, Barrel Select $12.00 (2)
Cabernet Sauvignon,'92, California, Valley Oaks $8.00 (4)
Cabernet Sauvignon,'92, North Coast, Barrel Select $12.00 (4)
Chardonnay,'92, Mendocino Co., Reserve $24.00 (7)
Chardonnay,'93, California, Sundial $8.00 (4)
Chardonnay,'93, Mendocino Co., Bonterra $9.00 (6)
Chardonnay,'93, North Coast, Barrel Select $11.00 (5)
Gewurztraminer,'94, California $7.00 (8)
Johannisberg Riesling,'93, California $7.00 (B-Dallas)
Johannisberg Riesling,'93, California, Reserve, LH (2)
Johannisberg Riesling,'94, California $7.00 (6)
Merlot,'93, California, Eagle Peak $8.00 (2)
Merlot,'93, Mendocino, Barrel Select $12.00 (3)
Petite Sirah,'91, Mendocino Co., Reserve $13.00 (7)
Pinot Noir,'92, Bien Nacido, Reserve $24.00 (4)
Pinot Noir,'92, North Coast, Barrel Select $13.00 (4)
Pinot Noir,'92, Olivet Vnd., Reserve $24.00 (4)
Sauvignon Blanc,'93, Mendocino Co. Fume $7.00 (4)
Sauvignon Blanc,'93, Mendocino Co., Barrel Sel. $10.00 (4)
Sauvignon Blanc,'94, Mendocino, Barrel Sel. $10.00 (B-San Fran)
White Zinfandel,'94, California $7.00 (8)
Zinfandel,'91, Mendocino Co., Reserve $13.00 (5)
Zinfandel,'92, Mendocino Co., Barrel Sel. $9.00 (5)

FIELD STONE

10075 Highway 128 Healdsburg 95448

Cabernet Sauvignon,'90, Alex. Vly., Hoot Owl $16.00 (B-Orange)

FIELDBROOK WINERY

4241 Fieldbrook Road Fieldbrook 95521

Cabernet Sauvignon,'92, Meredith Vnyd. $12.00 (B-State Fair)
Chardonnay,'94, Trinity Co., Meredith Vnyd. $12.00 (4)
Petite Sirah,'92, Mendocino, Pacini Vnyd. $14.00 (G-Orange)
Pinot Noir,'92, Napa Vly., Beard Vnyd. $18.00 (B-Orange)
Sauvignon Blanc,'94, Mendocino, Webb Vnyd. $11.00 (G-Orange)
Zinfandel,'92, Mendo., Pacini Vnyd. Res. $11.00 (S-San Fran)
Zinfandel,'93, Mendocino, Pacini Vnyd. $14.00 (Σ-San Fran)
Zinfandel,'94, Mendocino, Pacini Vnyd. $12.00 (S-San Fran)

FILSINGER VINEYARDS

39050 DePortola Rd. Temecula 92390

Cabernet Sauvignon,'91, Temecula $9.00 (S-Orange)

FIRESTONE VINEYARD

5017 Zaca Station Rd. Los Olivos 93441

Cabernet Sauvignon,'91, Santa Ynez Vly. $20.00 (2)
Cabernet Sauvignon,'92, Santa Ynez Vly. $12.00 (S-San Fran)
Chardonnay,'93, Santa Ynez Vly., Barrel Ferm. $12.00 (4)
Chardonnay,'94, Santa Ynez, Barrel Ferm. $12.00 (B-San Fran)
Gewurztraminer,'93, Santa Barbara Co. $9.00 (S-New World)
Johannisberg Riesling,'93, Santa Ynez $7.50 (S-Orange)
Johannisberg Riesling,'93, Santa Ynez Vly. $11.00 (3)
Merlot,'93, Santa Ynez Vly. $12.00 (2)
Red Meritage,'91, Santa Ynez Vly., Reserve $20.00 (2)
Red Meritage,'93, Santa Ynez Vly. $20.00 (B-State Fair)

FLORA SPRINGS WINE COMPANY

1978 W. Zinfandel Ln. St Helena 94574

Red Meritage,'91, Napa Vly., Trilogy $25.00 (4)
Sauvignon Blanc,'93, Napa Vly. $8.00 (B-W. Coast)

THOMAS FOGARTY WINERY

19501 Skyline Blvd. Portola Valley 94028

Cabernet Sauvignon,'90, Napa, Vallerga Vnyd. (S-New World)
Chardonnay,'92, Santa Cruz Mtns. $16.00 (3)
Chardonnay,'92, Santa Cruz Mtns., Reserve $18.00 (2)
Gewurztraminer,'93, Monterey, Ventana Vnyd. $12.00 (B-Dallas)
Gewurztraminer,'94, Monterey, Ventana Vnyd. $12.00 (6)
Pinot Noir,'92, Santa Cruz Mtns., Est. $22.00 (B-L.A.)

FOPPIANO VINEYARDS

12707 Old Redwood Hwy. Healdsburg 95448

Cabernet Sauvignon,'90, Russian River Vly. $9.50 (B-Farmers)
Merlot,'93, Russian River Vly. $10.00 (B-State Fair)
Petite Sirah,'91, Napa, Le Grande Reserve $19.50 (2)
Petite Sirah,'92, Sonoma Co. $10.00 (4)
Zinfandel,'93, Dry Creek Vly. $9.50 (2)

FOREST GLEN

6342 Bystrum Road Ceres 95307

Cabernet Sauvignon,'92, California, Barrel Select $10.00 (4)
Chardonnay,'93, California, Barrel Ferm. $10.00 (3)
Merlot,'93, California, Barrel Select $10.00 (5)
Merlot,'94, California $10.00 (B-San Fran)

FORESTVILLE VINEYARD

7010 Trenton-Healdsburg Rd. Forestville 95436

Cabernet Sauvignon,'92, California $6.00 (2)
Chardonnay,'93, California $6.00 (B-L.A.)
Gewurztraminer,'93, California $5.50 (3)
Johannisberg Riesling,'93, California $5.50 (B-Farmers)
Merlot,'93, California $6.00 (2)
Merlot,'94, California $6.00 (S-Orange)
Sauvignon Blanc,'93, California $5.50 (G-W. Coast)
White Zinfandel,'94, California $5.50 (B-W. Coast)
Zinfandel,'93, California $6.00 (3)

FOXEN

7200 Foxen Canyon Rd. Santa Maria 93454

Pinot Noir,'93, Bien Nacido Vnyd. $27.00 (S-Orange)
Pinot Noir,'93, Sanford & Benedict $30.00 (S-Orange)

FOXHOLLOW VINEYARDS

Address Not Available

Merlot,'93, California $10.00 (B-Farmers)

FRANCISCAN OAKVILLE ESTATE

1178 Galleron Road Rutherford 94573

Cabernet Sauvignon,'91, Napa Vly. $15.00 (4)
Cabernet Sauvignon,'92, Napa Vly. $15.00 (S-State Fair)
Chardonnay,'93, Napa Vly., Barrel Ferm. $12.00 (4)
Chardonnay,'93, Napa Vly., Cuvee Sauvage $30.00 (2)
Red Meritage,'90, Napa Vly., Magnificat $20.00 (2)
Red Meritage,'91, Napa Vly., Magnificat $22.00 (4)
Zinfandel,'93, Napa Vly. $11.00 (4)

FRANZIA BROTHERS WINERY

240 Stockton St. #800 San Francisco 94108

Cabernet Sauvignon,'NV, California $2.00 (2)
Chardonnay,'NV, California (B-New World)

FRATELLI PERATA WINERY

1595 Arbor Road Paso Robles 93446

Cabernet Sauvignon,'92, Paso Robles (B-L.A.)
Merlot,'93, Paso Robles, Est. $15.00 (3)

FREEMARK ABBEY

3022 St. Helena Hwy. No. St Helena 94574

Cabernet Sauvignon,'87, Napa Vly., Sycamore Vnyds. $20.00 (4)
Cabernet Sauvignon,'90, Napa Vly., Boche Vnyds. $25.00 (3)
Chardonnay,'92, Napa Vly. $16.00 (B-State Fair)

J. FRITZ WINERY

24691 Dutcher Creek Rd. Cloverdale 95425

Chardonnay,'93, Sonoma Co. $10.00 (3)
Merlot,'92, Dry Creek Vly. (S-San Diego)
Pinot Blanc,'94, Russian River Vly., Melon $10.00 (2)
Sauvignon Blanc,'93, Dry Creek Vly. $9.50 (G-New World)
Sauvignon Blanc,'94, Dry Creek Vly. $9.50 (2)
Zinfandel,'93, Dry Creek, 80 Yr. Old Vines $12.00 (4)
Zinfandel,'94, Dry Creek Vly., LH $14.00 (S-San Fran)

J. FURST

Address Not Available

Cabernet Sauvignon,'91, California $10.00 (B-W. Coast)
Chardonnay,'92, California $11.00 (4)
Pinot Noir,'91, Sonoma $8.00 (S-L.A.)
Pinot Noir,'93, Sonoma Co. $8.00 (S-W. Coast)

G

GAINEY VINEYARD

3950 East Hwy. 246 Santa Ynez 93460

Cabernet Sauvignon,'90, Santa Ynez Vly. $13.00 (5)
Chardonnay,'93, Santa Barbara Co. $14.00 (5)
Johannisberg Riesling,'94, Santa Ynez Vly. $8.00 (4)
Merlot,'91, Santa Ynez Vly. $14.00 (B-W. Coast)

Sauvignon Blanc,'93, Santa Ynez Vly. $9.00 (5)
Sauvignon Blanc,'94, Santa Ynez Vly. $9.00 (B-State Fair)

E. & J. GALLO

P. O. Box 1130 Modesto 95353

Cabernet Sauvignon,'90, Sonoma Co. $50.00 (B-Dallas)
Cabernet Sauvignon,'91, Northern Sonoma, Est. $50.00 (6)
Chardonnay,'93, Northern Sonoma $30.00 (4)
Chardonnay,'93, Sonoma $12.00 (B-San Fran)
Merlot,'92, Dry Creek Vly. (B-W. Coast)
Zinfandel,'90, Dry Creek, Frei Ranch (B-Dallas)
Zinfandel,'91, Dry Creek, Frei Ranch (B-Dallas)
Zinfandel,'92, Dry Creek, Frei Ranch (G-New World)

GAN EDEN

4950 Ross Road Sebastopol 95472

Cabernet Sauvignon,'89, Alexander Vly. $15.00 (2)
Chardonnay,'93, Sonoma Co. (B-New World)
Semillon,'93, Sonoma Co. $14.00 (5)

GEMELLO

9200 Highway 128 Philo 95466

Zinfandel,'92, Mendocino Co., 60th $16.00 (B-New World)

JOSEPH GEORGE

Address Not Available

Cabernet Sauvignon,'90, Stags Leap, Sig. Sel. $13.00 (B-San Fran)

GEYSER PEAK WINERY

22281 Chianti Rd. Geyserville 95441

Cabernet Sauvignon,'92, Alexander Vly., Reserve $20.00 (5)
Cabernet Sauvignon,'93, Alexander Vly. $10.00 (7)
Cabernet Sauvignon,'93, Alexander Vly., Reserve $20.00 (5)
Chardonnay,'93, Alexander Vly., Trione Res. $20.00 (8)
Chardonnay,'93, Sonoma Co. $10.00 (6)
Chardonnay,'94, Sonoma Co. $10.00 (2)
Gewurztraminer,'94, North Coast $6.00 (7)
Johannisberg Riesling,'93, Russian River Vly., LH $16.00 (6)
Johannisberg Riesling,'94, North Coast, Soft $6.00 (8)
Johannisberg Riesling,'94, Russian River Vly., LH $16.00 (6)
Merlot,'93, Alexander Vly. $12.00 (2)
Red Meritage,'92, Reserve Alexandre $25.00 (6)
Red Meritage,'93, Reserve Alexandre $25.00 (3)
Sauvignon Blanc,'94, Sonoma Co. $7.00 (5)
Semillon,'93, California $8.00 (B-Dallas)
Semillon,'94, California $8.00 (7)
Syrah,'92, Alexander Vly., Reserve $30.00 (5)
Syrah,'93, Alexander Vly. Shiraz $10.00 (3)
Syrah,'93, Alexander Vly., Reserve $30.00 (4)

GLASS MOUNTAIN

2812 St. Helena Hwy., N. St Helena 94574

Cabernet Sauvignon,'92, California $9.00 (2)

GLEN ELLEN WINERY

21468 - 8th Street E. Sonoma 95476

Cabernet Sauvignon,'92, California, Proprietor's Res. $5.00 (2)
Chardonnay,'93, Calif., Proprietor's Reserve $5.00 (B-New World)
Chardonnay,'94, Calif., Proprietor's Reserve $5.00 (S-L.A.)
Merlot,'93, California, Proprietor's Reserve $5.00 (4)

Sauvignon Blanc,'93, Calif., Prop. Res. $5.00 (B-W. Coast)
White Zinfandel,'94, California, Prop.Reserve $4.00 (6)

GOLD HILL VINEYARD

5660 Vineyard Lane Placerville 95667

Cabernet Franc,'90, El Dorado, Est. $12.00 (4)
Cabernet Sauvignon,'91, El Dorado, Estate $11.00 (3)

GOLDEN CREEK VINEYARD

4480 Wallace Road Santa Rosa 95404

Cabernet Sauvignon,'91, Sonoma Co., Reserve (2)
Merlot,'92, Sonoma Co., Reserve $15.00 (2)
Red Meritage,'92, Sonoma Caberlot, Reserve $15.00 (4)

RICHARD L. GRAESER WINERY

255 Petrified Forest Rd. Calistoga 94515

Cabernet Franc,'91, Napa Vly., Estate $15.00 (3)
Cabernet Sauvignon,'91, Godspeed Vnyd. (B-San Diego)
Cabernet Sauvignon,'91, Napa Vly., Estate $14.00 (3)

GRAND CRU VINEYARDS

1 Vintage Lane Glen Ellen 95442

Cabernet Sauvignon,'92, California $8.00 (S-Farmers)
Chardonnay,'93, California $8.00 (S-New World)
Gewurztraminer,'93, California $7.00 (2)
Johannisberg Riesling,'93, California $7.00 (2)
Merlot,'93, California $8.00 (3)
White Zinfandel,'94, California $7.00 (3)
Zinfandel,'92, California $7.00 (B-W. Coast)

GRANITE SPRINGS WINERY

6060 Granite Springs Rd. Somerset 95684

Cabernet Sauvignon,'93, El Dorado $10.00 (2)
Chenin Blanc,'94, Sierra Foothills $5.00 (G-L.A.)
Merlot,'93, El Dorado $14.00 (S-State Fair)
Petite Sirah,'93, El Dorado $10.00 (3)
Red Meritage,'92, El Dorado $12.00 (B-State Fair)
Zinfandel,'91, El Dorado, Est. $8.00 (S-San Diego)
Zinfandel,'92, El Dorado, Est. $8.00 (4)

GREENWOOD RIDGE VINEYARDS

5501 Highway 128 Philo 95466

Cabernet Sauvignon,'92, Anderson Vly., Estate $18.00 (6)
Johannisberg Riesling,'93, Anderson Vly., Estate $8.50 (4)
Merlot,'92, Anderson Vly., Estate $16.00 (S-Dallas)
Pinot Noir,'93, Anderson Vly., Roederer Vn. $15.00 (4)
Sauvignon Blanc,'93, Anderson Vly. $9.00 (5)
Zinfandel,'93, Sonoma, Scherrer Vnyd. $14.00 (8)

GRGICH HILLS CELLAR

1829 St. Helena Hwy. Rutherford 94573

Cabernet Sauvignon,'90, Napa Vly. $24.00 (4)
Chardonnay,'92, Napa Vly. $24.00 (2)
Johannisberg Riesling,'93, Napa Vly., LH $50.00 (2)
Sauvignon Blanc,'93, Napa Vly., Fume $13.00 (5)
Zinfandel,'91, Sonoma Co. $14.00 (3)
Zinfandel,'92, Sonoma Co. $14.00 (B-L.A.)

GROTH

750 Oakville Cross   Oakville   94562

Sauvignon Blanc,'94, Napa Vly. $9.00 (B-Orange)

GROVE STREET WINERY

4035 Westside Road   Healdsburg   95448

Cabernet Sauvignon,'92, California, Vineyard Select $7.00 (4)
Chardonnay,'93, Sonoma Co. $7.00 (3)
White Zinfandel,'93, California $4.50 (B-Dallas)
White Zinfandel,'94, California $4.50 (2)

GUEGLIELMO WINERY

1480 E. Main Avenue   Morgan Hill   95037

Zinfandel,'91, Santa Clara Vly., Reserve $9.00 (S-Farmers)

GUENOC WINERY

21000 Butts Canyon Rd.   Middletown   95461

Cabernet Franc,'91, Lake Co. $14.00 (6)
Cabernet Sauvignon,'91, Lake Co. $14.00 (5)
Cabernet Sauvignon,'91, Napa, Beckstoffer Vnyd, Res. $35.00 (3)
Cabernet Sauvignon,'92, California $11.00 (3)
Cabernet Sauvignon,'92, Lake Co. $14.50 (B-Orange)
Cabernet Sauvignon,'92, Napa Vly., Bella Vista Vnyd. $20.00 (5)
Cabernet Sauvignon,'92, Napa, Beckstoffer Vnyd., Res. $35.00 (4)
Chardonnay,'92, Genevieve Magoon Vnyd. $25.00 (G-Farmers)
Chardonnay,'93, Genevieve Magoon, Res. $25.00 (2)
Chardonnay,'93, Guenoc Vly., Estate $14.00 (2)
Chardonnay,'94, California $11.00 (B-W. Coast)
Chardonnay,'94, Genevieve Magoon Vnyd. $25.00 (B-State Fair)
Chardonnay,'94, Guenoc Vly. $14.00 (4)
Petite Sirah,'90, North Coast $13.00 (S-Dallas)
Petite Sirah,'91, North Coast $13.00 (8)
Petite Sirah,'92, North Coast $13.00 (5)
Red Meritage,'90, California, Langtry $35.00 (3)
Red Meritage,'91, California, Langtry $35.00 (7)
Red Meritage,'91, Lake Co. $15.00 (8)
Red Meritage,'92, Lake Co. $15.00 (3)
Sauvignon Blanc,'93, Guenoc Vly., Estate $11.00 (B-Orange)
Sauvignon Blanc,'94, California $8.00 (G-Orange)
Sauvignon Blanc,'94, Guenoc Vly., Est. $11.00 (4)
White Meritage,'93, Guenoc Vly., Langtry $17.00 (5)
White Meritage,'94, Guenoc Vly., Langtry $17.00 (3)
Zinfandel,'90, California $10.00 (B-Dallas)
Zinfandel,'91, California $10.00 (3)

GUNDLACH-BUNDSCHU WINERY

2000 Denmark St.   Sonoma   95476

Cabernet Franc,'92, Rhinefarm Vnyd. $14.00 (G-Dallas)
Cabernet Franc,'93, Sonoma Vly., Rhinefarm Vnyd. $14.00 (2)
Cabernet Sauvignon,'92, Sonoma, Rhinefarm Vnyd. $15.00 (4)
Chardonnay,'93, Sonoma Vly., Estate $12.00 (B-Orange)
Gewurztraminer,'93, Rhinefarm Vnyd. $8.00 (B-Dallas)
Gewurztraminer,'94, Sonoma, Rhinefarm Vnyd. $8.00 (3)
Johannisberg Riesling,'94, Sonoma Vly. $9.00 (B-W. Coast)
Merlot,'92, Sonoma Vly., Rhinefarm Vnyd. $16.00 (2)
Merlot,'93, Rhinefarm Vnyd. $15.00 (S-State Fair)
Zinfandel,'93, Sonoma, Rhinefarm Vnyd. $14.00 (5)

HACIENDA WINERY

1000 Vineyard Lane Sonoma 95476

Cabernet Sauvignon,'92, California $7.50 (B-Farmers)
Chardonnay,'93, California, Claire De Lune $7.50 (3)
Chenin Blanc,'94, California, Clare De Lune $7.00 (2)
Merlot,'93, California $7.50 (2)
White Zinfandel,'94, California $7.00 (S-W. Coast)

HAGAFEN CELLARS

P. O. Box 3035 Napa 94558

Cabernet Sauvignon,'88, Napa Vly., Reserve $28.00 (S-Orange)
Cabernet Sauvignon,'89, Napa Vly., Reserve $28.00 (2)
Cabernet Sauvignon,'90, Napa Vly. $20.00 (B-L.A.)
Cabernet Sauvignon,'90, Napa Vly., Reserve $28.00 (B-W. Coast)
Chardonnay,'92, Napa Vly. $14.00 (B-L.A.)
Johannisberg Riesling,'94, Napa Vly. $9.00 (5)
Pinot Noir,'94, Napa Vly., Harmonia $6.00 (G-State Fair)

HAHN ESTATES

37700 Foothill Rd. Soledad 93960

Cabernet Franc,'93, Santa Lucia Highlands $9.00 (3)
Cabernet Sauvignon,'92, Santa Lucia $9.00 (S-New World)
Merlot,'93, Santa Lucia Highlands $9.00 (B-W. Coast)

HANDLEY CELLARS

3151 Highway 128 Philo 95466

Chardonnay,'92, Anderson Vly. $11.00 (3)
Chardonnay,'92, Dry Creek Vly. $15.00 (6)
Gewurztraminer,'93, Anderson Vly. $8.00 (2)
Gewurztraminer,'94, Anderson Vly. $9.00 (3)
Sauvignon Blanc,'93, Dry Creek Vly. $8.00 (5)
Sparkling Wine,'89, Anderson Vly. Blanc De Blanc $18.50 (6)
Sparkling Wine,'89, Anderson Vly. Brut $15.00 (4)
Sparkling Wine,'91, Anderson Vly. Brut Rose $18.00 (3)

HANNA WINERY

4345 Occidental Rd. Santa Rosa 95401

Cabernet Sauvignon,'92, Alexander Vly. $16.00 (4)
Chardonnay,'93, Sonoma Co. $14.00 (3)
Merlot,'92, Alexander Vly. $16.00 (B-Dallas)
Merlot,'93, Alexander Vly. $16.00 (3)
Sauvignon Blanc,'94, Sonoma Co. $10.00 (5)

HARMONY CELLARS

3255 Harmony Vly. Rd. Harmony 93435

Chardonnay,'92, Paso Robles (S-New World)
Syrah,'93, Paso Robles, Sig. Series, LH $12.00 (B-Orange)

HART WINERY

P. O. Box 956 Temecula 92390

Merlot,'92, Temecula (S-San Diego)
Syrah,'93, Temecula, Estate (S-New World)

HAUTE CELLARS

Address Not Available

Cabernet Sauvignon,'NV, California $5.00 (B-Farmers)
Chardonnay,'NV, California $5.00 (3)
Sauvignon Blanc,'NV, California $4.00 (B-Farmers)

White Zinfandel,'NV, California $5.00 (B-Farmers)

HAVENS

Address Not Available

Merlot,'93, Napa Vly. $16.00 (B-Orange)

HAWK CREST

5766 Silverado Trail   Napa   94558

Cabernet Sauvignon,'92, California $9.00 (B-State Fair)

HAYWOOD WINERY

18701 Gehricke Rd.   Sonoma   95476

Cabernet Sauvignon,'92, California, Vintner's Select $8.00 (2)
Chardonnay,'93, California, Vintner's Select $8.00 (4)
Zinfandel,'91, Sonoma, Los Chamizal Vnyd. $14.00 (2)
Zinfandel,'92, Sonoma, Los Chamizal Vnyd. $14.00 (2)
Zinfandel,'92, Sonoma, Rocky Terrace, Est. $18.00 (2)

HEITZ WINE CELLARS

500 Taplin Road   St Helena   94574

Cabernet Sauvignon,'80, Bella Oaks Vnyd. $80.00 (B-San Fran)
Cabernet Sauvignon,'87, Martha's Vnyd. $78.00 (B-San Fran)
Cabernet Sauvignon,'90, Napa Vly. $18.00 (4)
Cabernet Sauvignon,'90, Napa Vly., Trailside Vnyd. $45.00 (3)

HESS COLLECTION WINERY

4411 Redwood Road   Napa   94558

Cabernet Sauvignon,'90, Mt. Veeder, Est. Res.   (B-San Diego)
Cabernet Sauvignon,'91, Napa Vly., Mt. Veeder, Est. $18.00 (9)
Cabernet Sauvignon,'92, California, Hess Select $9.50 (3)
Chardonnay,'93, California, Hess Select   (3)
Chardonnay,'93, Napa Vly. $15.00 (4)

HIDDEN CELLARS

1500 Ruddick-Cunningham Rd.   Ukiah   95482

Chardonnay,'92, Mendocino Co., Reserve $17.00 (B-Orange)
Chardonnay,'93, Mendocino $10.00 (B-Farmers)
Chardonnay,'93, Mendocino, Organic $10.00 (5)
Johannisberg Riesling,'93, Mendocino $8.00 (B-Farmers)
White Meritage,'92, Mendocino, Alchemy $20.00 (B-Farmers)
Zinfandel,'93, Mendo., McAdams Vnyd. $13.00 (S-San Fran)
Zinfandel,'93, Mendocino, Old Vines $10.00 (B-L.A.)
Zinfandel,'93, Mendocino, Organic $10.00 (2)

WILLIAM HILL WINERY

1761 Atlas Peak Road   Napa   94558

Cabernet Sauvignon,'91, Napa Vly. $14.00 (2)
Chardonnay,'93, Napa Vly. $12.00 (5)
Merlot,'92, Napa Vly.   (G-New World)
Sauvignon Blanc,'93, Napa Vly. $9.00 (3)

HOP KILN WINERY

6050 Westside Rd.   Healdsburg   95448

Cabernet Sauvignon,'91, Russian River Vly. $14.00 (4)
Cabernet Sauvignon,'92, Griffin Vnyds. $14.00 (S-State Fair)
Chardonnay,'93, Russian River, Griffin Vnyds. $15.00 (B-Orange)
Zinfandel,'92, Russian River Vly. $14.00 (2)
Zinfandel,'93, Sonoma Co., Primitivo $18.00 (5)
Zinfandel,'94, Russ. River, Griffin Vnyds., LH $12.00 (B-State Fair)

HOPE FARMS

2175 Arbor Road   Paso Robles   93447

Cabernet Sauvignon,'92, Paso Robles, Est. $13.00 (2)
Chardonnay,'93, Central Coast $10.00 (G-Orange)

ROBERT HUNTER WINERY

Address Not Available

Sparkling Wine,'91, Sonoma Vly., Brut De Noir $25.00 (4)

HUSCH VINEYARDS

4400 Highway 128   Philo   95466

Cabernet Sauvignon,'91, Mendocino, La Ribera Vnyd. $14.00 (3)
Cabernet Sauvignon,'92, La Ribera Ranch $14.00 (B-San Diego)
Cabernet Sauvignon,'92, La Ribera Red $8.00 (G-Farmers)
Cabernet Sauvignon,'92, Mendocino, No. Field Select $20.00 (3)
Chardonnay,'93, Mendocino $11.50 (2)
Chenin Blanc,'94, Mendocino Co., La Ribera $8.00 (9)
Gewurztraminer,'93, Anderson Vly. $9.00 (S-Dallas)
Gewurztraminer,'93, Anderson Vly., LH $14.00 (2)
Gewurztraminer,'94, Anderson Vly., Estate $9.00 (6)
Pinot Noir,'93, Anderson Vly., Est. $15.00 (3)
Sauvignon Blanc,'93, La Ribera Vnyd. $9.00 (B-New World)
Sauvignon Blanc,'94, Mendocino Co. $9.00 (2)

I

IMAGERY SERIES

1883 London Ranch Rd.   Glen Ellen   95442

Cabernet Franc,'92, Alex. Vly., Blue Rock Vnyd. $16.00 (7)
Petite Sirah,'92, Paso Robles, Shell Creek $16.00 (3)
Pinot Blanc,'93, Sonoma Mtn. $16.00 (5)
Sparkling Wine,'90, Carneros Brut $16.00 (2)
Sparkling Wine,'90, David Nash Brut (B-L.A.)

INDIAN SPRINGS VINEYARDS

16110 Indian Springs Rd.   Penn Valley   95946

Cabernet Sauvignon,'93, Nevada Co. $10.00 (5)
Chardonnay,'92, Anderson Vly. $10.00 (G-New World)
Merlot,'93, Nevada Co. $12.00 (5)
Semillon,'93, Nevada Co. $8.00 (3)

INGLENOOK

1991 St. Helena Hwy.   Rutherford   94573

Cabernet Sauvignon,'NV, California, Est. $4.00 (2)
Chardonnay,'91, Napa Vly. (G-New World)

IRON HORSE

9786 Ross Station Rd.   Sebastopol   95472

Cabernet Franc,'93, Alexander Vly., T-T Vnyd. $11.50 (S-Orange)
Red Meritage,'91, Alexander Vly., T-T Vnyd. $18.00 (2)
Sauvignon Blanc,'94, Alexander Vly., T-T Vnyd. $11.50 (B-Orange)
Sparkling Wine,'89, Sonoma, Blanc De Blanc $23.00 (S-Orange)
Sparkling Wine,'90, Sonoma, Sparkling Rose $25.00 (B-Orange)
Sparkling Wine,'91, Sonoma Co., Brut $22.00 (B-Orange)
Sparkling Wine,'92, Sonoma, Wedding Cuvee $22.00 (2)

J

JAEGER CELLAR

2125 Inglewood Ave. Rutherford 94573
Merlot,'89, Napa Vly., Inglewood Vnyd. $18.00 (2)

TOBIN JAMES CELLARS

P. O. Box 2459 Paso Robles 93447
Cabernet Sauvignon,'93, San Luis Obispo, Star Light $14.00 (2)
Merlot,'93, Paso Robles, Midnight $15.00 (2)
Zinfandel,'93, Blue Moon Flagship $14.00 (B-Orange)

JANKRIS VINEYARD

Rt. 2, Box 40 Templeton 93465
Chardonnay,'93, Paso Robles $10.00 (2)
Pinot Blanc,'93, Central Coast $8.50 (S-Orange)
Syrah,'93, Paso Robles $14.00 (B-Farmers)
Zinfandel,'93, Paso Robles, Est. $9.50 (2)

JARVIS WINERY

2970 Monticello Road Napa 94558
Chardonnay,'92, Napa Vly., Est. (G-L.A.)

JEKEL VINEYARDS

40155 Walnut Avenue Greenfield 93927
Cabernet Franc,'92, Arroyo Seco, Sanctuary Est. $13.00 (2)
Johannisberg Riesling,'93, Arroyo Seco, Gravelstone $6.00 (3)
Merlot,'93, Arroyo Seco, Sanctuary $13.00 (S-Orange)
Pinot Noir,'93, Arroyo Seco, Gravelstone $13.00 (2)
Red Meritage,'90, Arroyo Seco, Sanctuary Est. $13.00 (2)

JEPSON VINEYARDS

10400 So. Highway 101 Ukiah 95482
Chardonnay,'93, Mendocino, Estate $13.50 (G-New World)
Sauvignon Blanc,'93, Mendocino $8.50 (S-Orange)
Sparkling Wine,'89, Mendocino Blanc De Blanc $16.00 (4)

JORDAN VINEYARD & WINERY

P.O. Box 1919 Healdsburg 95448
Chardonnay,'92, Alexander Vly. $20.00 (4)
Sparkling Wine,'90, Sonoma Co. "J" $23.00 (8)

JOUILLIAN VINEYARDS

20300 Cachagua Rd. Carmel Valley 93924
Cabernet Sauvignon,'90, Carmel Vly. $14.00 (G-W. Coast)
Cabernet Sauvignon,'92, Carmel Vly. $14.00 (B-Orange)
Chardonnay,'93, Monterey $11.00 (4)
Sauvignon Blanc,'93, Carmel Vly. $8.50 (3)
Sauvignon Blanc,'94, Carmel Vly. $8.50 (2)

JUSTIN VINEYARDS

11680 Chimney Rock Rd. Paso Robles 93446
Cabernet Sauvignon,'92, San Luis Obispo, Justin Vnyds. $20.00 (2)
Red Meritage,'92, SLO, Isosceles Reserve $24.00 (3)

K

KARLY WINES

P. O. Box 729 Plymouth 95669
Petite Sirah,'93, Amador Co. $14.00 (B-San Fran)

KAUTZ IRONSTONE

1894 Six Mile Road Murphys 95247

Cabernet Sauvignon,'92, California, Triune $10.00 (B-San Fran)

KENDALL-JACKSON WINERY

421 Aviation Blvd. Santa Rosa 95403

Cabernet Franc,'92, California, Grand Reserve $20.00 (6)
Cabernet Sauvignon,'90, California, Grand Reserve $30.00 (3)
Cabernet Sauvignon,'91, California, Grand Reserve $30.00 (5)
Cabernet Sauvignon,'92, California, Vintner's Reserve $14.00 (4)
Chardonnay,'92, Santa Maria, Camelot Vnyd. $16.00 (4)
Chardonnay,'93, California, Grand Reserve $24.00 (3)
Chardonnay,'93, California, LH, R.S. 11.0% $15.00 (8)
Chardonnay,'93, California, Vintner's Reserve $14.00 (6)
Chardonnay,'93, Santa Maria., Camelot Vnyd. $16.00 (5)
Chardonnay,'94, California, Vintner's Reserve $14.00 (4)
Gewurztraminer,'94, California, Vintner's Reserve $10.00 (2)
Johannisberg Riesling,'93, California, SLH $15.00 (6)
Johannisberg Riesling,'93, California, Vintner's Reserve $10.00 (6)
Johannisberg Riesling,'94, California, Vintner's Reserve $10.00 (4)
Merlot,'92, California, Grand Reserve $30.00 (3)
Merlot,'92, California, Vintner's Reserve $15.00 (5)
Merlot,'93, California, Vintner's Reserve $15.00 (2)
Pinot Noir,'93, California, Grand Reserve $30.00 (8)
Pinot Noir,'93, California, Vintner's Reserve $9.00 (5)
Red Meritage,'90, California, Cardinale $50.00 (S-Dallas)
Red Meritage,'91, California, Cardinale $50.00 (S-Dallas)
Sauvignon Blanc,'93, California, Vintner's Reserve $9.00 (5)
Sauvignon Blanc,'94, California, Vintner's Reserve $9.00 (3)
Syrah,'91, California, Grand Reserve $20.00 (3)
White Meritage,'92, California, Royale $15.00 (S-Dallas)
Zinfandel,'89, Anderson Vly., Dupratt Vnyd. (B-Dallas)
Zinfandel,'92, California, Vintner's Reserve $13.00 (4)
Zinfandel,'92, California,Grand Reserve $20.00 (4)
Zinfandel,'93, California, Vintner's Reserve $13.00 (3)

KENWOOD VINEYARDS

9592 Sonoma Highway Kenwood 95452

Cabernet Sauvignon,'91, Jack London Vnyd. $20.00 (S-San Diego)
Cabernet Sauvignon,'91, Sonoma, Artist Series (S-San Diego)
Cabernet Sauvignon,'92, Sonoma, Jack London Vnyd. $20.00 (3)
Chardonnay,'93, Sonoma Vly., Beltane Ranch $18.00 (2)
Merlot,'92, Jack London Vnyd. $18.00 (3)
Pinot Noir,'93, Russian River Vly. $14.00 (3)
Sauvignon Blanc,'93, Sonoma Co. $9.50 (5)
Sauvignon Blanc,'94, Sonoma Co. $9.00 (2)
Zinfandel,'92, Sonoma Vly. $12.00 (4)
Zinfandel,'93, Sonoma Co., Mazzoni Vnyd. $15.00 (S-State Fair)

KINDERWOOD

737 Lamar Street Los Angeles 90031

Chardonnay,'94, Monterey Co. $6.00 (2)
Merlot,'93, California $6.00 (2)

KONRAD ESTATE WINERY

3620 Road B Redwood Valley 95470

Chardonnay,'92, Mendocino, Konrad Estate $11.00 (B-Orange)
Petite Sirah,'91, Mendocino Co., Est. $11.50 (3)

Red Meritage,'91, Mendocino, Melange A Trois $12.00 (2)

KORBEL CHAMPAGNE CELLARS

13250 River Road Guerneville 95446

Cabernet Sauvignon,'92, Alexander Vly. $18.00 (B-San Fran)
Chardonnay,'92, Sonoma Co. $15.00 (2)
Chardonnay,'93, Russian River Vly. $15.00 (S-San Fran)
Sparkling Wine,'90, California, Cuvee Pinot Noir (2)
Sparkling Wine,'90, California, Le Premier $20.00 (S-Orange)
Sparkling Wine,'91, California, Cuvee Chard, Res. $15.00 (2)
Sparkling Wine,'NV, California Brut Rose $11.00 (S-State Fair)
Sparkling Wine,'NV, California, Blanc De Noirs $10.00 (4)
Sparkling Wine,'NV, California, Brut $13.00 (B-Dallas)
Sparkling Wine,'NV, California, Natural $13.00 (5)
Sparkling Wine,'NV, California, Rouge $13.00 (6)

CHARLES KRUG WINERY

2800 St. Helena Hwy. St Helena 94574

Cabernet Sauvignon,'92, Napa Vly., Estate $12.00 (B-Orange)
Chardonnay,'92, Napa Vly., Carneros, Res. $18.00 (G-Orange)
Chardonnay,'93, Napa Vly. $11.00 (4)
Merlot,'92, Napa Vly. $13.00 (4)
Pinot Noir,'93, Napa Vly., Carneros $9.00 (3)

KUNDE ESTATE WINERY

10155 Sonoma Hwy. Kenwood 95442

Chardonnay,'94, Sonoma Vly. $14.00 (2)
Sauvignon Blanc,'94, Sonoma, Magnolia Lane $10.00 (B-Orange)
Zinfandel,'93, Sonoma Vly., Shaw Vnyd. (S-San Diego)

L

LA CREMA

8075 Martinelli Road Forestville 95436

Chardonnay,'93, California, Grand Cuvee $20.00 (7)
Chardonnay,'93, California, Reserve $12.50 (2)
Pinot Noir,'93, California, Grand Cuvee $20.00 (6)
Pinot Noir,'93, California, Reserve $13.50 (5)

LAKE SONOMA WINERY

9990 Dry Creek Rd. Geyserville 95441

Zinfandel,'93, Dry Creek Vly. $12.00 (B-State Fair)
Zinfandel,'93, Dry Creek, Old Vine Res. $14.00 (B-State Fair)

LAKEWOOD VINEYARDS

640 Mathews Rd. Lakeport 95453

Sauvignon Blanc,'93, Clear Lake $9.00 (3)
Semillon,'93, Clear Lake $12.00 (6)
White Meritage,'92, Clear Lake, Chevriot $12.00 (5)
White Meritage,'93, Clear Lake, Chevriot $12.00 (6)

LAMBERT BRIDGE WINERY

4085 W. Dry Creek Road Healdsburg 95448

Cabernet Sauvignon,'92, Sonoma Co. $15.00 (3)
Chardonnay,'93, Sonoma Co., Barrel Ferm. $13.00 (S-Orange)
Merlot,'93, Sonoma Co. $15.00 (3)

LANDMARK VINEYARDS

101 Adobe Canyon Rd. Kenwood 95452

Chardonnay,'93, Alexander Vly., Damaris Res. $19.00 (4)

Chardonnay,'93, Sonoma Co. $11.00 (2)
Chardonnay,'93, Sonoma Co., Overlook $13.00 (5)

LANG WINES

Address Not Available

Zinfandel,'92, El Dorado, Twin Rivers Vnyd. $8.00 (G-State Fair)

LAS VINAS WINERY

5573 W. Woodbridge Rd. Lodi 95242

Cabernet Sauvignon,'92, Napa Vly., Reserve $35.00 (B-State Fair)
Chardonnay,'93, California, Reserve $10.00 (B-Orange)

LATCHAM VINEYARDS

2860 Omo Ranch Rd. Mt Aukum 95656

Cabernet Franc,'91, Sierra Foothills $10.00 (B-L.A.)
Cabernet Franc,'93, Sierra Foothills $10.00 (Σ-State Fair)
Cabernet Sauvignon,'91, El Dorado $9.00 (3)
Petite Sirah,'92, El Dorado $10.00 (G-New World)
Petite Sirah,'93, El Dorado $10.00 (S-San Fran)
Zinfandel,'92, El Dorado, Reserve $10.00 (S-New World)
Zinfandel,'93, El Dorado, Reserve $10.00 (2)

LAURIER VINEYARDS

6342 Bystrum Road Ceres 95307

Chardonnay,'92, Sonoma Co. $15.00 (3)

LAVA CAP WINERY

2221 Fruitridge Rd. Placerville 95667

Cabernet Sauvignon,'91, El Dorado, Estate $12.00 (3)
Chardonnay,'93, El Dorado, Est., Reserve $15.00 (3)
Merlot,'93, El Dorado, Est. $14.00 (2)
Zinfandel,'93, El Dorado $12.00 (Σ-State Fair)

LEEWARD WINERY

2784 Johnson Dr. Ventura 93003

Cabernet Sauvignon,'92, Sonoma Co. $15.00 (3)
Chardonnay,'93, Central Coast $11.00 (2)
Merlot,'93, Napa Vly. $15.00 (4)
Pinot Noir,'93, Santa Barbara Co. $15.00 (3)

LEWIS CELLARS

Address Not Available

Cabernet Sauvignon,'92, Napa $30.00 (S-San Fran)

LOCKWOOD VINEYARD

1044 Harkins Road Salinas 93901

Cabernet Sauvignon,'91, Monterey, Partners Reserve $18.00 (3)
Cabernet Sauvignon,'92, Monterey $14.00 (4)
Cabernet Sauvignon,'92, Partner's Res. $18.00 (B-State Fair)
Chardonnay,'92, Monterey $14.00 (2)
Chardonnay,'92, Monterey, Reserve $17.00 (3)
Merlot,'92, Monterey $14.00 (S-New World)
Merlot,'93, Monterey $14.00 (B-State Fair)
Pinot Blanc,'93, Monterey $10.00 (4)

J. LOHR WINERY

1000 Lenzen Avenue San Jose 95126

Cabernet Sauvignon,'90, Paso Robles, VS#1 (S-San Diego)
Cabernet Sauvignon,'92, Paso Robles, Seven Oaks $12.00 (4)
Chardonnay,'93, Monterey, Riverstone $12.00 (2)
Johannisberg Riesling,'93, Monterey, B. Mist, LH $10.00 (6)

Johannisberg Riesling,'94, Monterey, Bay Mist $7.00 (6)

LOLONIS

1900 Road D Redwood Valley 95470

Petite Sirah,'91, Mendocino (G-New World)

Petite Sirah,'92, Mendocino, Reserve $15.00 (B-Orange)

LYETH

P. O. Box 414 Oakville 94562

Chardonnay,'93, Sonoma Co. $10.00 (B-Orange)

M

MAACAMA CREEK VINEYARDS

15001 Chalk Hill Road Healdsburg 95448

Cabernet Sauvignon,'92, Alexander Vly., Est. Reserve $12.00 (2)

MACKINAW

Address Not Available

Chardonnay,'93, California $11.00 (B-Orange)

MADDALENA VINEYARD

737 Lamar Street Los Angeles 90031

Chardonnay,'93, Central Coast $7.00 (B-Orange)

Gewurztraminer,'94, Central Coast $6.00 (B-Orange)

Merlot,'92, San Simeon Coll. $9.00 (B-Orange)

MADRONA VINEYARDS

P. O. Box 454, Gatlin Rd. Camino 95709

Cabernet Franc,'92, El Dorado $11.00 (4)

Cabernet Sauvignon,'91, El Dorado $11.00 (3)

Chardonnay,'92, El Dorado, Estate $10.00 (3)

Chardonnay,'93, El Dorado, Estate $10.00 (S-Orange)

Gewurztraminer,'94, El Dorado $9.00 (Σ-San Fran)

Johannisberg Riesling,'92, El Dorado $6.75 (2)

Johannisberg Riesling,'93, El Dorado $7.00 (2)

Johannisberg Riesling,'93, El Dorado, SLH $17.00 (G-State Fair)

Red Meritage,'92, El Dorado, Quintet Res. (B-San Diego)

Zinfandel,'92, El Dorado, Estate $8.50 (2)

Zinfandel,'93, El Dorado $9.00 (2)

MAISON DEUTZ WINERY

453 Deutz Dr. Arroyo Grande 93420

Sparkling Wine,'90, San Luis Obispo, Reserve Brut $23.00 (5)

Sparkling Wine,'NV, San Luis Obispo, Brut Cuvee $14.00 (5)

Sparkling Wine,'NV, San Luis Obispo, Brut Rose $18.00 (4)

Sparkling Wine,'NV, SLO/SB Blanc De Noirs $16.00 (4)

MAKOR WINERY

Address Not Available

Pinot Blanc,'94, Santa Barbara, Bien Nacido $11.00 (2)

MARK WEST VINEYARDS

7000 Trenton-Healdsburg Rd. Forestville 95436

Chardonnay,'92, Russian River, Sunrise (B-Dallas)

MARKHAM VINEYARDS

2812 St. Helena Hwy., N. St Helena 94574

Cabernet Sauvignon,'91, Napa Vly. $15.00 (4)

Chardonnay,'93, Napa Vly., Barrel Ferm. $14.00 (3)

MARTINI & PRATI WINERY

2191 Laguna Road Santa Rosa 95401

Zinfandel,'91, Sonoma Co. (G-L.A.)

LOUIS M. MARTINI

P. O. Box 112 St Helena 94574

Cabernet Sauvignon,'89, Napa Vly., Reserve $15.00 (2)
Cabernet Sauvignon,'90, Sonoma., Monte Rosso Vnyd. $23.00 (4)
Cabernet Sauvignon,'91, Monte Rosso Vnyd. $23.00 (B-State Fair)
Cabernet Sauvignon,'92, North Coast $8.50 (3)
Chardonnay,'92, Napa Vly. $9.00 (3)
Gewurztraminer,'93, Russian River Vly. $9.00 (4)
Gewurztraminer,'94, Russian River Vly. $8.00 (B-State Fair)
Merlot,'90, Los Vinedos Del Rio Vnyd. $15.00 (B-San Diego)
Merlot,'92, North Coast $9.00 (5)
Petite Sirah,'91, Napa Vly., Reserve (2)
Pinot Noir,'92, Napa Vly., Carneros $7.50 (2)
Sauvignon Blanc,'93, Napa Vly. $8.00 (B-W. Coast)
Sauvignon Blanc,'94, Napa Vly. $8.00 (2)
Zinfandel,'92, Sonoma Vly. $8.00 (S-Farmers)

MARTY'S SELECTION

Address Not Available

Cabernet Sauvignon,'89, Napa Vly. (B-Dallas)

MARTZ VINEYARD

20799 Highway 128 Yorkville 95494

Zinfandel,'91, Mendocino (B-New World)

MASTANTUONO WINERY

100 Oak View Road Templeton 93465

Chenin Blanc,'94, Central Coast $6.00 (2)

MATANZAS CREEK

6097 Bennett Valley Rd. Santa Rosa 95404

Sauvignon Blanc,'93, Sonoma Co. $14.00 (2)

MAYACAMAS

1155 Lokoya Road Napa 94558

Sauvignon Blanc,'93, Napa Vly. $10.00 (B-Orange)

MAZZOCCO VINEYARDS

1400 Lytton Springs Rd. Healdsburg 95448

Cabernet Sauvignon,'91, Sonoma Co. $18.00 (4)
Merlot,'91, Dry Creek Vly. $15.00 (B-Dallas)
Red Meritage,'90, Dry Creek Vly., Matrix $28.00 (B-Dallas)
Red Meritage,'91, Dry Creek., Matrix, Estate $28.00 (4)
Zinfandel,'92, Sonoma Co. $14.00 (2)
Zinfandel,'93, Sonoma Co. $14.00 (2)

MC DOWELL VALLEY VINEYARDS

14100 Mtn. House Road Hopland 95449

Syrah,'92, Mendocino, Estate $16.00 (B-San Fran)

MC ILROY WINES

8375 Westside Road Healdsburg 95448

Chardonnay,'93, Russian Riv., Aquarius Ranch $15.00 (6)
Red Meritage,'92, Russian River Vly. $15.00 (S-Farmers)
Zinfandel,'93, Russian Riv.., Porter Bass Vnyd. $15.00 (6)

MC KEON-PHILLIPS

Address Not Available

Cabernet Sauvignon,'92, Santa Barbara Co. $17.00 (B-Farmers)

MEEKER VINEYARD

9711 W. Dry Creek Rd. Healdsburg 95448

Cabernet Sauvignon,'91, Dry Creek., Gold Leaf Cuvee $14.00 (4)
Cabernet Sauvignon,'91, Scharf Family Vnyd. (G-New World)
Zinfandel,'92, Sonoma Co., Third Rack $8.00 (3)
Zinfandel,'93, Dry Creek, Gold Leaf Cuvee $13.00 (4)
Zinfandel,'93, Sonoma Co., Cuvee $10.00 (2)

MERIDIAN VINEYARDS

7000 Hwy. 46 East Paso Robles 93447

Cabernet Sauvignon,'92, Paso Robles $12.00 (6)
Chardonnay,'93, Edna Vly. $14.00 (4)
Chardonnay,'93, Santa Barbara Co. $10.00 (2)
Pinot Noir,'92, Santa Barbara Co. $14.00 (2)
Pinot Noir,'93, Santa Barbara $14.00 (S-San Fran)
Pinot Noir,'93, Santa Barbara, Res. $17.00 (G-San Fran)
Sauvignon Blanc,'93, California $9.00 (3)
Syrah,'92, Paso Robles $13.00 (S-Farmers)
Zinfandel,'90, Paso Robles $13.00 (2)

MERRYVALE VINEYARDS

3640 Buchanan St. San Francisco 94123

Cabernet Sauvignon,'91, Napa Vly. $23.00 (2)
Cabernet Sauvignon,'92, Napa Vly. $23.00 (B-W. Coast)
Chardonnay,'93, Napa Vly., Starmont $16.00 (3)
Merlot,'92, Napa Vly. (G-Dallas)
Sauvignon Blanc,'93, Napa Vly. $10.00 (B-W. Coast)

MICHEL-SCHLUMBERGER WINERY

4155 Wine Creek Rd. Healdsburg 95448

Cabernet Sauvignon,'90, Dry Creek Vly., Reserve $30.00 (4)
Cabernet Sauvignon,'91, Dry Creek Vly. $18.00 (2)
Chardonnay,'92, Dry Creek, Benchland Est. $18.00 (3)
Merlot,'92, Dry Creek Vly. $18.00 (B-New World)
Merlot,'93, Dry Creek Vly. $18.00 (B-L.A.)

MIETZ CELLARS

602 Limerick Lane Healdsburg 95448

Merlot,'93, Sonoma Co. $16.50 (3)

MILANO WINERY

14594 So. Highway 101 Hopland 95449

Zinfandel,'93, Mendo., Sanel Vly. Vnyd. $10.00 (S-State Fair)

MILL CREEK VINEYARDS

1401 Westside Rd. Healdsburg 95448

Chardonnay,'93, Dry Creek Vly., Estate $12.00 (3)
Gewurztraminer,'94, North Coast $8.00 (2)
Merlot,'92, Dry Creek, Est. $14.00 (G-W. Coast)
Merlot,'93, Dry Creek Vly. $14.00 (B-State Fair)
Sauvignon Blanc,'93, Dry Creek Vly. $8.00 (S-New World)
Sauvignon Blanc,'94, Dry Creek Vly. $8.00 (G-L.A.)

MILLAIRE WINERY

276 Main Street Murphys 95247

Cabernet Sauvignon,'92, Sierra Foothills $15.00 (B-State Fair)

Zinfandel,'92, El Dorado, Robert's Cuvee, LH $14.00 (B-State Fair)
Zinfandel,'94, Sierra Foothills, Jeunesse $6.00 (S-State Fair)

MIRABELLE CELLARS

Address Not Available

Sparkling Wine,'NV, North Coast, Brut $12.00 (2)

MIRASSOU VINEYARDS

3000 Aborn Rd. San Jose 95135

Cabernet Franc,'92, California, Family Sel. $7.00 (3)
Cabernet Sauvignon,'91, Family Sel. $9.00 (B-New World)
Cabernet Sauvignon,'91, Monterey, Harvest Reserve $12.00 (3)
Cabernet Sauvignon,'92, Harvest Res. $12.00 (S-State Fair)
Cabernet Sauvignon,'92, Monterey, Family Sel. $9.00 (B-State Fair)
Chardonnay,'92, Monterey Co., Harvest Res. $12.00 (2)
Chardonnay,'93, Monterey, Family Sel. $9.00 (B-Farmers)
Chardonnay,'93, Monterey, Harvest Reserve $12.00 (5)
Chenin Blanc,'93, Monterey, Family Selection $6.00 (2)
Johannisberg Riesling,'93, Family Sel. $6.00 (B-San Diego)
Merlot,'92, Central Coast, Harvest Res. $12.00 (B-W. Coast)
Petite Sirah,'92, Monterey, Anniversary Sel. $13.50 (2)
Petite Sirah,'92, Monterey, Family Sel. $9.00 (6)
Pinot Blanc,'92, Monterey, Harvest Reserve $7.00 (S-W. Coast)
Pinot Blanc,'93, Monterey, Harvest Reserve $12.00 (2)
Pinot Blanc,'93, Monterey, Wt. Burgundy $7.00 (5)
Pinot Noir,'91, Monterey, Harvest Reserve $12.00 (B-San Diego)
Pinot Noir,'92, Monterey, Family Sel. $7.00 (B-W. Coast)
Pinot Noir,'92, Monterey, Harvest Reserve $12.00 (3)
Sauvignon Blanc,'93, California $5.00 (4)
Sparkling Wine,'89, Monterey Co., Reserve Brut $15.00 (2)
Sparkling Wine,'89, Monterey, Au Naturel $15.00 (3)
Sparkling Wine,'91, Monterey Co. Brut $12.00 (4)
Sparkling Wine,'91, Monterey, 5th Gen. Cuvee $12.00 (6)
Zinfandel,'91, Santa Clara, 5th Gen. Res. $12.00 (S-Orange)
Zinfandel,'92, Central Coast, Family Sel. $6.00 (2)

MISSION CANYON CELLARS

Address Not Available

Chenin Blanc,'93, Santa Barbara $5.50 (2)

MISSION VIEW VINEYARDS

13350 N. River Road San Miguel 93451

Sauvignon Blanc,'94, Paso Robles, Fume $9.00 (2)
Zinfandel,'93, Paso Robles $12.00 (2)

CHARLES B. MITCHELL VINEYARDS

8221 Stoney Creek Rd. Somerset 95684

Chenin Blanc,'94, El Dorado $6.00 (B-State Fair)

ROBERT MONDAVI WINERY

7801 St. Helena Hwy. Oakville 94562

Cabernet Sauvignon,'91, California, Coastal (B-New World)
Cabernet Sauvignon,'92, Napa Vly., Unfiltered $16.00 (B-Orange)
Cabernet Sauvignon,'92, North Coast $11.00 (B-Dallas)
Cabernet Sauvignon,'93, North Coast $11.00 (2)
Chardonnay,'93, California, Barrel Aged $7.00 (B-Orange)
Chardonnay,'93, Napa Vly. $14.00 (S-State Fair)
Pinot Noir,'92, Napa Vly, $15.00 (2)
Pinot Noir,'93, Napa Vly., Unfiltered $15.00 (G-State Fair)

Sauvignon Blanc,'93, Napa Vly., To-Kalon Res. $18.50 (B-Orange)

MONT ST. JOHN

5400 Old Sonoma Rd. Napa 94558

Cabernet Sauvignon,'91, Napa Vly. $14.00 (2)
Chardonnay,'93, Carneros, Est. $13.00 (B-Farmers)
Pinot Noir,'93, Carneros, Estate $14.00 (4)

MONTEREY VINEYARDS

800 S. Alta Street Gonzales 93926

Cabernet Sauvignon,'92, Monterey Co., Classic $6.00 (B-Farmers)
Cabernet Sauvignon,'93, Monterey Co. $6.00 (B-San Fran)
Merlot,'93, Monterey, Classic $6.00 (S-Farmers)
White Zinfandel,'94, Central Coast, Classic $5.00 (B-Orange)

MONTERRA WINERY

12001 S. Hwy. 99 Manteca 95336

Merlot,'92, Monterey, Sand Hill $10.00 (G-State Fair)
Petite Sirah,'91, Monterey $10.00 (2)
Petite Sirah,'92, Monterey $10.00 (B-San Fran)

MONTEVINA WINERY

P. O. Box 1000 Plymouth 95669

Sauvignon Blanc,'93, California, Fume $7.00 (5)
White Zinfandel,'94, Amador Co. $6.50 (2)
Zinfandel,'91, Amador Co., Reserve $12.00 (S-New World)
Zinfandel,'93, Amador Co. $7.00 (6)
Zinfandel,'93, Amador Co., Brioso $7.50 (2)

MONTICELLO VINEYARDS

4242 Big Ranch Road Napa 94558

Chardonnay,'92, Napa Vly., Corley Est. Res. (B-San Diego)
Merlot,'92, Napa, Corley Fam, Vnyds. $18.00 (2)

MONTPELLIER VINEYARDS

P. O. Box 789 Ceres 95307

Cabernet Sauvignon,'92, California $8.00 (3)
Chardonnay,'93, California $8.00 (2)
Merlot,'93, California $8.00 (2)
Pinot Noir,'93, California $8.00 (3)
White Zinfandel,'94, California $7.00 (2)
Zinfandel,'93, California $7.00 (B-Farmers)

Z. MOORE

3364 River Road Santa Rosa 95401

Johannisberg Riesling,'93, Monterey Co., Quaff $6.50 (S-Orange)

MOSHIN VINEYARDS

Address Not Available

Pinot Noir,'92, Russian River Vly. $15.00 (2)

MOUNT KONOCTI

4350 Thomas Drive Kelseyville 95451

Cabernet Franc,'93, Lake Co. $10.00 (6)
Chardonnay,'93, Lake/Mendocino Co. $10.00 (B-W. Coast)
Johannisberg Riesling,'94, Lake Co., White $8.00 (3)
Merlot,'93, Lake Co. $10.00 (B-Dallas)
Sauvignon Blanc,'93, Lake Co. Fume $8.00 (4)
Sauvignon Blanc,'93, Lake Co. Fume, Reserve $10.00 (2)

MOUNT MADRONA WINERY

8440 St. Helena Hwy. Rutherford 94573

Cabernet Sauvignon,'91, Napa Vly. $14.00 (4)
Chardonnay,'92, Napa Vly. $14.00 (2)

MOUNT PALOMAR WINERY

33820 Rancho Calif. Rd. Temecula 92591

Syrah,'93, California, Rey Sol $8.00 (5)

MOUNT VEEDER WINERY

1999 Mt. Veeder Rd. Napa 94558

Cabernet Sauvignon,'91, Mt. Veeder $40.00 (B-San Fran)
Red Meritage,'91, Napa Vly., Reserve $40.00 (3)

MOUNTAIN VIEW VINTNERS

1480 E. Main Avenue Morgan Hill 95037

Chardonnay,'93, Monterey $6.00 (S-Orange)

MUMM NAPA VALLEY

8445 Silverado Trail Rutherford 94573

Sparkling Wine,'89, Carneros, Winery Lake Brut $23.00 (5)
Sparkling Wine,'90, Carneros, DVX Brut $32.00 (4)
Sparkling Wine,'NV, Cuvee Napa Blanc De Noirs $14.00 (7)
Sparkling Wine,'NV, Cuvee Napa, Brut Prestige $14.00 (3)

MURPHY-GOODE ESTATE WINERY

4001 Highway 128 Geyserville 95441

Chardonnay,'93, Alexander Vly. $11.00 (2)
Chardonnay,'94, Alexander Vly., Barrel Ferm. $12.50 (B-Orange)
Merlot,'93, Alex. Vly., Murphy Ranch $15.00 (B-San Diego)
Pinot Blanc,'93, Melon De Bourgogne $12.50 (G-Orange)
Pinot Blanc,'94, Alexander Vly., Est. $12.00 (2)
Sauvignon Blanc,'93, Alexander Vly. Fume, Res. $15.00 (3)
Sauvignon Blanc,'94, Alexander Vly., Fume $10.00 (4)

N

NAPA CELLARS

7481 St. Helena Hwy. Oakville 94562

Chardonnay,'93, Napa Vly. $7.00 (B-Orange)

NAPA CREEK WINERY

1001 Silverado Trail St Helena 94574

Cabernet Sauvignon,'91, Napa Vly. $10.00 (2)
Chardonnay,'92, Napa Vly. $10.00 (2)
Pinot Noir,'92, Napa Vly. (S-New World)

NAPA RIDGE WINERY

2000 Main Street St Helena 94574

Cabernet Sauvignon,'91, North Coast, Reserve $13.00 (5)
Cabernet Sauvignon,'92, Central Coast $8.00 (5)
Cabernet Sauvignon,'93, North Coast $8.00 (B-San Fran)
Chardonnay,'93, Central Coast $8.00 (S-New World)
Chardonnay,'93, Napa Vly., Reserve $13.00 (7)
Chardonnay,'94, Central Coast $8.00 (2)
Gewurztraminer,'93, Central Coast $5.00 (2)
Gewurztraminer,'94, Central Coast $5.00 (2)
Merlot,'92, North Coast $9.00 (3)
Pinot Noir,'93, North Coast $9.00 (4)
Sauvignon Blanc,'93, North Coast $5.00 (4)

White Zinfandel,'94, Lodi $5.00 (4)

NAPA-VILLAGES

5225 Solano Avenue Napa 94558

Chardonnay,'92, Napa Vly. $10.00 (B-Orange)

NAVARRO VINEYARDS

5601 Highway 128 Philo 95466

Cabernet Franc,'92, Mendocino $16.00 (B-San Fran)
Cabernet Sauvignon,'90, Mendocino $16.00 (2)
Cabernet Sauvignon,'91, Mendocino $17.00 (2)
Chardonnay,'93, Anderson Vly. (B-New World)
Chardonnay,'93, Anderson Vly., Reserve $15.00 (4)
Chardonnay,'93, Mendocino $11.00 (3)
Gewurztraminer,'93, Anderson Vly. $10.00 (5)
Johannisberg Riesling,'93, Anderson Vly. $8.50 (2)
Johannisberg Riesling,'93, Anderson Vly., LHCS $20.00 (4)
Johannisberg Riesling,'93, Melange A Trois (G-New World)
Johannisberg Riesling,'94, Anderson Vly., LH $14.00 (S-State Fair)
Pinot Noir,'91, Anderson Vly. $15.00 (4)
Pinot Noir,'92, Anderson Vly. $15.00 (B-San Fran)
Pinot Noir,'93, Anderson Vly. $9.00 (2)
Sauvignon Blanc,'93, Mendo., Cuvee 128 $11.00 (G-New World)
Sauvignon Blanc,'94, Mendocino, Cuvee 128 $11.00 (Σ-State Fair)
Semillon,'93, North Coast $11.00 (2)
Zinfandel,'93, Mendocino $15.00 (4)

NELSON ESTATE VINEYARD

Address Not Available

Cabernet Franc,'90, Sonoma Co. $15.00 (S-Dallas)

NEVADA CITY WINERY

321 Spring St. Nevada City 95959

Cabernet Franc,'93, Nevada Co. $12.00 (G-Orange)
Cabernet Sauvignon,'92, Sierra Foothills $12.00 (B-State Fair)
Chardonnay,'93, Nevada Co., Barrel Ferm. $10.00 (2)
Gewurztraminer,'93, Sonoma Co. $8.00 (B-Orange)
Zinfandel,'93, Sierra Foothills $10.00 (2)

NEWLAN VINEYARDS

5225 Solano Avenue Napa 94558

Cabernet Sauvignon,'89, Napa Vly. $10.00 (B-W. Coast)
Cabernet Sauvignon,'91, Napa Vly. $16.00 (2)
Chardonnay,'92, Napa Vly. $10.00 (S-W. Coast)
Johannisberg Riesling,'93, Napa Vly., LH $11.00 (B-Orange)
Pinot Noir,'93, Napa Vly. $18.00 (2)

NEWTON

2555 Madrona Ave. St Helena 94574

Red Meritage,'92, Napa Vly. $11.00 (S-Orange)

NICHELINI VINEYARDS

2300 Lower Chiles Rd. St Helena 94574

Cabernet Sauvignon,'89, Napa Vly. $12.00 (2)
Merlot,'92, Napa Vly., Nichelini Vnyd. $20.00 (B-State Fair)
Zinfandel,'91, Napa Vly., Nichelini Vnyd. $12.00 (4)

NICHOLS WINERY

Address Not Available

Chardonnay,'93, Arroyo Grande, Talley Vnyd. $21.00 (B-Orange)

Pinot Noir,'93, Santa Barbara, Madre Vnyd. $24.00 (2)

NORMAN VINEYARDS

7450 Vineyard Dr. Paso Robles 93446

Cabernet Sauvignon,'92, Paso Robles $13.00 (3)
Chardonnay,'93, Paso Robles (B-San Diego)
Zinfandel,'94, Paso Robles, LH $15.00 (B-State Fair)

O

OAK FALLS

9140 Owens Mt. Ave. Chatsworth 91311

Cabernet Sauvignon,'93, Napa Vly. $8.00 (2)
Chardonnay,'93, Napa Co. $6.00 (S-New World)
Pinot Noir,'93, Sonoma (S-New World)

OAKVILLE RANCH VINEYARDS

7781 Silverado Trail Napa 94558

Cabernet Sauvignon,'92, Napa Vly. $24.00 (B-Orange)
Chardonnay,'93, Napa Vly., Vista Vnyd. $18.00 (B-San Fran)

OBESTER

12341 San Mateo Rd. Half Moon Bay 94019

Gewurztraminer,'93, Anderson Vly. $8.00 (B-W. Coast)
Johannisberg Riesling,'94, Mendocino Co. $7.00 (2)

OLIVET LANE ESTATE

P. O. Box 2386 So San Francisco 94083

Chardonnay,'93, Russian River $13.00 (B-Farmers)
Pinot Noir,'93, Russian River Vly. $13.00 (4)

ORFILA VINEYARDS

13455 San Pasqual Rd. Escondido 92025

Gewurztraminer,'93, California $10.00 (B-Farmers)
Merlot,'91, California (B-Dallas)
Merlot,'92, California (S-Dallas)
Merlot,'92, San Diego, Reserve $25.00 (B-Dallas)

P

PACIFIC RIM

10 Pine Flat Road Santa Cruz 95060

Chenin Blanc,'94, California $8.00 (B-Orange)
Johannisberg Riesling,'94, California $8.00 (S-Orange)

PAHLMEYER

P. O. Box 2410 Napa 94558

Red Meritage,'91, Napa Vly., Estate $32.00 (B-Orange)

PARADISE RIDGE WINERY

4545 Thomas Lake Harris Dr. Santa Rosa 95403

Chardonnay,'93, Sonoma Co. $15.00 (S-State Fair)

PARAISO SPRINGS VINEYARDS

38060 Paraiso Springs Rd. Soledad 93960

Gewurztraminer,'93, Santa Lucia Highlands $7.00 (B-Farmers)
Johannisberg Riesling,'93, Santa Lucia Highlands $7.00 (3)
Johannisberg Riesling,'94, Santa Lucia $7.00 (B-San Fran)
Pinot Blanc,'93, Santa Lucia Highlands $9.00 (B-San Diego)

PARDUCCI WINE CELLARS

501 Parducci Road Ukiah 95482

Cabernet Franc,'93, Mendocino Co. $9.00 (B-State Fair)
Cabernet Sauvignon,'91, Mendocino Co. $8.00 (3)
Cabernet Sauvignon,'92, Mendocino Co. $8.00 (B-State Fair)
Cabernet Sauvignon,'93, Mendo., Cellar Sel. $15.00 (S-State Fair)
Chardonnay,'93, Mendocino Co. $8.00 (B-New World)
Chardonnay,'94, Mendocino Co. $8.00 (G-State Fair)
Merlot,'93, North Coast $8.00 (3)
Petite Sirah,'91, Mendocino Co. $7.00 (2)
Petite Sirah,'92, Mendocino Co. $7.00 (2)
Petite Sirah,'93, California $7.00 (Σ-L.A.)
Pinot Noir,'93, Mendocino Co. $7.00 (2)
White Zinfandel,'94, California $5.00 (B-San Fran)
Zinfandel,'93, Mendocino $7.00 (S-San Fran)

FESS PARKER WINERY

6200 Foxen Canyon Rd. Los Olivos 93441

Chardonnay,'93, Santa Barbara Co. $13.00 (3)
Chardonnay,'93, Santa Barbara Co., Res. $18.00 (4)
Merlot,'93, Santa Barbara Co. $16.00 (B-Orange)
Pinot Noir,'93, Santa Barbara Co. $15.00 (6)
Pinot Noir,'93, Santa Barbara Co., Reserve $20.00 (8)
Syrah,'93, Santa Barbara Co. $15.00 (2)

PEACHY CANYON WINERY

Rt. 1, Box 115C Paso Robles 93446

Cabernet Sauvignon,'93, Central Coast $18.00 (S-Orange)
Zinfandel,'93, Paso Robles, Dusi Ranch $20.00 (G-Orange)

PEDRONCELLI WINERY

1220 Canyon Road Geyserville 95441

Cabernet Sauvignon,'92, Alexander Vly., Fay Vnyd. $14.00 (2)
Cabernet Sauvignon,'92, Dry Creek Vly. $9.50 (2)
Chardonnay,'92, Dry Creek Vly. $9.00 (B-New World)
Chardonnay,'93, Dry Creek Vly. $9.00 (S-L.A.)
Merlot,'92, Dry Creek Vly. (G-New World)
Pinot Noir,'92, Dry Creek Vly. $9.50 (S-Orange)
Sauvignon Blanc,'93, Dry Creek Vly. Fume $8.00 (2)
Zinfandel,'93, Dry Creek, Mother Clone $10.00 (B-San Fran)
Zinfandel,'93, Dry Creek, Pedroni-Bushnell $12.00 (2)
Zinfandel,'94, Sonoma Co. $6.00 (S-State Fair)

PEIRANO ESTATE VINEYARDS

3862 Peninsula Ct. Stockton 95219

Zinfandel,'92, Lodi, Est. $10.00 (3)
Zinfandel,'93, Lodi $10.00 (B-Orange)

PEJU PROVINCE

8466 St. Helena Hwy. Rutherford 94573

Cabernet Sauvignon,'91, Napa Vly., H.B. Vnyd. $35.00 (2)
Cabernet Sauvignon,'92, Napa Vly., HB Vnyd. $35.00 (B-W. Coast)
Chardonnay,'93, Napa Vly., Barrel Ferm. $16.00 (2)
Red Meritage,'92, Napa Vly. $30.00 (2)

ROBERT PEPI WINERY

7585 St. Helena Hwy. Oakville 94562

Cabernet Sauvignon,'89, Napa Vly., Vine Hill Ranch $18.00 (4)
Cabernet Sauvignon,'91, Napa Vly., Vine Hill Ranch $18.00 (4)

Chardonnay,'91, Napa, Puncheon Ferm. $15.00 (3)
Chardonnay,'92, Napa Vly., Puncheon Ferm. $15.00 (6)
Sauvignon Blanc,'92, Napa Vly., Reserve Sel. $20.00 (4)
Sauvignon Blanc,'93, Napa Vly., Reserve Sel. $20.00 (4)
Sauvignon Blanc,'93, Napa, Two Heart Canopy $11.00 (3)
Sauvignon Blanc,'94, Napa, Two Heart Canopy $11.00 (2)

PEPPERWOOD GROVE

8440 St. Helena Hwy. Rutherford 94573

Cabernet Franc,'92, California, Cask Lot 2 (2)
Pinot Noir,'93, California $6.00 (B-Orange)

MARIO PERELLI-MINETTI

1443 Silverado Trail, N. St Helena 94574

Cabernet Sauvignon,'91, Napa Vly. $14.00 (G-L.A.)
Chardonnay,'91, Napa Vly. (S-L.A.)

PERRY CREEK VINEYARDS

7400 Perry Creek Road Somerset 95684

Cabernet Franc,'92, El Dorado $11.50 (2)
Cabernet Sauvignon,'92, El Dorado $10.00 (3)
Chardonnay,'94, El Dorado $9.00 (3)
Johannisberg Riesling,'94, El Dorado $6.00 (3)
Sauvignon Blanc,'94, El Dorado $7.00 (G-San Fran)
White Zinfandel,'94, Sierra Foothills (B-W. Coast)
Zinfandel,'92, El Dorado $9.00 (B-W. Coast)
Zinfandel,'93, El Dorado $9.00 (S-San Fran)

PESENTI WINERY

2900 Vineyard Drive Templeton 93465

Johannisberg Riesling,'NV, San Luis Obispo $6.00 (B-State Fair)

PETERSON WINERY

Address Not Available

Cabernet Sauvignon,'92, Dry Creek Vly. (S-New World)
Zinfandel,'93, Dry Creek Vly. (B-New World)

JOSEPH PHELPS VINEYARDS

200 Taplin Road St Helena 94574

Cabernet Sauvignon,'92, Napa Vly. $20.00 (3)
Gewurztraminer,'93, California $13.00 (S-Orange)
Merlot,'92, Napa Vly. $18.00 (B-Orange)
Red Meritage,'91, Napa Vly., Insignia $50.00 (3)

R. H. PHILLIPS VINEYARD

26836 County Rd. 12A Esparto 95627

Cabernet Sauvignon,'92, Calif., Barrel Cuvee $7.50 (B-New World)
Cabernet Sauvignon,'93, California, Barrel Cuvee $7.50 (2)
Chardonnay,'93, California, Barrel Cuvee $8.00 (G-New World)
Chardonnay,'94, Dunnigan Hills, Cuvee $7.00 (3)
Chenin Blanc,'93, California, Dry $5.00 (3)
Sauvignon Blanc,'93, California $6.00 (S-W. Coast)
White Zinfandel,'94, Calif., Night Harvest (B-Dallas)

PINE RIDGE

5901 Silverado Trail Napa 94558

Chardonnay,'93, Napa, Knollside Cuvee. $14.00 (G-Orange)
Chardonnay,'93, Napa, Stags Leap Dist. $23.50 (S-Orange)
Merlot,'93, Napa Vly., Selected Cuvee $18.00 (G-Orange)

PIPER SONOMA

11447 Old Redwood Hwy. Healdsburg 95448

Pinot Noir,'93, Russian River, Bearboat $18.00 (S-San Fran)
Sparkling Wine,'85, Sonoma, Tete De Cuvee $28.00 (G-Orange)
Sparkling Wine,'90, Sonoma Co., Sparkling Rose $19.00 (2)
Sparkling Wine,'NV, Sonoma Co. Blanc De Noir $13.50 (3)
Sparkling Wine,'NV, Sonoma Co. Brut $13.50 (4)

PLAM VINEYARDS

6200 Washington St. Yountville 94599

Cabernet Sauvignon,'92, California $30.00 (B-New World)
Chardonnay,'94, Napa Vly. $18.00 (S-San Fran)

POALILLO VINEYARDS

Address Not Available

Zinfandel,'92, Paso Robles, Westside $13.00 (G-Orange)

POPPY HILL CELLARS

5400 Old Sonoma Rd. Napa 94558

Cabernet Sauvignon,'92, California, Calif. Selection $8.00 (3)
Cabernet Sauvignon,'92, Napa Vly., Founders Sel. $10.00 (5)
Chardonnay,'93, California $8.00 (B-New World)
Merlot,'93, Napa Vly., Founder's Sel. $11.00 (2)

PRESTON VINEYARDS & WINERY

9282 W. Dry Creek Rd. Healdsburg 95448

Petite Sirah,'92, Dry Creek Vly., Est. (B-L.A.)
Sauvignon Blanc,'93, Dry Creek, Cuvee De Fume $9.50 (2)
Sauvignon Blanc,'93, Dry Creek, Est., Organic $12.00 (B-Orange)
Semillon,'93, Dry Creek Vly. $13.00 (2)
Syrah,'92, Dry Creek Vly., Est. $18.00 (4)
Zinfandel,'93, Dry Creek Vly., Est. $12.00 (4)

PRIDE MOUNTAIN VINEYARDS

4026 Spring Mtn. Road St Helena 94574

Cabernet Franc,'93, Sonoma Co. $20.00 (2)
Merlot,'93, Napa Vly. $20.00 (2)

Q

QUAIL RIDGE CELLARS

1055 Atlas Peak Road Napa 94558

Cabernet Sauvignon,'89, Napa Vly., Eisele Vnyd., Res. $30.00 (3)
Cabernet Sauvignon,'90, Napa Vly. $12.00 (2)
Chardonnay,'92, Napa Vly. $12.00 (B-San Diego)
Merlot,'91, Napa Vly. $14.00 (2)
Sauvignon Blanc,'92, Napa Vly. $9.00 (S-Orange)
Sauvignon Blanc,'93, Napa Vly. $9.00 (2)

QUIVIRA VINEYARDS

4900 W. Dry Creek Rd. Healdsburg 95448

Red Meritage,'91, Dry Creek Vly., Cuvee $15.00 (6)
Sauvignon Blanc,'93, Dry Creek Vly. $10.00 (2)
Zinfandel,'93, Dry Creek Vly. $14.00 (6)

R

RABBIT RIDGE VINEYARDS

3291 Westside Rd. Healdsburg 95448

Cabernet Sauvignon,'90, Sonoma Co., Est. Reserve $20.00 (5)

Chardonnay,'93, Rabbit Ridge Reserve $16.00 (B-Orange)
Chardonnay,'94, Sonoma Co. $10.00 (B-Orange)
Merlot,'92, Carneros, Sangiacomo Vnyd. $15.00 (3)
Syrah,'92, Sonoma Co. $16.00 (G-State Fair)
Zinfandel,'93, Dry Creek Vly. $10.00 (4)
Zinfandel,'93, San Lorenzo Reserve $18.00 (S-State Fair)

A. RAFANELLI WINERY

4685 W. Dry Creek Rd. Healdsburg 95448

Cabernet Sauvignon,'91, Dry Creek Vly. $18.00 (B-New World)
Cabernet Sauvignon,'92, Dry Creek Vly., Unfiltered $18.00 (6)
Zinfandel,'92, Dry Creek Vly. $13.00 (2)
Zinfandel,'93, Dry Creek Vly. $13.00 (4)

RANCHO SISQUOC WINERY

6600 Foxen Canyon Rd. Santa Maria 93454

Cabernet Sauvignon,'92, Santa Maria Vly., Est. $15.00 (4)
Chardonnay,'93, Santa Maria Vly., Est. $15.00 (B-Farmers)
Johannisberg Riesling,'94, Santa Maria Vly. $8.00 (2)
Johannisberg Riesling,'94, Santa Maria Vly. $10.00 (B-L.A.)
Red Meritage,'91, Santa Maria, Cellar Sel. $30.00 (B-Farmers)
Sauvignon Blanc,'93, Santa Maria Vly., Est. $12.00 (B-San Diego)

RAVENSWOOD

21415 Broadway Sonoma 95476

Cabernet Sauvignon,'92, Sonoma $13.00 (S-Orange)

RAYMOND VINEYARD & CELLAR

849 Zinfandel Lane St Helena 94574

Cabernet Sauvignon,'90, Napa Vly., Reserve $26.00 (5)
Cabernet Sauvignon,'91, California, Amberhill $9.00 (2)
Cabernet Sauvignon,'91, Napa Vly. $17.00 (4)
Cabernet Sauvignon,'92, California, Amberhill $9.00 (B-W. Coast)
Chardonnay,'92, Napa Vly. $13.00 (5)
Chardonnay,'92, Napa Vly., Reserve $18.00 (2)
Chardonnay,'93, California, Amberhill $11.00 (4)
Merlot,'92, Napa Vly. $17.00 (5)
Pinot Noir,'92, Napa Vly. $17.00 (3)
Red Meritage,'90, Napa Vly., Reserve $40.00 (2)
Sauvignon Blanc,'93, Napa Vly. $9.00 (3)

RENAISSANCE VINEYARD

P. O. Box 1000 Renaissance 95962

Cabernet Sauvignon,'91, North Yuba, Estate $13.00 (S-L.A.)
Sauvignon Blanc,'91, North Yuba, SLH $13.00 (B-Dallas)

RENWOOD WINERY

12225 Steiner Rd. Plymouth 95669

Syrah,'92, Amador Co. (B-New World)
Zinfandel,'92, Amador, Old Vines $15.00 (S-San Diego)
Zinfandel,'93, Amador, Old Vines $15.00 (S-L.A.)
Zinfandel,'93, Grand-pere Vnyd. $22.00 (S-Orange)

RETZLAFF VINEYARDS

1356 S. Livermore Ave. Livermore 94550

Cabernet Sauvignon,'92, Livermore Vly., Est. $16.00 (2)

RICHARDSON VINEYARDS

2711 Knob Hill Rd. Sonoma 95476

Cabernet Franc,'93, Sonoma Vly., Giles Vnyd. $14.50 (2)

Merlot,'93, Carneros, Sanciacomo Vnyd. $18.00 (5)
Pinot Noir,'93, Sangiacomo Vnyd. (B-San Diego)

RIVER RUN VINTNERS

65 Rogge Lane Watsonville 95076

Merlot,'93, California $15.00 (4)
Syrah,'93, Monterey, Ventana Vnyd. $15.00 (5)
Zinfandel,'92, California (2)
Zinfandel,'93, California, LH, R.S. 7.0% $15.00 (4)

ROCHIOLI VINEYARD

6192 Westside Road Healdsburg 95448

Pinot Noir,'93, Russian River Vly. $18.00 (3)
Sauvignon Blanc,'94, Russian River Vly., Est. $13.00 (5)

ROMBAUER VINEYARDS

3522 Silverado Trail St Helena 94574

Chardonnay,'93, Carneros (G-Dallas)
Red Meritage,'88, Napa, Le Meilleur Du Chai $35.00 (B-Orange)

ROSENBLUM CELLARS

2900 Main Street Alameda 94501

Cabernet Sauvignon,'92, Napa, Holbrook Mitchell $15.00 (2)
Merlot,'92, Russian River Vly. (B-Dallas)
Petite Sirah,'92, Napa Vly. (B-Dallas)
Red Meritage,'92, Napa, Holbrook Mitchell Trio $23.00 (S-Dallas)
Red Meritage,'93, Napa, Holbrook Mitchell Trio $23.00 (B-San
Zinfandel,'93, Alex. Vly., Harris-Kratka Vnyd. $15.00 (2)
Zinfandel,'93, Contra Costa Co. $11.00 (6)
Zinfandel,'93, Mt. Veeder, Brandlin Ranch $19.00 (4)
Zinfandel,'93, Paso Robles, R. Sauret Vnyd. $11.50 (2)
Zinfandel,'93, Sonoma Co., Old Vines $13.00 (5)
Zinfandel,'NV, California, Cuvee X $8.00 (3)

ROUND HILL VINEYARDS

1680 Silverado Trail St Helena 94574

Cabernet Sauvignon,'90, Napa Vly., Reserve $14.00 (3)
Cabernet Sauvignon,'91, California $8.00 (B-New World)
Cabernet Sauvignon,'92, California $8.00 (B-Orange)
Chardonnay,'93, California $8.00 (2)
Chardonnay,'93, Napa Vly., Reserve $14.00 (B-San Diego)
Merlot,'92, Napa Vly., Reserve $13.00 (2)
Merlot,'93, California $8.00 (2)
Sauvignon Blanc,'94, Napa Vly. $8.00 (B-W. Coast)
Zinfandel,'92, Napa Vly. $8.00 (3)

RUBISSOW-SARGENT WINE CO.

2413 Fourth Street Berkeley 94710

Merlot,'92, Napa Vly., Mt. Veeder $16.00 (S-Orange)
Red Meritage,'90, Napa, Les Trempettes $18.00 (2)

RUTHERFORD ESTATE CELLARS

P. O. Box 402 Rutherford 94573

Cabernet Sauvignon,'91, Napa Vly. $7.00 (2)
Cabernet Sauvignon,'92, Napa Vly. $7.00 (2)
Chardonnay,'92, Napa Vly. $7.00 (3)
Merlot,'92, Napa Vly. $7.00 (Σ-San Diego)
Sauvignon Blanc,'92, Napa Vly. $7.00 (S-San Diego)
White Zinfandel,'94, California $6.00 (3)

RUTHERFORD HILL WINERY

200 Rutherford Hill Rd. Rutherford 94573

Chardonnay,'92, Napa Vly., Jaeger Vnyd. $12.00 (S-Orange)
Chardonnay,'92, Napa Vly., Reserve (B-Dallas)
Merlot,'92, Napa Vly., Reserve XVS $21.00 (4)

RUTHERFORD RANCH VINEYARDS

1680 Silverado Trail St Helena 94574

Cabernet Sauvignon,'91, Napa Vly. $11.00 (3)
Cabernet Sauvignon,'91, Napa Vly., Lot 2 $10.00 (2)
Chardonnay,'93, Napa Vly. $9.00 (S-New World)
Merlot,'93, Napa Vly. $11.00 (S-State Fair)
Red Meritage,'90, Napa Vly., Quintessence $20.00 (5)
Sauvignon Blanc,'93, Napa Vly. $9.00 (2)

RUTHERFORD VINEYARDS

Address Not Available

Cabernet Sauvignon,'92, Napa Vly. (B-New World)
Chardonnay,'93, Napa Vly. (B-New World)

RUTHERFORD VINTNERS

Address Not Available

Sauvignon Blanc,'93, Napa Vly., Fume $8.00 (S-Orange)

RUTZ WINERY

Address Not Available

Cabernet Sauvignon,'91, Napa Vly. $22.50 (B-Orange)

S

SADDLEBACK CELLARS

P. O. Box 141 Oakville 94562

Pinot Blanc,'93, Napa Vly., Estate $9.00 (B-Orange)

SALAMANDRE

108 Don Carlos Drive Aptos 95003

Merlot,'92, Arroyo Seco $14.00 (B-Orange)

SAN MARTIN WINERY

12001 S. Hwy. 99 Manteca 95336

Chardonnay,'94, California $5.00 (B-State Fair)
Sauvignon Blanc,'93, California $5.00 (3)
White Zinfandel,'94, California $5.00 (2)

SAN SABA VINEYARD

P. O. Box 2526 Salinas 93902

Cabernet Sauvignon,'90, Monterey (B-New World)
Cabernet Sauvignon,'92, Monterey (S-L.A.)
Merlot,'92, Monterey Co., Bocage (B-Dallas)

SANFORD WINERY

7250 Santa Rosa Rd. Buellton 93427

Pinot Noir,'92, Santa Barbara Co. $18.00 (B-Dallas)
Pinot Noir,'93, Santa Barbara Co. $18.00 (3)

SANTA BARBARA WINERY

202 Anacapa St. Santa Barbara 93101

Chardonnay,'92, Santa Ynez, Reserve $20.00 (B-Dallas)
Chardonnay,'93, Santa Ynez, Reserve $20.00 (S-Orange)
Chenin Blanc,'91, Santa Ynez, Barrel Ferm. $8.00 (B-Orange)
Johannisberg Riesling,'93, Santa Ynez Vly. $8.50 (B-Orange)

Sauvignon Blanc,'93, Santa Ynez, Barrel Ferm. $8.00 (B-Orange)
Sauvignon Blanc,'93, Santa Ynez, LH, R.S. 18.5% $14.00 (2)
Sauvignon Blanc,'93, Santa Ynez, Reserve $12.00 (S-Orange)
Zinfandel,'92, Santa Ynez, La Fond Vnyd. $11.00 (2)

SANTA YNEZ WINERY

343 N. Refugio Road Santa Ynez 93460

Sparkling Wine,'84, Reserve De Cave Brut $20.00 (S-Orange)

SANTINO WINES

12225 Steiner Rd. Plymouth 95669

Johannisberg Riesling,'82, El Dorado, DBS $30.00 (3)
Johannisberg Riesling,'89, Sonoma Co., DBSH $11.00 (2)
White Zinfandel,'94, Amador Co., White Harvest $6.00 (2)
Zinfandel,'89, Amador Co., Dry Berry Select $11.00 (3)

V. SATTUI WINERY

1111 White Lane St Helena 94574

Cabernet Sauvignon,'91, Napa Vly. $15.00 (3)
Cabernet Sauvignon,'91, Napa Vly., Mario's Reserve $35.00 (7)
Cabernet Sauvignon,'91, Napa Vly., Preston Vnyd. $25.00 (5)
Cabernet Sauvignon,'91, Napa Vly., Suzanne's Vnyd. $20.00 (3)
Cabernet Sauvignon,'92, Napa Vly., Preston Vnyd. $17.00 (2)
Cabernet Sauvignon,'92, Napa Vly., Suzanne's Vnyd. $20.00 (2)
Chardonnay,'93, Napa Vly., Carsi Vnyd. $17.50 (2)
Johannisberg Riesling,'93, Napa Vly. Dry $10.00 (B-Dallas)
Johannisberg Riesling,'93, Napa Vly., Off Dry $10.00 (B-New World)
Johannisberg Riesling,'94, Napa Vly., Dry $10.00 (6)
Johannisberg Riesling,'94, Napa Vly., Off Dry $10.00 (2)
Sparkling Wine,'92, Napa Vly., Carsi Estate $15.00 (6)
White Zinfandel,'94, California $8.00 (6)
Zinfandel,'91, Napa Vly., Howell Mtn. $16.00 (2)
Zinfandel,'92, Howell Mtn. $16.00 (S-State Fair)
Zinfandel,'92, Napa, Suzanne's Vnyd. $13.00 (B-W. Coast)

SAUCELITO CANYON VINEYARD

1600 Saucelito Creek Rd. Arroyo Grande 93420

Cabernet Sauvignon,'92, Arroyo Grande Vly. $12.00 (B-Orange)
Zinfandel,'93, Arroyo Grande $14.00 (S-State Fair)

SAUSAL WINERY

7370 Hwy. 128 Healdsburg 95448

Cabernet Sauvignon,'92, Alexander Vly. $14.00 (2)
Zinfandel,'93, Alexander Vly. $9.00 (4)

SCHRAMSBERG VINEYARDS

1400 Schramsberg Rd. Calistoga 94515

Sparkling Wine,'87, Napa Vly., Blanc De Noirs $24.00 (2)
Sparkling Wine,'89, Blanc De Blanc $22.00 (S-L.A.)
Sparkling Wine,'89, Napa Vly., J. Schram $50.00 (2)
Sparkling Wine,'90, Napa, Blanc De Blanc $22.00 (S-Orange)
Sparkling Wine,'90, Napa, Cuvee De Pinot $22.00 (G-New World)
Sparkling Wine,'91, Napa Vly., Cuvee De Pinot $22.00 (2)
Sparkling Wine,'NV, Brut (B-L.A.)

SCHUETZ OLES

Address Not Available

Petite Sirah,'93, Napa, Rattlesnake Acres $15.00 (B-State Fair)

SCHUG CARNEROS ESTATE WINERY

602 Bonneau Road Sonoma 94576

Pinot Noir,'93, Carneros $16.00 (2)

SEBASTIANI VINEYARDS

389 Fourth St. E. Sonoma 95476

Cabernet Sauvignon,'91, Sonoma Vly. Cherryblock $25.00 (4)
Cabernet Sauvignon,'92, Sonoma Co. $10.00 (5)
Chardonnay,'93, Russian River, Dutton Ranch $18.00 (4)
Chardonnay,'93, Sonoma Co. $10.00 (4)
Chardonnay,'94, Sonoma Co. $10.00 (G-L.A.)
Merlot,'93, Sonoma Co. $11.00 (2)
Sparkling Wine,'91, Richard Cuneo Cuvee $15.00 (3)

SEGHESIO WINERY

14730 Grove Street Healdsburg 95448

Pinot Noir,'93, Sonoma Co., Home Ranch (2)
Sauvignon Blanc,'94, Sonoma Co. $7.00 (2)
Zinfandel,'93, Sonoma Co., Home Ranch $9.00 (2)

SEQUOIA GROVE VINEYARDS

8338 St. Helena Hwy. Napa 94558

Cabernet Sauvignon,'92, Napa Vly., Est. Reserve $18.00 (4)
Chardonnay,'92, Napa Vly., Estate Res. $18.00 (S-San Diego)
Chardonnay,'92, Napa, Carneros, Calif. Sel. (B-San Diego)
Chardonnay,'93, Napa Vly., Barrel Sel. $16.00 (2)
Chardonnay,'93, Napa Vly., Est. Reserve $18.00 (2)

SHAFER VINEYARDS

6154 Silverado Trail Napa 94558

Cabernet Sauvignon,'91, Napa Vly., Stag's Leap $22.00 (2)
Cabernet Sauvignon,'92, Stag's Leap Dist. $22.00 (5)
Chardonnay,'93, Napa Vly., Barrel Select $16.00 (4)
Merlot,'92, Napa Vly. $23.00 (S-New World)
Merlot,'93, Napa Vly. $23.00 (5)

SHENANDOAH VINEYARDS

12300 Steiner Rd. Plymouth 95669

White Zinfandel,'94, Amador Co. $5.00 (B-State Fair)
Zinfandel,'93, Amador Co., Reserve $8.00 (S-State Fair)

SIERRA VISTA WINERY

4560 Cabernet Way Placerville 95667

Cabernet Sauvignon,'92, El Dorado, Est. $12.00 (3)
Cabernet Sauvignon,'92, El Dorado, Five Star Reserve $22.00 (2)
Sauvignon Blanc,'94, El Dorado, Estate, Fume $8.00 (2)
Syrah,'92, El Dorado, Estate $16.00 (4)
Zinfandel,'93, El Dorado, Est. $10.00 (3)
Zinfandel,'94, El Dorado $7.00 (B-State Fair)

SILVER HORSE VINEYARDS

2995 Pleasant Road San Miguel 93441

Pinot Noir,'94, Paso Robles $14.00 (B-State Fair)
Zinfandel,'92, Paso Robles $12.00 (3)

SILVER OAK

915 Oakville Cross Rd. Oakville 94562

Cabernet Sauvignon,'91, Alexander Vly. $32.00 (B-Orange)
Cabernet Sauvignon,'91, Napa Vly. $36.00 (B-Orange)

SILVER RIDGE VINEYARDS

Address Not Available

Chardonnay,'92, California, Barrel Ferm. $10.00 (2)
Merlot,'92, California $10.00 (2)

SILVERADO VINEYARDS

6121 Silverado Trail Napa 94558

Cabernet Sauvignon,'92, Napa Vly. $19.00 (3)
Chardonnay,'93, Napa Vly. $15.00 (4)
Merlot,'92, Napa Vly. $17.00 (2)
Sauvignon Blanc,'93, Napa Vly. $9.50 (S-W. Coast)
Sauvignon Blanc,'94, Napa Vly. $10.00 (B-San Fran)

SIMI WINERY

16275 Healdsburg Ave. Healdsburg 95448

Cabernet Sauvignon,'91, Alexander Vly. $15.00 (S-Orange)
Chardonnay,'92, Mendo/Sonoma/Napa $13.00 (2)
Sauvignon Blanc,'93, Sonoma Co. $9.00 (2)

SINGLE LEAF VINEYARDS

7480 Fairplay Road Somerset 95684

Cabernet Sauvignon,'92, El Dorado, De Casabel $11.00 (2)
White Zinfandel,'94, El Dorado $6.00 (2)
Zinfandel,'92, El Dorado $8.50 (B-W. Coast)

SMITH & HOOK WINERY

37700 Foothill Rd. Soledad 93960

Merlot,'92, Santa Lucia Highlands $18.00 (5)

SMITH-MADRONE VINEYARDS

4022 Spring Mt. Road St Helena 94574

Johannisberg Riesling,'93, Napa Vly., Estate (B-San Diego)

SOBON ESTATE

14430 Shenandoah Rd. Plymouth 95669

Syrah,'93, Shenandoah Vly. $10.00 (B-State Fair)

SODA CANYON

4130 Silverado Trail Napa 94558

Chardonnay,'92, Napa Vly. $10.00 (B-W. Coast)

SOLIS WINERY

3920 Hecker Pass Rd. Gilroy 95020

Merlot,'93, Santa Clara Co. $14.00 (B-State Fair)

SONOMA CREEK WINERY

23355 Millerick Road Sonoma 95476

Cabernet Sauvignon,'92, Sonoma Co., Reserve $17.00 (6)
Cabernet Sauvignon,'93, Sonoma Co. $10.00 (S-W. Coast)
Chardonnay,'92, Carneros, Estate $10.00 (B-Dallas)
Chardonnay,'93, Sonoma Vly., Carneros Res. $16.00 (3)
Chardonnay,'93, Sonoma, Carneros $10.00 (S-L.A.)
Pinot Noir,'93, Sonoma Co. $10.00 (3)
Zinfandel,'93, Sonoma Co. $10.00 (4)
Zinfandel,'93, Sonoma Vly., Old Vines (2)

SONORA WINERY

17500 Rt. 5 Road Sonora 95370

Zinfandel,'92, Sonoma, Passalacqua Vnyd. $10.00 (2)
Zinfandel,'93, Sierra Foothills, TC Vnyd. $13.00 (S-San Fran)

ST. CLEMENT VINEYARDS

2867 St. Helena Hwy. N. St Helena 94574

Cabernet Sauvignon,'92, Napa Vly. $23.00 (4)
Chardonnay,'93, Napa, Carneros $18.00 (S-San Fran)
Merlot,'92, Napa Vly. $21.00 (5)
Red Meritage,'93, Napa Vly., Oroppas $30.00 (3)
Sauvignon Blanc,'94, Napa Vly. $11.00 (3)

ST. FRANCIS VINEYARDS

8450 Sonoma Highway Kenwood 95452

Cabernet Sauvignon,'91, Sonoma, Reserve $24.00 (S-New World)
Cabernet Sauvignon,'93, Sonoma Vly. $10.00 (3)
Merlot,'92, Sonoma Vly. $18.00 (3)
Zinfandel,'93, Sonoma Vly., Old Vines $16.00 (2)

ST. SUPERY VINEYARDS

8440 St. Helena Hwy. Rutherford 94573

Cabernet Sauvignon,'91, Napa, Dollarhide Ranch $14.00 (4)
Chardonnay,'93, Napa, Dollarhide Ranch $13.00 (2)
Merlot,'92, Napa Vly., Dollarhide Ranch $14.50 (3)
Sauvignon Blanc,'93, Napa Vly. $8.50 (B-W. Coast)

STAG'S LEAP WINERY

5766 Silverado Trail Napa 94558

Cabernet Sauvignon,'92, Napa Vly., Fay Vnyd. $35.00 (S-San Fran)
Chardonnay,'93, Napa Vly. $19.00 (G-Orange)
Johannisberg Riesling,'94, Napa Vly. $9.00 (B-Orange)
Petite Sirah,'92, Napa Vly., Petite Syrah $25.00 (B-San Diego)

STAGLIN FAMILY VINEYARD

1570 Bella Oaks Lane Rutherford 94573

Cabernet Sauvignon,'92, Napa Vly. $28.00 (B-Orange)

P. & M. STAIGER

1300 Hopkins Gulch Rd. Boulder Creek 95006

Cabernet Sauvignon,'92, Santa Cruz Mtns. $14.00 (B-San Fran)

STE. CLAIRE

18700 Geyserville Ave. Geyserville 95441

Cabernet Sauvignon,'92, California $11.00 (3)
Chardonnay,'92, California, Barrel Select $11.00 (4)
Sauvignon Blanc,'91, Lake Co. $8.00 (B-W. Coast)

STELTZNER

5998 Silverado Trail Napa 94558

Cabernet Sauvignon,'90, Napa, Stags Leap $19.00 (B-Orange)
Red Meritage,'92, Napa, Stags Leap Dist. $11.00 (B-Orange)

ROBERT STEMMLER WINERY

3805 Lambert Bridge Rd. Healdsburg 95448

Pinot Noir,'91, Sonoma Co. $20.00 (2)

STERLING VINEYARDS

1111 Dunaweal Ln. Calistoga 94515

Cabernet Sauvignon,'91, Napa, Diamond Mt. Ranch $17.00 (3)
Cabernet Sauvignon,'92, Napa Vly. $14.00 (B-Orange)
Chardonnay,'93, Carneros, Winery Lake Vnyd. $19.00 (3)
Merlot,'91, Napa, 3 Palms Vnyd. $22.00 (S-New World)
Merlot,'92, Napa Vly. $14.00 (B-State Fair)
Pinot Noir,'93, Carneros, Winery Lake Vnyd. $18.00 (4)

Red Meritage,'91, Napa Vly., Reserve $40.00 (4)
Sauvignon Blanc,'93, Napa Vly. $9.00 (B-San Fran)

STEVENOT WINERY

2690 San Domingo Rd. Murphys 95247

Cabernet Sauvignon,'92, Calaveras Co., Reserve $10.00 (2)
Chardonnay,'93, Calaveras Co. $9.00 (3)
Merlot,'93, Sierra Foothills, Reserve $10.00 (3)
Zinfandel,'90, El Dorado Co., LH $12.00 (S-State Fair)

STONE CELLARS

9140 Owens Mt. Ave. Chatsworth 91311

Cabernet Sauvignon,'93, Napa Vly. $8.00 (B-State Fair)

STONE CREEK WINES

9380 Sonoma Highway Kenwood 95452

Cabernet Sauvignon,'90, Napa Vly., Chairman's Res. $15.00 (3)
Cabernet Sauvignon,'93, California, Spec. Sel. $7.00 (B-Dallas)
Merlot,'92, Napa, Chairman's Res. $16.50 (S-Orange)
Sauvignon Blanc,'94, Napa, Special Sel. Fume $7.00 (B-Orange)
White Zinfandel,'94, California, Special Sel. $6.00 (B-Orange)

STONESTREET WINERY

4611 Thomas Road Healdsburg 95448

Cabernet Sauvignon,'91, Alexander Vly. $22.00 (6)
Cabernet Sauvignon,'92, Alexander Vly. $22.00 (G-State Fair)
Chardonnay,'92, Sonoma Co. $20.00 (5)
Chardonnay,'93, Sonoma Co. $21.00 (7)
Chardonnay,'93, Sonoma Co., Reserve $30.00 (2)
Gewurztraminer,'93, Anderson Vly. $13.00 (2)
Merlot,'92, Alexander Vly. $22.00 (4)
Pinot Noir,'92, Sonoma Co. $21.00 (6)
Red Meritage,'91, Alexander Vly., Legacy $35.00 (6)
Red Meritage,'92, Alexander Vly., Legacy $35.00 (6)

STONY RIDGE WINERY

4948 Tesla Road Livermore 94550

Cabernet Franc,'91, Napa Vly. (B-New World)
Cabernet Sauvignon,'93, Napa, Mt. Veeder, Ltd. Rel. $14.00 (3)
Johannisberg Riesling,'94, Monterey, Ltd. Rel. $7.00 (B-State Fair)
Sauvignon Blanc,'93, Sonoma Co. (G-New World)

STORRS WINERY

303 Potrero St. #35 Santa Cruz 95060

Chardonnay,'93, S. Cruz, Vanumanutagi $17.00 (B-Orange)
Merlot,'93, San Ysidro Dist. $17.00 (2)
Petite Sirah,'93, Santa Cruz Mtns. $16.00 (4)
Zinfandel,'92, Beauregard Ranch $15.00 (4)
Zinfandel,'93, Santa Cruz Mtns. $16.00 (3)

STORY VINEYARDS WINERY

10525 Bell Road Plymouth 95669

Zinfandel,'83, Shenandoah Vly. $29.00 (B-State Fair)
Zinfandel,'92, Shenandoah Vly., Reserve $19.00 (S-State Fair)

STORYBOOK MOUNTAIN VINEYARDS

3835 Highway 128 Calistoga 94515

Zinfandel,'91, Napa Vly., Est. Reserve $25.00 (G-San Diego)
Zinfandel,'92, Napa Vly. $14.00 (3)

STRAUS

498 Franz Vly. School Rd. Calistoga 94515

Merlot,'91, Napa Vly. $15.00 (B-Orange)

RODNEY STRONG VINEYARDS

11455 Old Redwood Hwy. Healdsburg 95448

Cabernet Sauvignon,'91, No.Sonoma, Alex. Crown $20.00 (4)
Cabernet Sauvignon,'91, Northern Sonoma, Reserve $30.00 (5)
Cabernet Sauvignon,'92, Sonoma Co. $10.00 (3)
Chardonnay,'93, Chalk Hill Vnyd. $14.00 (3)
Chardonnay,'93, Sonoma Co. $11.00 (3)
Merlot,'92, Sonoma Co. $14.00 (5)
Pinot Noir,'93, River East Vnyd., Estate $15.00 (5)
Zinfandel,'92, Russian Riv., River West Vnyd. $14.00 (2)

SUNSTONE VINEYARDS

125 N. Refugio Road Santa Ynez 93460

Merlot,'93, Santa Ynez Vly. $18.00 (B-Orange)

SUTTER HOME WINERY

277 St. Helena Hwy. So. St Helena 94574

Cabernet Sauvignon,'91, Napa Vly., Reserve $12.00 (2)
Chenin Blanc,'93, California $4.50 (2)
Zinfandel,'90, Amador Co., Reserve (2)

SWANSON VINEYARDS

1271 Manley Lane Rutherford 94573

Chardonnay,'93, Napa Vly., Carneros $20.00 (5)
Merlot,'92, Napa Vly., Est. $16.00 (3)
Syrah,'92, Napa Vly. $25.00 (3)

SYLVESTER VINEYARDS

5115 Buena Vista Dr. Paso Robles 93446

Cabernet Sauvignon,'92, Paso Robles, Kiara Reserve $8.00 (2)
Chardonnay,'93, Paso Robles, Kiara Reserve $8.00 (2)

T

T-VINE

Address Not Available

Chardonnay,'94, Monterey $11.00 (B-Orange)

TAFT STREET

2030 Barlow Lane Sebastopol 95472

Cabernet Sauvignon,'92, California $9.00 (S-Orange)
Chardonnay,'93, Sonoma Co. $11.00 (S-New World)
Sauvignon Blanc,'94, Sonoma $7.00 (B-San Fran)

IVAN TAMAS

5565 Tesla Road Livermore 94550

Chardonnay,'92, Livermore, Reserve (B-New World)

TANTALUS CELLARS

Address Not Available

Red Meritage,'91, Sonoma, Tantalus $15.00 (B-L.A.)

TEMECULA CREST WINERY

Address Not Available

Cabernet Sauvignon,'92, Temecula $13.00 (2)
Johannisberg Riesling,'93, Temecula (2)
Sauvignon Blanc,'94, Temecula $8.00 (B-Farmers)

THORNTON WINERY

32575 Rancho Calif. Rd. Temecula 92592

Chardonnay,'93, Brindiamo, Calif., Ltd. (B-New World)
Pinot Noir,'93, Brindiamo, Edna Vlly. $10.00 (2)
Sparkling Wine,'87, Culbertson, Brut Rose $16.00 (4)
Sparkling Wine,'88, Culbertson, Brut Reserve $18.00 (2)
Sparkling Wine,'88, Culbertson, Natural $16.00 (2)
Sparkling Wine,'94, Culbertson, Artist Ser. Cuvee $12.00 (2)
Sparkling Wine,'NV, Culbertson, Blanc De Noir $10.00 (2)
Sparkling Wine,'NV, Culbertson, Brut $10.00 (3)
Sparkling Wine,'NV, Culbertson, C. De Frontignan $10.00 (3)

TOPAZ WINES

1937 Waverly Street Napa 94558

Red Meritage,'91, Napa Vly., Rouge De Trois $16.00 (2)

TREFETHEN VINEYARDS

1160 Oak Knoll Ave. Napa 94558

Cabernet Sauvignon,'89, Napa Vly., Est. Res. $30.00 (B-L.A.)
Chardonnay,'87, Napa Vly., Library Sel. $30.00 (2)
Chardonnay,'93, Napa Vly. $19.00 (B-State Fair)

TRELLIS VINEYARDS

Address Not Available

Cabernet Sauvignon,'93, Sonoma $10.00 (B-San Fran)
Chardonnay,'93, Sonoma Co. $8.00 (4)
Sauvignon Blanc,'93, Sonoma Co. $6.00 (2)

TRENTADUE WINERY

19170 Geyserville Ave. Geyserville 95441

Merlot,'92, Alexander Vly., Estate (B-Dallas)
Petite Sirah,'92, Sonoma Co. $11.00 (3)
Zinfandel,'93, Sonoma $11.00 (S-San Fran)

TRIBAUT

427 Bush Street San Francisco 94108

Sparkling Wine,'NV, California, Blanc De Blanc $9.00 (3)
Sparkling Wine,'NV, California, Brut $9.00 (2)

TROUT GULCH VINEYARDS

18426 Chelmsford Dr. Cupertino 95014

Chardonnay,'93, Santa Cruz Mtns. $14.00 (B-San Fran)
Pinot Noir,'91, Santa Cruz Mtns. $16.00 (3)
Pinot Noir,'92, Santa Cruz Mtns. $16.00 (S-San Diego)

TRUCHARD VINEYARDS

3234 Old Sonoma Rd. Napa 94559

Cabernet Sauvignon,'91, Carneros $18.00 (2)
Merlot,'92, Carneros $18.00 (2)
Pinot Noir,'92, Carneros $18.00 (2)
Syrah,'93, Napa Vly., Carneros $18.00 (4)

TULOCAY WINERY

1426 Coombsville Napa 94558

Cabernet Sauvignon,'92, Napa Vly., Cliff Vnyd. $15.00 (3)
Zinfandel,'92, Napa Vly., Casanova Vnyd. $11.00 (3)

TWIN HILLS RANCH

2025 Nacimiento Lake Dr. Paso Robles 93446

Zinfandel,'92, Paso Robles $9.00 (B-State Fair)

Zinfandel,'NV, Paso Robles $6.00 (B-State Fair)

V

M. G. VALLEJO WINERY

21468 - 8th Street E. Sonoma 95476

Cabernet Sauvignon,'92, California $6.00 (2)
Chardonnay,'93, California $6.00 (S-New World)
Chardonnay,'94, California $6.00 (2)
Merlot,'93, California $6.00 (5)
White Zinfandel,'93, California $5.00 (G-New World)
White Zinfandel,'94, California $5.00 (3)

VAN ROEKEL VINEYARDS

Address Not Available

Cabernet Sauvignon,'93, Temecula $9.00 (B-W. Coast)
Chardonnay,'94, Temecula, A Boire $8.00 (2)
Pinot Blanc,'93, Temecula $8.00 (6)
Sauvignon Blanc,'93, Temecula, Fume $7.00 (2)
Syrah,'93, Temecula, Estate $6.00 (4)
White Zinfandel,'94, Temecula $5.00 (B-W. Coast)

VENDANGE

389 4th St. E. Sonoma 95476

Cabernet Sauvignon,'NV, California, Autumn Harvest $6.00 (2)
Chardonnay,'94, Calif., Autumn Harvest $6.00 (S-L.A.)
Merlot,'NV, Calif., Autumn Harvest $6.00 (S-Orange)
White Zinfandel,'94, Calif., Autumn Harvest $6.00 (B-State Fair)
Zinfandel,'NV, Calif., Autumn Harvest $6.00 (B-L.A.)

VENEZIA

22281 Chianti Rd. Geyserville 95441

Cabernet Sauvignon,'93, Alexander Vly. $20.00 (2)
White Meritage,'94, Alex. Vly., Nuovo Mondo $20.00 (3)

VENTANA VINEYARDS & WINERY

2999 Monterey-Salinas Hwy. Monterey 93940

Cabernet Sauvignon,'93, Monterey, Est. $12.00 (B-Farmers)
Chardonnay,'91, Monterey, Gold Stripe $12.00 (3)
Chardonnay,'92, Monterey, Est., Gold Stripe $12.00 (2)
Chenin Blanc,'93, Monterey, Estate $8.00 (2)
Johannisberg Riesling,'93, Monterey White Riesling $8.00 (3)
Sauvignon Blanc,'93, Monterey $9.00 (B-W. Coast)

VICHON WINERY

1595 Oakville Grade Oakville 94562

Cabernet Sauvignon,'91, Napa Vly. $16.00 (2)
Cabernet Sauvignon,'92, California, Coastal Sel. $8.50 (B-Dallas)
Cabernet Sauvignon,'92, Napa Vly. $16.00 (S-State Fair)
Chardonnay,'93, California, Coastal Sel. $9.00 (4)
Chardonnay,'93, Napa Vly. $14.00 (2)
Merlot,'92, Napa Vly. $18.00 (2)
White Meritage,'93, Napa Vly. $9.00 (B-Dallas)

VILLA MT. EDEN

620 Oakville Cross Rd. Oakville 94562

Cabernet Sauvignon,'91, Calif., Cellar Select $8.00 (S-Dallas)
Cabernet Sauvignon,'91, Napa Vly., Grand Reserve $14.00 (5)
Cabernet Sauvignon,'92, California, Cellar Select $8.00 (4)
Chardonnay,'92, Carneros, Grand Res. $14.00 (B-Dallas)

Chardonnay,'93, California, Cellar Select $8.00 (4)
Chardonnay,'93, Carneros, Grand Reserve $14.00 (5)
Merlot,'92, Napa Vly., Grand Reserve $14.00 (3)
Pinot Blanc,'93, Santa Maria, Grand Res. $14.00 (2)
Pinot Noir,'93, California, Cellar Select $8.00 (2)
Pinot Noir,'93, Los Carneros, Grand Reserve $14.00 (6)
Zinfandel,'92, California, Cellar Select $8.00 (2)
Zinfandel,'93, California, Cellar Select $8.00 (3)
Zinfandel,'93, Napa Vly., Grand Res. $14.00 (B-Farmers)

VITA NOVA

Address Not Available

Cabernet Franc,'93, Santa Barbara Co. $12.00 (B-Orange)

VOSS VINEYARDS

Address Not Available

Chardonnay,'92, Napa Vly. $14.00 (G-Orange)
Merlot,'92, Napa Vly. $14.00 (3)
Sauvignon Blanc,'94, Napa Vly. $10.00 (2)
Zinfandel,'92, Alexander Vly. $13.00 (S-New World)

W

WEINSTOCK CELLARS

308-B Center Street Healdsburg 95448

Cabernet Sauvignon,'93, Alexander Vly. $9.00 (5)
Chardonnay,'93, Napa Co. $9.00 (B-New World)
Sauvignon Blanc,'93, Alexander Vly. $9.00 (S-New World)
White Zinfandel,'94, California $7.00 (7)

WELLINGTON VINEYARDS

11600 Dunbar Road Glen Ellen 95442

Cabernet Sauvignon,'91, Napa Vly., Mt. Veeder Dist. $16.00 (2)
Cabernet Sauvignon,'92, Mohrhardt Ridge $14.00 (B-W. Coast)
Merlot,'92, Sonoma Co. $15.00 (3)

WENTE BROS. WINERY

5565 Tesla Road Livermore 94550

Cabernet Sauvignon,'92, Livermore Vly. (G-Dallas)
Chardonnay,'92, Arroyo Seco, Riva Ranch $13.00 (3)
Chardonnay,'93, Central Coast, Est. $7.50 (B-Farmers)
Chenin Blanc,'93, Central Coast, Spec. Sel. $5.00 (G-State Fair)
Johannisberg Riesling,'93, Arroyo Seco Vnyd. $18.00 (5)
Sauvignon Blanc,'93, Livermore Vly., Est. $7.00 (4)
Semillon,'91, Livermore Vly. $6.50 (B-W. Coast)
Sparkling Wine,'NV, Arroyo Seco, Grande Brut $10.00 (4)

WESTOVER VINEYARDS

Address Not Available

Cabernet Sauvignon,'93, Kalthoff Vnyd. Res. $12.50 (S-Orange)
Pinot Blanc,'93, Monterey Co., Reserve $8.00 (B-Orange)

WHALER VINEYARD

6200 East Side Road Ukiah 95482

Zinfandel,'92, Mendocino $10.00 (G-Orange)

WHEELER WINERY

650 Fifth St., #403 San Francisco 94107

Cabernet Sauvignon,'91, Norse Vnyd. Reserve (G-Dallas)
Sauvignon Blanc,'92, Sonoma Co., Fume (B-Dallas)

Zinfandel,'91, Dry Creek Vly. $10.00 (B-Orange)

WHITE OAK VINEYARDS

208 Haydon Street Healdsburg 95448

Chardonnay,'93, Sonoma Co. (B-Dallas)
Zinfandel,'92, Sonoma Co. $9.00 (2)

WHITE ROCK VINEYARDS

1115 Loma Vista Dr. Napa 94558

Red Meritage,'91, Napa Vly. $22.00 (B-San Fran)

WHITEHALL LANE WINERY

1563 St. Helena Hwy. St Helena 94574

Cabernet Sauvignon,'91, Napa Vly., Reserve $24.00 (4)
Cabernet Sauvignon,'92, Napa Vly., Reserve $24.00 (S-San Fran)
Merlot,'92, Knight's Vly. $16.00 (2)
Merlot,'93, Napa Vly. $18.00 (G-San Fran)
Merlot,'93, Napa Vly., Leonardini Vnyd. $28.00 (2)
Red Meritage,'91, Napa Vly. $16.00 (B-Dallas)
Sauvignon Blanc,'93, Napa Vly., Barrel Ferm. (B-Dallas)

WHITFORD CELLARS

4047 E. Third Street Napa 94558

Chardonnay,'90, Haynes Vnyd., Est. $12.00 (S-L.A.)

WILD HORSE WINERY

P. O. Box 638 Templeton 93465

Cabernet Franc,'91, San Luis Obispo Co. (G-San Diego)
Cabernet Sauvignon,'92, San Luis Obispo $12.00 (3)
Cabernet Sauvignon,'93, San Luis Obispo Co $12.00 (S-L.A.)
Chardonnay,'94, Central Coast $13.00 (2)
Merlot,'92, Central Coast $15.00 (G-New World)
Merlot,'93, Central Coast $15.00 (B-L.A.)
Pinot Blanc,'93, Monterey $13.00 (S-Dallas)
Pinot Blanc,'94, Monterey $13.00 (5)
Pinot Noir,'93, Central Coast $30.00 (Σ-Farmers)
Pinot Noir,'93, Paso Robles, Chev. Sauvage $14.00 (3)

WILDHURST VINEYARDS

11171 Highway 29 Lower Lake 95457

Chardonnay,'92, Sonoma, Reserve $12.00 (B-New World)
Chardonnay,'93, Sonoma Co., Reserve $12.00 (3)
Merlot,'92, Lake Co. $16.00 (B-State Fair)
Sauvignon Blanc,'93, Clear Lake, Fume $11.00 (2)
Zinfandel,'92, Clear Lake $9.00 (2)

WINDSOR VINEYARDS

11455 Old Redwood Hwy. Healdsburg 95448

Cabernet Sauvignon,'91, Mendocino Co. $12.00 (4)
Cabernet Sauvignon,'91, River West Vnyd. $14.00 (2)
Cabernet Sauvignon,'91, Sonoma Co., Signature Series $18.00 (3)
Cabernet Sauvignon,'92, Mendocino $12.00 (S-San Fran)
Cabernet Sauvignon,'92, Sonoma Co. $10.00 (4)
Chardonnay,'92, Alex. Vly., Murphy Ranch $12.00 (2)
Chardonnay,'93, Russian River Vly., Res. $14.00 (4)
Chardonnay,'93, Russian River, Preston Ranch $12.50 (3)
Chardonnay,'93, Sonoma Co. $9.00 (B-L.A.)
Chardonnay,'93, Sonoma Co., Signature Series $15.00 (5)
Chenin Blanc,'93, Alexander Vly. $7.00 (3)
Gewurztraminer,'94, Sonoma Co., Winemaster Sel. $7.00 (3)

Johannisberg Riesling,'93, California $7.00 (S-State Fair)
Johannisberg Riesling,'94, Le Baron Vnyd., Est. $7.00 (3)
Merlot,'92, River West Estate $14.00 (S-New World)
Merlot,'92, Sonoma, Shelton Sig. Series $20.00 (4)
Merlot,'93, Sonoma Co., Reserve $14.00 (2)
Petite Sirah,'92, North Coast $10.00 (5)
Pinot Noir,'92, Calif.Shelton Signature $14.00 (B-Dallas)
Pinot Noir,'93, Calif.Shelton Signature $15.00 (B-San Fran)
Red Meritage,'92, Sonoma Co. $16.00 (3)
Sauvignon Blanc,'93, Sonoma Co. Fume $8.00 (4)
Sauvignon Blanc,'94, Alexander Vly. Fume, Res. $10.00 (2)
Sparkling Wine,'88, Sonoma Co. Blanc De Noir $13.00 (5)
Sparkling Wine,'88, Sonoma Co. Brut $12.50 (2)
Sparkling Wine,'90, Sonoma, Lib. Reserve Brut $16.00 (2)
Sparkling Wine,'NV, California, Lot 2, Extra Dry $8.00 (2)
Zinfandel,'91, Sonoma, Shelton Sig. Series $14.00 (G-Dallas)
Zinfandel,'92, Sonoma Co. $8.00 (2)
Zinfandel,'92, Sonoma, Shelton Sig. Series $14.00 (4)

WINDWALKER VINEYARD

7360 Perry Creek Road Somerset 95684

Chardonnay,'94, El Dorado, Est. $9.00 (2)
Chenin Blanc,'93, El Dorado, Estate $6.00 (2)

WINTERBROOK WINES

4851 Buena Vista Rd. Ione 95640

Cabernet Sauvignon,'91, Napa, Grand Res. (B-Dallas)

WOODBRIDGE

4614 W. Turner Rd. Lodi 95640

Chardonnay,'93, California (B-New World)
Zinfandel,'93, Calif., Barrel Aged $5.00 (S-State Fair)

WOODSIDE VINEYARDS

340 Kings Mtn. Road Woodside 94062

Cabernet Sauvignon,'91, Calif., Kings Mountain (S-San Diego)
Zinfandel,'91, Santa Cruz Mtns., Est. $14.00 (S-San Diego)

Y

YORK MOUNTAIN WINERY

Rt. 2, Box 191 Templeton 93465

Cabernet Sauvignon,'89, San Luis Obispo $14.00 (B-San Diego)
Chardonnay,'93, San Luis Obispo $12.00 (3)
Merlot,'91, San Luis Obispo $12.00 (B-San Fran)
Pinot Noir,'91, San Luis Obispo Co. $10.00 (3)
Zinfandel,'91, San Luis Obispo Co. $9.00 (3)

YORKVILLE CELLARS

Address Not Available

Merlot,'92, Mendocino Co. $14.00 (B-San Diego)

YVERDON VINEYARDS

3787 Spring Mtn. Road St Helena 94574

Cabernet Sauvignon,'79, Napa, Library $35.00 (B-San Fran)
Cabernet Sauvignon,'80, Napa, Library $35.00 (B-San Fran)
Cabernet Sauvignon,'81, Napa, Library $35.00 (S-San Fran)
Cabernet Sauvignon,'82, Napa, Library $35.00 (B-San Fran)
Cabernet Sauvignon,'83, Napa, Library $35.00 (B-San Fran)
Cabernet Sauvignon,'84, Napa, Library $35.00 (B-San Fran)

Z D WINES

8383 Silverado Trail Napa 94558

Cabernet Sauvignon,'92, Napa Vly. $25.00 (7)
Chardonnay,'93, California $22.00 (3)
Pinot Noir,'93, Napa Vly., Carneros $23.00 (3)

ZACA MESA WINERY

6905 Foxen Canyon Rd. Los Olivos 93441

Chardonnay,'93, S. Barbara, Chapel Vnyd. $18.00 (3)
Chardonnay,'94, Santa Barbara, Zaca Vnyd. $13.00 (2)
Syrah,'92, S. Barbara, Zaca Vnyds. $12.00 (B-San Diego)
Syrah,'93, Santa Barbara, Zaca Vnyds. $12.00 (2)

STEPHEN ZELLERBACH VINEYARD

2150 McNab Ranch Rd. Ukiah 95482

Cabernet Sauvignon,'93, California $7.00 (2)
Chardonnay,'94, Calif., Robert Alison Vnyd. $8.00 (2)
Chardonnay,'94, California $8.00 (2)
Chardonnay,'94, Sonoma Co. $11.00 (S-Orange)
Sauvignon Blanc,'93, California, Sweet $7.00 (B-L.A.)
Sauvignon Blanc,'93, Sonoma Co. $7.00 (3)